Prince Charming Goes West
The Story of the E.P. Ranch

The Prince of Wales, "all duded up" on his ranch.

Prince Charming Goes West

The Story of the E.P. Ranch

by

Simon M. Evans

University of Calgary Press

University of Calgary Press
2500 University Drive N.W.
Calgary, Alberta, Canada T2N 1N4

Canadian Cataloguing in Publication Data

Evans, Simon M.
　　Prince charming goes west

　　Includes bibliographical references and index.
　　ISBN 1-895176-34-4

　　1. E.P. Ranch (Pekisko, Alta.). 2. Windsor, Edward,
Duke of, 1894–1972. 3. Ranch life—Alberta—Pekisko—
History. I. Title.

FC3699.P44E93 1993　　636.2'01'0971234　　　C93-091374-4
F1079.5.P44E93 1993

The Alberta
Foundation
for the Arts

Financial support provided by the Alberta Foundation for the Arts,
a beneficiary of the Lottery Fund of the Government of Alberta

Cover design by Jon Paine
Printed in Canada by Kromar Printing Limited

♾ This book is printed on acid-free paper.

Contents

To the saints at

Trinity Episcopal School for Ministry

Ambridge, Pennsylvania

List of Illustrations

Unless otherwise indentified, the photographs listed below are from the collections at the Glenbow Archives, Calgary.

Maps and Figures

Acknowledgements

It is a pleasure to remember and to acknowledge with gratitude those who have contributed to the completion of this book. I must start by thanking Lynn Cartwright, who showed me round the E.P. Ranch before the project was started, and who has supported me with her knowledge and hospitality ever since. She has played a key role in restoring and maintaining the ranch house, and has introduced a whole generation of Albertans to an interesting chapter of their history through the operation of the Prince of Wales Tea House. Without her vision and enthusiasm the building might have disappeared.

The staff at the Glenbow Library and Archives were patient and professional. Doug Cass, in particular, must have built up quite a file of inquiries from me over a six-year period, and yet he was always good humoured and helpful. In rather the same way, the staff of the reference service at the National Archives of Canada prepared me so well, that I could make the most of the relatively short periods I was able to work there. My research in Britain was aided by the courtesy and interest of Dr. G. Haslam, Archivist to the Duchy of Cornwall.

Ironically, I now live just about as far away from Southern Alberta as it is possible to get and still remain in Canada. This might have been an obstacle if it had not been for the generosity of David and Betty Watson, who provided me with a home away from home in Calgary. Chip and Jeanne Beaty did the same for me in Lethbridge. Howard and Tamara Palmer convinced me early on that the topic was worth pursuing. Don Smith and my colleague Elizabeth Behrens were kind enough to read part of the manuscript and provide useful suggestions. Dale LeDrew and Sylvia Fudge retyped the manuscript cheerfully. During the later stages of completing the manuscript, the staff at the University of Calgary Press have been a pleasure to work with, and John King, the production editor, has been imaginative and indefatigable. Thanks too to Bill Matheson, who did the cartography and to copyeditor Peter Enman.

It is abundantly clear that the very foundation of this book is the body of scholarship concerning Prince Edward which has been published over the years. In particular, Philip Ziegler, as the official biographer of Edward VII, had unprecedented access to the Royal Archives. His book is therefore almost a "primary source" for those of us who follow after him. Frances Donaldson's brilliant biography was the first one I read on Edward, and her insights and evaluations remain definitive. Michael Bloch, too, has used the Duke and Duchess of Windsor's Paris papers with skill and passion to present an alternative view of their life together in exile. The contribution of these and other scholars is made explicit in the frequent references made to their work, but I should like to add my own less formal but heartfelt expression of gratitude.

I am indebted to all those who shared with me their memories of H.R.H. Edward, Duke of Windsor, and the E.P. Ranch. In particular, Mary Diebel, John Little, Roy Griswold, Nita Maga, and Albert Shimbashi, filled in some gaps, and breathed life into the text with their reminiscences.

Memorial University of Newfoundland provided me with financial assistance to complete the manuscript, while the community at Trinity Episcopal School for Ministry, Ambridge, Pennsylvania, to whom the book is dedicated, sustained me during the writing of it. Thank you all very much.

This book has been published with the help of a grant from the Social Science Federation of Canada, using funds provided by the Social Sciences and Humanities Research Council of Canada.

Introduction

In the spring of 1985, I had the pleasure of planning and leading a field trip through the foothills country of southern Alberta as part of the annual meeting of the Canadian Association of Geographers, which was hosted that year by the University of Calgary. One of the themes on which we were focusing was "the ranching frontier," and it seemed fitting that we should have our picnic lunch at the "Prince of Wales Teahouse," on the site of the E.P. (Edward Prince) Ranch, at Pekisko, Alberta. Our hostess, Lynn Cartwright, explained that the elegant reception room and glassed in porch in which we were entertained had been rebuilt from the original plans when the old building had become unsafe some years before. We had a chance to see how carefully the restoration had been accomplished as we compared photographs in scrapbooks with the existing rooms. We also wandered through the assemblage of buildings, barns, and corrals which fringed Pekisko Creek. The Party was impressed with the tranquil beauty of the site, and the sense of the continuity of settlement which it conveyed. There was even an original homestead which had survived as a chicken house! One colleague remarked that the history of the E.P. Ranch would provide an interesting "backbone" on which to hang a study of the region. This book has been written in response to that challenge.

In 1919, Edward, Prince of Wales, visited Canada. This was the first of a series of trips round the British Empire designed to strengthen relationships between the mother country and colonies after the stresses of the First World War. The Canadian tour was an outstanding success. While in Alberta the Prince spent some time on the Bar U Ranch near High River. On his return eastward from Vancouver he made arrangements to purchase a small ranch close to the Bar U. Edward owned the E.P. Ranch for the next forty-three years, and often remarked that it was the only property he owned.

With an infusion of capital, expertise, and prize winning livestock from the Duchy of Cornwall estates, the original ranch was transformed into a centre of breeding excellence which had international significance. The ongoing contribution of the Prince to the welfare of agriculture in Alberta, indeed in Canada, was justly lauded. The onset of the great depression coincided with the development of new interests by Prince Edward, and led to a down-scaling of activities at the ranch during the 1930s. During his brief reign and subsequent abdication, attempts were made to dispose of the property. However, during the Second World War, Edward, now the Duke of Windsor, was serving as Governor of the Bahamas and had real hopes that oil might be discovered on the ranch. He visited the E.P. with the Duchess in 1941, and invested in an exploratory well in 1945. Unfortunately, the wildcat well proved to be dry. The later 1950s saw the ranch revitalized with new infusions of capital. Once more it was to be used as a link between the pedigree bloodstock of the United Kingdom and the farms and ranches of western Canada. The management of this new enterprise proved to be too unwieldy to grasp the real opportunities which existed, and the ranch was still costing the Duke and his friends money when he reluctantly decided to sell it to a local rancher in 1962.

The aim of this book is to tell the story of the E.P. Ranch. It is a story of an extraordinary man and a place of unusual beauty and charm. Its telling will involve an attempt to get behind the facade of a royal figurehead, so that we can get to know Edward better both as a person, and as Prince, King, and ex-monarch. It will also mean exploring the foothills carefully, and becoming familiar with the way in which this region was occupied and transformed by European settlement. The history of the ranch is naturally interwoven with the history of the foothills region as a whole.

Contemporary newspaper accounts of the Prince's Canadian visits depict him as a one-dimensional "Prince Charming," the golden haired youth who seemed to embody "Britain's imperishable glory." Both the style and the content of this coverage reflected a respectful, even unctuous attitude toward the monarchy which reads somewhat strangely in the 1990s.[1] Likewise, the biographical works written by people who accompanied the Prince of Wales on his journeys were panegyrical, and failed entirely to capture the multi-faceted personality of a highly strung young man who was being subjected to immense pressures by his "job." The ongoing and penetrating biographical dissection to which Edward has been subjected during the past two decades now enables us to make connections between his Canadian appearances and his behaviour at the

---

1 There is a great deal of similarity in the language used in some of the official "booster" literature of the time and that employed to discuss the Prince and his contribution to "Empire building." See, for example, R. Douglas Francis, *Images of the West* (Saskatoon: Prairie Books, 1989), especially "The West, the Nation and the Empire," p. 73ff.

ranch, on the one hand, and the development of his personality, on the other.[2] The decisions he made can be interpreted in the context of the life he was leading and the concerns which were uppermost in his mind. For example, the Prince's determination to purchase the ranch in 1919 may be interpreted as an attempt on his part to establish a pied-à-terre far from his father's disapproving frown.

This body of modern biographical work allows us to enter into a relationship with a real person rather than to view a cardboard cut-out of a royal silhouette from a decorous distance. It was by coming out from behind the veil of majesty and by projecting his own personality that Edward achieved his greatest triumphs. It was his refusal to recognize that the monarchy existed quite apart from the person who temporarily held the office, and that kingship imposed limits on what he could and could not do as a private person, which brought him low. Those who have struggled to get to know Edward, and to communicate their views of his character to us, disagree with each other and often contradict themselves as they grapple with his chameleon-like personality. "No man is consistent, yet more than most he seems to have been a kaleidoscope of conflicting elements; his character is evanescent, bewildering, rippling and swirling like a mountain stream."[3] The modern reader would find some of his attitudes hateful, even bigoted, but he cannot be understood, and should not be judged, outside the context of his times. His views differed not one whit from those of his social set and political stripe. His intimate correspondence with Wallis Simpson reveals an abject dependence in the relationship which we may find difficult to admire or even sympathize with.[4] And yet in this relationship at least he was steadfast and unswerving throughout the remainder of his life. It would be presumptuous to suggest that a detailed investigation of the purchase and subsequent management of the E.P. Ranch "throws new light on Edward's character." It does, however, provide some revealing footnotes to *A King's Story*.[5] The converse of this idea, that knowledge of the owner is an essential point of departure for any understanding of the history of the ranch, is undoubtedly true.

---

2 This literature will be introduced later, but mention should be made now of the two most important contributions, Frances Donaldson, *Edward VIII* (London: Weidenfield and Nicolson, 1974); and Philip Ziegler, *Edward VIII: The Official Biography* (London: Collins, 1990).

3 Ziegler, *Edward VIII*, p. 560.

4 Michael Bloch (ed.), *Wallis and Edward: Letters; 1931–1937* (New York: Simon and Schuster, 1986).

5 H.R.H. Edward, Duke of Windsor, *A King's Story: The Memoirs of the Duke of Windsor* (New York: G.P. Putnam, 1952).

Those who served the royal household were, almost without exception, both loyal and discrete. However, time has passed, and today letters and diaries are available which would not have been published in the past. For example, the letters of Alan Lascelles to his wife give a lively and down-to-earth account of happenings at the ranch in 1924 which contrast amusingly with the bland press releases issued.[6]

Three men, a professor, a lawyer, and a shepherd, served the E.P. Ranch with devotion and resolution. Taken together their years of service add up to almost three-quarters of a century. Professor Carlyle managed the ranch from its establishment in 1920 until 1941; Alick Newton acted as an executive link between Edward and his ranch, and became the Duke of Windsor's trusted Canadian advisor; while William Elliott joined the staff in the early 1920s and stayed until the mid–1950s. He was responsible for implementing Carlyle's ideas, and he took over management in 1941. The letters between these men and the Prince provide some of the most useful primary sources for this study.

The foothills of southern Alberta constitute a distinctive sub-region within the Prairies. This separate identity is based on both physical geography and history. The broken terrain, the frequency of Chinook winds during the winters, and the reliable streams flowing from the mountains, make this ideal ranching country. For more than a decade, during the late 1870s and 1880s, the Canadian government recognized this regionalization and did all in its power to encourage the establishment of a large-scale cattle industry in what was designated "the Grazing Country."[7] Eastern Canadian and British capital investment was lured to the region by the passage of legislation which made available large acreages of pasture land at nominal rents. The creation of a "cattle kingdom" was congruent with the immediate aims of the National Policy, for ranchers would occupy Canadian territory effectively, and provide freight for the projected transcontinental railway. Moreover, Canadian parliamentarians and businessmen alike were excited by the "beef bonanza" which was sweeping the Great Plains of the United States. They sought to capture for Canada a share in the rapidly expanding meat market of Great Britain.

Thus it was the cattlemen, not homesteading wheat farmers, who initiated European settlement in the foothills and valleys of the Canadian Rockies, and explored the short grass Prairie to the east. During their brief period of unchallenged occupation they put their brand on the region, and the subsequent decades, although they have been accompanied by far-reaching economic, technological, and social changes,

---

6 Duff Hart-Davis (ed.), *In Royal Service: The Letters and Journals of Sir Alan Lascelles, 1920–1936*, Vol. 2 (London: Hamish Hamilton, 1988).

7 This is the title of a map produced by the Canadian Department of the Interior in 1881.

have never entirely eradicated their initial impact. The core area of the ranching country, reaching northward from Fort Macleod and the Oldman River, round the flanks of the Porcupine Hills, up to Millarville, Priddis, and Cochrane in the Bow Valley, still retains proudly some of the characteristics which made it distinct in the past. This is a region where continuity of settlement is the norm, where land is handed down from generation to generation. There is a tradition of breeding excellence and innovation. Investment in ranch infrastructure is often out of proportion to potential monetary returns, suggesting that "psychic income" is important. Today, as in the past, the links with Calgary are very close, and through Calgary knowledge of and connections with the global economy and culture are strong. This is a clannish but certainly not an insular society.

The ranching period in western Canada has been subjected to careful reappraisal during the past twenty years. The work of L.G. Thomas and D.H. Breen has challenged the assumption that the cattlemen's frontier in Canada was merely the result of gradual diffusion from the northern grasslands of the United States.[8] These historians have stressed the development of a social milieu, cemented by common background and by shared enjoyment of outdoor activities, which differed markedly from the stereotypical "wild west" of Montana and Wyoming. My own work has argued the importance of a spatial component in any attempt to grapple with the complex reality of the Canadian ranching industry.[9] While parts of the foothills were dominated by an Anglo-Canadian "cattle compact," the extensive short grass prairies reaching eastward to the Cypress Hills and beyond were occupied from time to time by major cattle companies from the United States, and by innumerable small scale ranchers from Montana. This intrusion profoundly influenced the impressions which incoming settlers formed of ranching around the turn of the century. Moreover, most of the technology of the open range was borrowed wholesale from south of the border, and it could be argued that several of the dominant ranches owed their economic success to knowledgeable foremen from Montana. Thus, the general outline of the ranching period in western Canada has been sketched in, but much

---

8 L.G. Thomas, "The Ranching Period in Southern Alberta" (unpublished M.A. Thesis, University of Alberta, 1935); Patrick A. Dunae (ed.), *Ranchers' Legacy* (Edmonton: University of Alberta Press, 1986); and D.H. Breen, *The Canadian Prairie West and the Ranching Frontier, 1874–1924* (Toronto: University of Toronto Press, 1983).

9 Simon M. Evans, "The Passing of a Frontier: Ranching in the Canadian West, 1882–1912" (unpublished Ph.D. Dissertation, University of Calgary, 1976); "American Cattlemen on the Canadian Range, 1874–1914," *Prairie Forum*, Vol. 4 (Spring 1979), pp. 121–35; and "The Origins of Ranching in Western Canada: American Diffusion or Victorian Transplant?" in L.A. Rosenvall and S.M. Evans (eds.), *Essays on the Historical Geography of the Canadian West* (Geography Department, University of Calgary, 1987).

remains to be done. If the historiographical model followed in the United States is anything to go by, it seems likely that the next phase of inquiry in Canada will involve in-depth study of individual ranch enterprises.[10] As these case studies multiply they will enable the general descriptive models which have been established to be refined.

The purchase of a ranch in the heart of the foothills country by an heir to the British throne seemed like the culmination of a thirty-year period during which ties to the mother country had been particularly strong. A way of life had been implanted in the shadow of the Rockies which was fast disappearing "at home." However, this carefree society of privileged immigrants was undergoing profound changes during the first decade of the new century, and was shattered by the First World War. Many young men returned to their regiments, and foothills war memorials witness to the disproportionate numbers from the area who subsequently died at the western front. Economic power and social leadership passed to the hands of the Canadian born and to a new generation of self-made entrepreneurs. The Prince of Wales seems to have been fascinated by the western mystique popularized by "westerns" and exemplified by the Calgary Stampede. It was roping, steer-wrestling, and bronco-busting which interested him, rather than hunting, polo, and horse racing, which had been the favoured activities of expatriate Britons. Moreover, he sought out archetypical westerners like George Lane and Pat Burns, who could regale him with stories of their pioneering days. He relished western Canada because it was new and free, and different from the kind of society he was used to.

In each era, the E.P. Ranch was caught up in the warp and weft of the fascinating region in which it was located. During the 1920s the cattle industry underwent profound technological and organizational changes. Old markets had disappeared and new ones demanded higher quality meat. Operating from a more limited deeded landbase, ranchers intensified their operations and improved their herds. The E.P. Ranch played a role in encouraging this process both by acting as a progressive model, and as a source of pedigree livestock. The impact of the depression on the prairie provinces in general has been scrupulously documented.[11]

---

10 H.R. Mothershead, *The Swan Land and Cattle Company Ltd.* (Norman: University of Oklahoma Press, 1971); and W.M. Pearce, *The Matador Land and Cattle Company* (Norman: University of Oklahoma Press, 1964). In Canada, a start has been made; see S. Jameson, *Ranchers, Cowboys and Characters: Birth of Alberta's Western Heritage* (Calgary: Glenbow-Alberta Institute, 1987), and Henry C. Klassen, "The Conrads in the Alberta Cattle Business, 1875–1911," *Agricultural History* 64:3 (1990).

11 W.A. Mackintosh and W.L.G. Joerg (eds.), *Canadian Frontiers of Settlement* (in nine volumes; Toronto: MacMillan, 1934–40); J. Gray, *Men Against the Desert* (Saskatoon: Western Producer, 1967); Barry Broadfoot, *Ten Lost Years* (Toronto: Doubleday Canada, 1973); D. Francis and H. Ganzevoort (eds.), *The Dirty Thirties in Prairie Canada*

The worst devastation of drought, dust storm, and grasshoppers was suffered by those who had recently occupied the semi-arid short-grass prairies of Palliser's Triangle. What was the depression like on the ranches and in the small communities of the foothills? The local newspapers and the E.P. Ranch papers and account books suggest that this well-established area survived better than most. It was the collapse of the market and falling prices rather than the physical parameters which most affected people in this region. The discovery of oil at Turner Valley and the subsequent exploration for oil and natural gas within the foothills introduced new infrastructure, new settlements, and a new, if transitory, element into society.[12] The Prince of Wales obtained sub-surface rights to his property and carried out geological exploration during the last years of the Second World War. His correspondence conveys vividly the roller-coaster of hopes and disappointments which was the common lot of all those engaged in the "oil patch." The aims and dreams of the newly constituted "E.P. Ranch Company," and of its manager, Colonel Kennedy, were somewhat ahead of their time. New breeds of animals and innovative genetic and feeding techniques were at the experimental stage, and on the threshold of adoption. But was it reasonable to attempt to do so much on one small ranch? The vision which had captivated the Duke of Windsor and his European friends once more proved to be a mirage. Finally, the sale of the E.P. Ranch to the Cartwright family in 1962 contributed to the emergence of one of the largest ranches in the foothills.

This book, then, is about a ranch and its owner: a person and a place. In pursuing these dual objectives, it has been something of a problem to preserve a balance between them. Some readers, already familiar with the life and times of Prince Edward, may find the biographical material redundant. It has been included so that those who are not versed in the history of the British monarchy in the twentieth century can follow the various stages of His Royal Highness' career, and see how his changing fortunes affected his attitude to his ranch. Others may enjoy getting to know the royal protagonist, and be less interested in the foothills and the ranch. The choice of what to put in and what to leave out was sometimes a hard one, but in many instances it was made simpler by the presence or absence of archival material. The documents which have survived in the archives tend to be official letters and reports. As the Duke of Windsor aged and became a more private figure, so archival material on

---

(Vancouver: Tantalus Research, 1980); and Pierre Berton, *The Great Depression, 1929–1939* (Toronto: McClelland and Stewart, 1990).

12 J.J. Barr, "The Impact of Oil on Alberta: Retrospect and Prospect," in A.W. Rasporich (ed.), *The Making of the Modern West: Western Canada Since 1945* (University of Calgary Press, 1984).

the ranch became thinner. It is ironic that it is easier to piece together the history of the great ranches of the late nineteenth and early twentieth centuries, than it is to find accounts of the evolving life and work patterns in the foothills during the 1940s and 1950s. Perhaps the short-comings of this account may spur some readers to realize that they have lived "history," and that the documentary evidence of their experiences—letters, photographs, diaries, account books, and artifacts—make up the indispensable materials from which we can forge an image of ourselves, and the place we occupy and have made our own.

I

The Prince of Wales' Canadian Tour

A boy, a man, a gentleman, a soldier, a statesman,
and an ideal future king of Britain.[1]

Finally, the war to end all wars ground to a halt. The economic system was slow to adjust, and the logistical problems of demobilization, massive unemployment, and inadequate housing meant that there was unrest at home and throughout the Empire. India was seething, in Canada the resistance of French Canadians to wartime conscription had left scars; Australia resounded to radical and labour unrest; while South Africa had its racial problems. The Prime Minister, Lloyd George, thought to deploy the war-hero Prince of Wales to cement imperial relationships before the wartime camaraderie had dissipated. He felt that "the appearance of the popular Prince of Wales might do more to calm the discord than half a dozen solemn imperial conferences."[2] The Prince accepted this charge with enthusiasm. Even before the war he had remonstrated with his father that, as he had "neither the mind nor the will for books," the experience of going up to Oxford would be wasted on him. Would it not be better he argued, for him to be sent on a world tour? That way he could learn about people and places at first hand.[3]

In August 1919, the Prince left for Canada on H.M.S. Renown. The ship's chronicle remarks that the Prince of Wales was:

All that has ever been said of him—very young looking, he is nearer seventeen in his appearance than his correct age of twenty-five; he is almost crazy about exercise. ... We had a semi-organized "rag" afterwards (dinner, in the wardroom) quite the leading spirit was

1 PAC RG7 G21 Vol. 594, 26371, Lt. Col. A.E. Belcher, Past President of Veterans of 1866.

2 Frances Donaldson, *Edward VIII* (London: Weidenfeld and Nicolson, 1986), p. 63; and Philip Ziegler, *King Edward VIII: The Official Biography* (London: Collins, 1990), p. 114.

3 Christopher Warwick, *Abdication* (London: Sidewick and Jackson, 1986), p. 31.

H.R.H., who finished the evening about 12:30 a.m. looking very hot and dishevelled, rather dirty about the shirt sleeves, with something round his neck that might once have been a collar.[4]

He stepped ashore in the New World at St. John's, Newfoundland, Britain's oldest colony, where he passed through a triumphal arch, "largely composed of drums of cod-liver oil, and hung with the carcases of dried cod-fish."[5] In spite of poor weather, the crowds were enormous and responded to the Prince with warmth and enthusiasm, especially when he mentioned the exemplary war record of the Newfoundland Regiment. A few days later he landed in Canada at St. John, New Brunswick, and, in his first speech on Dominion soil he articulated a theme to which he would return again and again:

> This is a red letter day for me, a day to which I have eagerly looked forward and which I can never forget. At the same time I do not feel that I have come to this great dominion as a stranger, since I have been so closely associated with dominion troops throughout the war. . . . I want Canada to look upon me as Canadian, if not actually by birth, yet certainly in mind and spirit, for this, as the eldest son of the ruler of the great British Empire, I can assure you that I am.[6]

He moved across the country on a tidal wave of patriotic euphoria. Not only were the crowds bigger than they had ever been, but their mood and psychology was different from that of pre-war crowds. As the Prince was to recollect later:

> The crowds proved so volatile and vigorous as to constitute at times an almost terrifying phenomenon. Uncontrolled, almost ferocious in their determination to satisfy their curiosity about me, they again and again broke through and swamped police lines. They snatched my handkerchief; they tried to tear the buttons off my coats.[7]

Frederick Griffin, a young newspaperman who was to follow all the Prince's visits to Canada for the *Toronto Star*, commented that the crowds in Montreal were particularly dense and noisy:

---

4 Hector Bolitho, *King Edward VIII: An Intimate Biography* (New York: Literary Guild of America, Inc., 1937), p. 98.

5 H.R.H. Edward, Duke of Windsor, *A King's Story: The Memoirs of the Duke of Windsor* (Toronto: Thomas Allen, 1951; New York: G.P. Putnam, 1952), p. 140.

6 Basil Maine, *The King's First Ambassador* (London: Hutchinson, 1935), p. 53.

7 Edward, *King's Story*, p. 141.

Signing the guest book in Halifax. The smile was brought on by somebody
in the crowd shouting, "Careful, sir, you're signing the pledge!"

If the Police had not been lusty, the Prince might have been suffocated
or clawed to death. The police, frightened, had excuse for being brutal.
Scratches on the Prince's neck showed where people had caught him
with their finger nails in their eagerness to touch him.[8]

Old Sir Joseph Pope, who was supposed to be in charge of the royal
tour because of his pre-war experience, had arranged for the Prince to
ride to a review in Toronto in a horse-drawn vehicle. As soon as the
Prince appeared the veterans broke ranks, and there was considerable
danger that the horses would panic and cause injuries. Eventually
Edward was lifted up and passed over the crowd to the podium from

---

8 Frederick Griffen, *Variety Show: Twenty Years of Watching the News Parade* (Toronto:
MacMillan, 1936), p. 70.

which he was to speak. Godfrey Thomas, H.R.H.'s private secretary, reported to his mother Queen Mary, "These were the most extraordinary days I have ever seen . . . half the people seemed to have taken leave of their senses."[9] Sir Joseph exclaimed, "I simply cannot understand what has come over the Canadian people, Sir! This utter lack of control, it is not at all what I had expected."[10] He had failed to grasp what the twenty-five year old Prince had intuitively understood, that relationships between monarch and people had been changed for ever. Prince Edward was never a remote figure, a marionette mechanically bowing and waving, but rather a golden-haired young man who moved among the people and made you feel as you shook his hand that, for a moment at least, he was genuinely delighted to have the opportunity of meeting you. He felt that his role was to give the aloof and mysterious institution of monarchy a new, popular, and "more democratic" image. Of course he already knew thousands of Canadians, having worked with the Canadian Corps in Flanders. *The Times* correspondent caught the spirit of these occasions well in an account of a ceremony at which the Prince bestowed decorations on returning soldiers or on their nearest relations:

> For each old mother or father, all of whom seemed to look into his face as if he himself was their son, for each pathetic widow, for each wounded soldier, he had an especial word of sympathy and praise and understanding, and not a short one either, so that before he gave them his left hand to shake after pinning on the medal won in the great struggle, he never stopped talking for a moment . . . for him and for the Empire this gift of human sympathy and kindliness is a great and valuable possession.[11]

A member of the royal party commented on the same ability in a larger context:

> . . . his happy way of making crowds no less than individuals feel that he meets them halfway. It is always quite obvious somehow that the huge masses of people who have thronged his movements everywhere feel his heart goes out to them as much as theirs to him, and the effect is (I use the word literally) indescribable.[12]

The Prince and his entourage moved across the country in a special train. At all the big cities he attended functions, and at innumerable

---

9 Ziegler, *Edward VIII*, p. 117.
10 Edward, *King's Story*, p. 141.
11 *Times*, September 4, 1919.
12 Ziegler, *Edward VIII*, p. 118.

country stations along the route he held impromptu socials off the back of the train. At Nipigon he spent a few days roughing it in a fishing camp with Indian guides. In Saskatoon, having watched a rodeo, he joined in the action by mounting a bronco and leading the cowboys in a gallop around the arena.[13]

The Prince was accompanied by a hastily assembled staff. In June, he wrote to the Duke of Devonshire, the Governor General of Canada, about the forthcoming tour:

> The question of Chief of Staff is still under discussion and I cannot as yet give his name. Several Generals and others have been suggested and two or three have been approached, but, up to the present, Lord Stanfordham has failed to get anybody to consent to go with me. However, by the end of this week we should be able to rope in somebody suitable.[14]

In spite of the hurry, it is interesting that several of those pressed into royal service at this time found themselves in it for life. This was certainly true of Admiral Halsey, who was finally appointed "Chief of Staff" to the Prince, and Captain of the Renown. He had had a distinguished career in the Royal Navy, including action ashore in the Boer War in the defence of Ladysmith, where he commanded a battery of 4.7-inch guns. He had fought in all the North Sea battles of the First World War. In 1919, Halsey was forty-seven, and his appointment reflected a desire on the part of King George V to have some mature advisors of the old school on his son's staff. Halsey had had some experience as a financial manager, and, as captain of the new battle cruiser New Zealand, and later the cruiser Australia, he had established a close association with those dominions. Indeed, during naval engagements he had worn a robe of kiwi feathers over his uniform, which had been given to him for protection by a Maori chief. Halsey's transparent honesty and good humour made him a valuable counsellor for the Prince, who would sometimes accept unpalatable advice from a mentor with such an obviously high sense of duty. Sir Charles Elliott recalled one such episode during the royal visit to Japan in 1922:

> But my most vivid recollection of him is a night interview on the Renown at which Admiral Halsey was present and gave him some sound advise as to behaviour in which I endeavoured occasionally to join. H.R.H. was sitting in a large high-backed armchair close to the wall, and as the sermon proceeded gradually wriggled upwards until he

---

13 W. Douglas Newton, *Westward with the Prince of Wales* (London: D. Appleton, 1920), p. 190.

14 PAC RG7 G23(2), H.R.H. to Duke of Devonshire, June 9, 1919.

"Joining the action" at a rodeo in Saskatoon, 1919.

squatted on the top of the back and from that elevation he regarded his two elderly monitors with a most impish and incredulous smile.[15]

Admiral Halsey was affectionately known as "the old salt" by the royal household. As the Prince's controller during the 1930s, it was his unpleasant duty to protest the extravagant bills being run up by Mrs. Simpson, and to point out to his royal master that the British public

15 Warwick, *Abdication*, p. 60.

would not accept her as Queen. He was sacked, provoking Lord Mountbatten—who had been Halsey's flag lieutenant—to exclaim: "the old salt fired? Its not true . . . I admire that marvellous man more than anyone I know."[16]

Godfrey Thomas was another important member of the party who remained on Edward's staff for many years. Unlike most of the Prince's intimates, he was a quiet man whose interests were of an intellectual kind. The Prince described him as "my greatest friend and the one man I can trust and who really understands me."[17] He remained as private secretary until Edward's accession to the throne. At that time he was offered the key position of private secretary to the new King. He declined the honour, perhaps because he was becoming increasingly alarmed with his "master's" extravagances and his secret plans for Mrs. Simpson. However, he did stay in royal service and remained a loyal friend to Edward. Some of the new appointees were already familiar and reassuring faces. Captain Piers Legh and Captain Lord Claude Hamilton had both served in the Grenadier guards during the war, and had spent some time acting as equerries to the Prince. In a letter to his mother from the front Edward had confided that Hamilton and Legh were, "my 2 great friends who are and have been real friends to me; I'm devoted to them."[18]

Lieutenant Colonel Edward Grigg was also a guardsman, and an inspired choice as speech writer. He was a brilliant man and had a deep interest in imperial affairs. For a decade he had been the editor in charge of reporting on colonial affairs at the *Times* of London, and he knew Canada well. On the one hand he avoided wounding Canadian susceptibilities, while on the other he "was able to inject that permissible amount of humour into the speeches he prepared for the Prince that they became the youthful utterances to be expected from a charming young man."[19] After touring Canada in 1919, and Australia and New Zealand the following year, he joined the staff of the Prime Minister. In 1925 he was appointed Governor of Kenya, and invited the Prince of Wales to visit him there in 1928.

The party was rounded out by Walter Peacock, who worked for the Duchy of Cornwall. He was not a "courtier" in the sense that the others were, but he played a key role in the establishment of the E.P. Ranch. He

---

16 J. Bryan III and Charles J.V. Murphy, *The Windsor Story* (New York: William Morrow, 1979), p. 183.

17 Lord Birkenhead, *Walter Monckton* (London: Weidenfield and Nicholson, 1969), p. 154.

18 Ziegler, *Edward VIII*, p. 75.

19 *Winnipeg Telegram*, December 3, 1919.

The Prince of Wales arrives at Calgary, to be greeted by Lieutenant
Governor Brett. Rear Admiral Sir Lionel Halsey looks on.

visited the ranch on several occasions, and looked after the ranch manager when he visited Britain.

On Sunday, September 14, the Prince arrived at Calgary, after spending an hour shooting gophers from the train on the way down from Edmonton! He attended church at the Pro-Cathedral and lunched at the country club. The fulsome rhetoric of the Calgary Herald is rather typical of the way in which his every move was reported:

> King George has done the supremely right thing in sending the Prince ... at this portentous period of the Empire's history, and the ready acquiescence of the gallant young Prince is just what might be expected of one who thus early in his predestined career of greatness, has gained, not only the respect, but the affection of the British People by his fine character and his most engaging qualities.[20]

Rather different qualities were displayed at the dinner given that night at the Ranchmen's Club. Colonel Henderson reported:

> The Provincial government saw fit to accord a special dispensation as to the liquor laws. The ranchmen rose to the occasion, and at one moment during the evening a judge of the Provincial supreme court saw fit to rise and sing a little song, the chorus of which runs: "another little drink won't do us any harm." The chairman, feeling that the evening was becoming a little too hilarious, caught my eye and obviously intended to quell the concert. I motioned to him, however, that he had a guest on his right who was by no means the least vociferous of those who were singing.[21]

On Monday morning there was a huge military parade at the Stampede Grounds and veterans, V.A.D.s, Cadets, boy scouts, and disabled war veterans were all inspected.

> It was a thrilling and inspiring sight—the wind whipped flags and bunting, the glorious old red, white and blue of the Union Jacks forming the background for the gorgeous royal standard floating above the platform, and the hot September sunshine of a perfect Calgary day pouring its benediction upon the tribute to Britain's imperishable glory, embodied in the person of the grave young man who stood at the salute. ... His radiant smile, infectious good-humour, genuine enjoyment, together with the perfect weather and loyal hearts, combine to make a day always to be remembered in Calgary's history.[22]

---

20 *Calgary Herald*, September 12, 1919.

21 PAC RG7 G23 Vol. 17(4) No. 29, Henderson to Duke of Devonshire, September 24, 1991.

22 *Calgary Herald*, September 15, 1919.

After this exacting morning and formal lunch, the royal entourage was able to leave Calgary to travel by train to High River, a small town some fifty kilometres south of the city. The Prince had asked that he should have the opportunity to learn how Canadians made their living, and he had been visiting factories, mines, and farms on his tour. He was fascinated by what he saw and retained information in the same way that he remembered the names of people he met. A few years later, a visitor to Fort Belvedere, who had no particular regard for the Prince, admitted that he was astounded at "the consummate knowledge he revealed of every remote corner of the Empire as he showed off a wall of framed maps in his living room."[23] Here, in the foothills of the Rocky Mountains, a visit had been arranged to the famous Bar U Ranch. This side trip was also designed to give the Prince a brief respite from the gruelling round of official engagements. Before the tour had begun, the Prince had written somewhat diffidently to the Governor General:

> I hope you won't mind my saying that I should very much appreciate an occasional free day, particularly when I go west or when visiting some district where there would be a chance of some form of sport or recreation. I am by nature rather a crank on exercise and get very stale if I have to go a long time without getting any at all.[24]

That this request was reasonable was proved by the fact that the Prince was dangerously close to collapse by the time he left Toronto, and desperately needed to spend a few days at a more relaxed pace. Edward's exhaustion was added to by his refusal to relax when he did have a chance. He reacted to stress by staying up later and later, talking and smoking incessantly. His friend and advisor Thomas berated the Prince for his lack of common sense:

> It is inconceivable to me that anyone who has got such sound, if perhaps somewhat exaggerated ideas about health from the point of view of exercise . . . should be so utterly insane and unreasonable about the elementary rules of health as regards other things. How you survived in Canada I cannot imagine . . . you are highly strung and nervous to begin with. You never allowed yourself a moment's rest the whole time. You sat up every night, often quite unnecessarily, 'til godless hours . . . you smoke far too much and drink a great deal too much whisky.[25]

23 Alastair Cooke, *Six Men* (London: Bodley Head, 1977), p. 51.

24 PAC RG7 G23(2), H.R.H. to Duke of Devonshire, June 9, 1919. For arrangements see PAC RG7 G23(5) No. 30–42, Lane to Henderson, June 27, 1919, and Henderson to Lane, August 25, 1919.

25 Ziegler, *Edward VIII*, p. 123.

Before the Prince could "escape" to the ranch, he had one more series of duties to perform in High River. The town was festooned with bunting and streamers, and there was a triumphal arch, two bands, and massed choirs . . . veterans were reviewed and a tree planted. "The Prince, by his thoroughly democratic appearance in both dress and manners, immediately enthroned himself in the hearts of the large crowd."[26]

Finally, duty done, the Prince entered a car and, followed by three others filled with royal staff, guns, and fishing tackle, they bumped and plunged the twenty or so kilometres to the Bar U. They arrived at about 6 p.m., and had time to explore the stables, and to pot a few ducks, before the light failed completely.

The Prince's host was George Lane, one of the most respected of the so called "cattle kings" and a co-founder of the Calgary Stampede. He was sixty-three when he welcomed the Prince of Wales to his ranch. His tall gaunt frame was somewhat stooped, and his long drooping moustache gave him rather a mournful air in contemporary photographs. However, he was reputed to have had a dry sense of humour and considerable wit and charm. There was absolutely no pretentiousness about him. He was always natural and sometimes this would come across as brusqueness. He was used to giving orders and did not suffer fools gladly.[27]

His career, which took him from young cowboy to become one of the acknowledged leaders of the Canadian cattle industry, seems almost too much of a romantic stereotype to be real. He was born in Des Moines, Iowa in 1856, and followed his father northward to the Montana goldfields as a teenager. He worked as cowboy, teamster, and Indian scout during the 1870s. In 1884, Fred Stimson, the energetic and able manager of the fledgling North West Cattle Company, wrote to the Montana Stock Growers' Association and asked them to recommend a good man to run his range operations. The Association suggested Lane, and he signed on as foreman of the Bar U. As was so often the case among cowboys, Lane started to run cattle on his own account, and by the early 1890s he was in a position to purchase his own place. First, he bought the Flying E Ranch in the Porcupine Hills, and later the YT on the Little Bow River. In 1902 The North West Cattle Company wound up its affairs on the death of the principal shareholder, Andrew Allen, and the Bar U was sold to a company organized by Lane. The deal involved thousands of acres of land, leases, stock, and buildings, and was one of

---

26 *High River Times*, September 18, 1919.

27 C.I. Ritchie, "George Lane, One of the Big Four," *Canadian Cattlemen*, Vol. 3, No. 2 (September, 1940); Edward Brado, *Cattle Kingdom: Early Ranching in Alberta* (Vancouver: Douglas and McIntyre, 1984), p. 124; and Newton, *Westward with the Prince*, p. 203.

Watching cowboys at work, the corral at the Bar U.
Archie McLean, George Lane, and the Prince of Wales.

the biggest ranch transactions in the North West to that date. Lane now owned the ranch on which he had once worked for $100 a month.

As Lane's fortunes rose so did his role as a leader of the cattlemen's interests. As Vice-President of the Western Stock Grower's Association he visited Ottawa in 1912 and lobbied the Prime Minister and the Minister of the Interior to establish a commission to investigate conditions in the ranch industry. His submission to that commission shows his firm grasp of contemporary problems. In 1919, Lane was the driving force behind the establishment of the Cattlemen's Protective Association of Western Canada. This banding together of the major interests in the range cattle industry took over the role of the defunct Western Stock Grower's Association and formally amalgamated with that body in 1920. The new association quickly became an effective modern lobby group.

Thus the Prince's host knew the cattle business from end to end. He had demonstrated both practical skills and managerial acumen, and had also gained the support of his peers. A number of anecdotes are told about Lane's relationship with the Prince of Wales; they centre round his refusal to be awed by the future king. Probably they have gained in the

Cutting out cattle, Bar U. H.R.H., A.E. Cross, and George Lane.

telling and do not bear repeating; however, two things are beyond dispute: first, Lane always addressed H.R.H. as "Prince," and second, this did not prevent the old rancher and the young "royal" from establishing a friendly relationship based on mutual respect.

His first morning on the ranch the Prince got up early and slipped from the house unnoticed for a run. It seems likely that he went southward from the ranch house to climb the rounded hills from which he would have been able to look down on the Bedingfeld Ranch, the winding wooded valley of Pekisko Creek, and the shining Rocky Mountains illuminated in the morning sun.

After breakfast the party rode to the foothills and watched the round-up and fall branding of some Bar U cattle. The Prince rode Mrs. Alex Flemming's horse with young Mr. Ives' saddle. He is reported to have

Watching branding at the Bar U. Professor Carlyle is to the left of H.R.H.

shown "horsemanship that was delightful to see."[28] He remarked that he was "darn glad he wasn't a calf!" and declined to have a go at branding because, he said, "I don't understand the work and I might inflict some unnecessary suffering on the beast."[29] The incident that impressed the locals most occurred late in the morning when there was a severe shower. The Prince was offered a ride back to the ranch in a car, but declined and road home soaking wet to lunch. In the afternoon he still had the energy to go for a stiff walk to shoot "prairie chickens." He left the ranch at about 6 p.m., having written "some ranch" in the guest book, and having let it be known that he had enjoyed his stay enormously. "I spent 24 hours at the ranch, I wish it could have been 24 years." As the Prince passed once again through the triumphal arch at High River to climb into his railway car "Killarney," he was heard to remark that he was going to return. The party arrived back in Calgary in time to attend a big dance at the armoury that evening. The Prince's stamina was truly amazing.

---

28 *High River Times*, September 18, 1919.

29 *Calgary Herald*, September 17, 1919.

Next day the Prince went off to Banff to meet the Stoney Indians and to become "Chief Morning Star," while the bunting was cleared up at High River; the children returned to their lessons; and the town elders congratulated themselves on a job well done. However, as he travelled through the Rockies to Field and Golden, and on to Vancouver and Victoria, the Prince was mulling over his ranching experience. He wrote to his mother that he would love to work on a ranch for a few months, "that's a real life."[30] One witness, Mrs. Yule, suggested that the Prince had already talked to her father, Professor Carlyle, as they overlooked the Bedingfeld Ranch, and said how much he would like to own a place like that.[31] Colonel Henderson, who, as an aide to the Governor General, was responsible for insuring that the tour ran smoothly, also claimed credit for suggesting the purchase of the ranch to the Prince:

> The visit to the Bar U was an unqualified success. I am more than pleased with this in that some of the party were rather bored with the idea of going there. As a result of the visit H.R.H. is today intimating to His Majesty confidentially that he proposes to purchase a ranch in this vicinity, and the telegram is so worded that it does not give his Royal Highness (the king) much opportunity of saying that he thinks it inadvisable . . . the scheme emanated from myself, and it is roughly that a Pedigree shorthorn herd be established, together with the introduction of a few thoroughbred horses for the purpose of breeding a high class horse suitable for range work, with the ultimate idea of breeding a polo pony type of horse.[32]

On September 29 or 30, the Prince telegraphed George Lane and asked him to meet the royal train at Fort Macleod as it headed back east. Lane just had time to contact the Bedingfelds to confirm that they were prepared to sell before hurrying south to the station. Apparently a deal was struck; Lane would purchase the ranch on the Prince's behalf, and Professor Carlyle (a distinguished veterinarian working for Lane) would run it for him.[33] On October 7, a deed of sale was executed between Frank Bedingfeld and his mother Agnes on the one hand and George Lane on the other. It involved 1,440 freehold acres at $25 an acre and a half share in 41,440 acres of leased land. There were also 400 head of horses and 150 cattle. The total price was $130,000.[34] The Prince

---

30 Ziegler, *Edward VIII*, p. 119.

31 GA M3973 f. 16, Typescript of interview by George Gooderham of Mrs. Helen (Charles) Yule, daughter of Professor W.L. Carlyle.

32 PAC RG7 G23 Vol. 17(4) No. 29, Henderson to Duke of Devonshire, September 24, 1919.

33 PAC RG7 G23 Vol. 19(10) No. 80–90, Henderson to Halsey, n.d.

34 GA M2398 f. 162, Agreement for Sale and Purchase, 1919.

"Chief Morning Star," Banff, 1919.

announced his purchase in his farewell speech in Winnipeg.

> I shall not say goodbye to western Canada, but only au revoir. I think this western spirit must be very catching, at least I know I've caught it very badly. I feel so much at home here by this time that I want to have a permanent home among the people of the west, a place where I can come sometimes and live for a while. To this end I recently purchased a small ranch in southern Alberta and I shall look forward to developing it and making it my own . . . the atmosphere of western Canada appeals to me intensely, the free, vigorous, hopeful spirit of westerners not only inspires me, but makes me feel happy and at home.[35]

It is important to put this purchase in context. It was not something that the Prince did all the time. In fact he was often to remark that the ranch was the only property he owned. On later tours to Australia and New Zealand, India, or South Africa, he never made any moves to acquire a pied-à-terre. Why now? What were the pressing motives which drove the Prince to take an action which he knew would be questioned by his father? Thirty years later in his autobiography, *A King's Story,* Edward recalled his motives like this:

> the fact is, my impulse in making this investment . . . was far removed from imperial politics. In the midst of that majestic countryside I had suddenly been overwhelmed by an irresistible longing to immerse my-self, if only momentarily, in the simple life of the western Prairies. There, I was sure, I would find occasional escape from the sometimes too confining too well ordered island life of Great Britain.[36]

Certainly, the ranch was in a beautiful setting. In September a profusion of flowers and shrubs were blooming around the house, while the trees along the creek were beginning to turn colour. The Prince was not the first British visitor to become intoxicated with the beauty of the foothills country. Many upper-middle class English men and women, and several titled individuals, had settled in the area, and part of the lure was undoubtedly the aesthetic appeal of the region. Author Ronald Rees steeped himself in the letters, poems, and art work, of newcomers to the foothills and concluded that "probably no pioneer country elicited so much praise from settlers and visitors alike."[37]

At first, it seemed likely that the Prince's immediate attraction to the area might have been due in part to his recognition of a familiar social

---

35 *High River Times,* October 16, 1919.

36 Edward, *King's Story,* p. 152.

37 Ronald Rees, *New and Naked Land: Making the Prairies Home* (Saskatoon: Western Producer, 1988), p. 137.

The Prince of Wales riding at the Bar U.

environment. The neighbourhood of the ranch had been settled by "gentlemen immigrants" who had re-created many of the attributes of English country life. However, there is no evidence of the Prince attending race meetings, hunts, polo, or even church. His new Albertan friends like Lane, Burns, and Newton were not expatriates or particularly "upper crust." Rather, the Prince seems to have been drawn to the mystique of the "wild west": branding, roping, and calf-wrestling. He even organized a rodeo on one of his visits.

Undoubtedly, the Prince saw the ranch as a get-away where he could pursue a number of his favourite activities. There were unlimited opportunities for walking, fishing, shooting, and above all for riding.

During his teens the young Prince had had to be pushed into learning to ride by his father. However, during his time at Oxford he hunted regularly, and on his return to England after purchasing the ranch, hunting became a passion with him. There is no doubt that he always enjoyed riding and helping to work cattle on the ranch.

On a deeper level, the purchase of the ranch may have been linked to the Prince's relationship with his father, which was generally strained and unhappy. George V is reported to have said, "My father was frightened of his mother; I was frightened of my father; and I am damn well going to see that my children are frightened of me."[38] He was certainly successful in inspiring fear in his sons. The story is told that, when Prince Henry arrived late for breakfast, he was so nervous that one furious look from the King was enough to make him faint. Walter Monckton recalls an interesting conversation with Edward's brother, George VI. The King explained:

> It was difficult for David. My father was so inclined to go for him. I always thought that it was a pity that he found fault with him over unimportant things, like what he wore. This only put David's back up. But it was a pity that he did things which he knew would annoy my father. The result was that they did not discuss the important things quietly.[39]

On one memorable occasion a courtier overheard the King bellow at the Prince of Wales, "You dress like a cad. You act like a cad. You are a cad. Get out!"[40] The Prince's longtime friend and confidant, Freda Dudley Ward, commented:

> His (the king's) strictness only chafed David and led to rows. He became more bitter—David I mean—and more and more despondent as time passed, and the rows became hotter. He was a grown man now and he resented his father ordering him to button his jacket or straighten his tie.[41]

Just before leaving for Canada the Prince had insisted on moving out of Buckingham Palace, and had established himself at York House. "I'm not going to be wet-nursed or interfered with any more."[42] Perhaps the

---

38 Brian Inglis, *Abdication* (New York: MacMillan, 1966), p. 9. This oft-cited quotation may be apocryphal; see Kenneth Rose, *King George V* (London: Papermac, 1983), p. 57.

39 Birkenhead, *Monckton*, p. 124.

40 Bryan and Murphy, *Windsor Story*, p. 69.

41 Bryan and Murphy, *Windsor Story*, p. 69.

42 Ziegler, *Edward VIII*, p. 170.

purchase of the ranch was also an act of defiant independence—another attempt to distance himself from his hectoring father.

The Prince's difficulties with his father were closely linked to the way he viewed his "job." "The King loved everything old, the Prince loved everything new (possibly in reaction) and they were separated by a generation gap that had been unnaturally widened by the war."[43] George V, consciously or unconsciously, had reacted to his father's flamboyant lifestyle and insured that his court was dull, respectable, and governed by an unchanging and traditional round of events and activities. He became the guardian of standards of piety and behaviour that had become "old fashioned" to many of the younger generation.[44] A sense of duty and the responsibility of his position were so deeply imbued in his character that he would never have dreamt of questioning his lot. The Prince of Wales, on the other hand, was often to rail against his royal station. During the war he had resented being kept, as he saw it, "in a glass case." He "disliked intensely those humiliating precautions which were the due badge of his rank, and craved instead the still higher privilege of sharing the common lot."[45] Back in peacetime London, and humiliated to the point of tears by his father's bullying, he exclaimed:

> I want no more of this Princing! I want to be an ordinary person. I must have a life of my own. . . . What does it take to be a good king? You must be a figurehead, a wooden man! Do nothing to upset the Prime Minister or the Court or the Archbishop of Canterbury! Show yourself to the people! Mind your manners! Go to church! What modern man wants that kind of life?[46]

Later he spoke to his friend and confidant, Walter Monckton, about the prospect of becoming king. He could not bear to feel that he would be cooped up in Buckingham Palace all the time within iron bars. The people must take him as he was, a man different from his father and determined to be himself.[47]

During his almost constant interaction with soldiers during the war, and in the steady stream of post-war engagements which he carried out, Prince Edward began to develop a way of discharging his public duties which was in keeping with his personality. Of course, he faced disapproval from the royal establishment. The Victorian view of kingship

---

43 Donaldson, *Edward VIII*, p. 60.

44 Hector Bolitho, *A Century of British Monarchy* (London: Longmans and Green, 1951), p. 182.

45 Inglis, *Abdication*, p. 13.

46 Bryan and Murphy, *Windsor Story*, p. 69.

47 Birkenhead, *Monckton*, p. 127.

was summarized by the political journalist Walter Bageshot. "Above all things your royalty is to be reverenced and if you begin to poke about it, you cannot reverence it, we must not let in daylight upon magic."[48] When the Prince of Wales asked Sir Frederick Ponsonby, Keeper of the Privy Purse, how he thought he was getting on, Ponsonby replied:

> If I may say so, Sir, I think there is a risk in your making yourself too accessible. The monarchy must always retain an element of mystery. A Prince should not show himself too much. The monarchy must remain on a pedestal.[49]

The Prince replied that times had changed since the war, and he felt that one of his tasks was to bring the institution nearer the people. "To hell with precedents!! They won't wash nowadays."[50] These were somewhat revolutionary sentiments, and the tensions which they created must have been hard to bear. Before leaving for Canada the Prince visited the Countess of Airlie, who had been his mother's lady in waiting for fifty years, and she commented shrewdly on his state of mind:

> He sat for over an hour on a stool in front of the fire smoking one cigarette after another and talking his heart out. He was nervous and frustrated, pulled this way and that. The Queen had told me that she was urging the King to keep him in England, "to learn how to govern" as she put it, and make up for the gap in his constitutional experience caused by the war. Mr. Lloyd George on the other hand had evolved a plan for a series of Empire tours for the heir to the throne, to strengthen relations with the peoples of the Commonwealth. The King was inclining to this idea, and the Prince himself preferred it.[51]

The overwhelming success of his Canadian tour helped to mature and develop the Prince's character. It "gave him self-confidence when he most needed it. . . . Canada helped to confirm and give point to his character."[52] As H.R.H. wrote years later:

> My first days in Canada were in some ways the most exhilarating that I have ever known . . . my private evaluation of my own worth had

48 Tom MacDonell, *Daylight Upon Magic: The Royal Tour of Canada, 1939* (Toronto: MacMillan, 1989), p. 91.

49 This story is widely reported; see Philip Ziegler, *Crown and People* (London: Collins, 1978), p. 34. Ponsonby hardly mentions the Prince of Wales in his memoirs: Sir Frederick Ponsonby, *Recollections of Three Reigns* (London: Eyre and Spottiswoode, 1951).

50 Ziegler, *Edward VIII*, p. 110.

51 Donaldson, *Edward VIII*, p. 66.

52 Maine, *King's First Ambassador*, p. 54.

previously not been particularly high, but the Canadians in their kindly enthusiasm almost convinced me that they liked me for myself, an act of openheartedness that did my ego no end of good.[53]

Elsewhere he wrote, "I do like these Canadians so much, they are charming and so kind and hospitable if one takes them the right way and if they take to you."[54] That Canadians had taken to him was obvious, one astute observer concluded:

> It almost takes one's breath away. It is not merely loyalty to the crown, but the expression of a deep, spontaneous affection for the young man who is heir to the oldest throne in the world. . . . The Prince has something to offer that can come from no other human being. He symbolizes the unity of the whole Empire, and does it with the joyousness and courage that belongs to youth.[55]

But the tour was not only a personal triumph; to the Prince it was a vindication of his perception of kingship. The western spirit which he mentioned in his speech at Winnipeg as being, "free, vigourous, and hopeful," accorded perfectly with his vision of a new kind of monarchy. He wanted to create something new and he dreamt that his ranch could be both a get-away from the pressures of princehood and the carping criticism of his father, and also a symbol of a new and exciting relationship with the peoples of the emerging commonwealth of nations, which was evolving from the more rigid structure of the "Empire."

As the royal entourage sailed home in H.M.S. Renown, the Prime Minister was able to boast of the outcome of his plan to use the Prince of Wales to bind the Dominions more firmly to the mother country:

> The throne means a great deal to this country. It means even more to the Empire. Throughout all climes, through all continents, there is no institution, Parliament, laws, ecclesiastical organizations, not even language, of which it can be said that it is common to the whole Empire. But the throne unites them all. You have only to read what happened in Canada to see that the Empire is stronger today for that tour. The welcome was not an organized one; it welled from the hearts of a brave people, and you can see it in every line that comes from Canada and in

53 Edward, *King's Story*, p. 143. His words echo those of his father on the occasion of his Silver Jubilee in May 1935. See Bolitho, *Century of British Monarchy*, p. 183. It is ironic that a tour of Canada was to play a similar role in giving Edward's brother, George VI, a new confidence in his ability to fill the part that had been thrust upon him. "That tour made us!" Queen Elizabeth was to tell Mackenzie King. MacDonell, *Daylight Upon Magic*, p. 268.

54 Ziegler, *Edward VIII*, p. 120.

55 Ziegler, *Edward VIII*, p. 120.

every word you hear of what happened there. The Prince of Wales struck the right note. He greeted Canada as a nation, as a nation which had won the spurs of nationhood in the great conflict of the nations for freedom and civilization, and that was part of his success.[56]

It did not escape the Prince that it was precisely by ignoring the conventional views of his father and the old guard and going his own way, that he had made a success of his tour beyond anything which had been seen before.[57]

56 Warwick, *Abdication*, p. 53.

57 Donaldson, *Edward VIII*, p. 74.

II

The Physical and Historic Setting of the E.P. Ranch

Faith! 'tis a land as green as the sea,
That rolls as far and rolls as free
with drifts of flowers, so many there be,
where the cattle roam and rest.[1]

The purchase of a ranch in southern Alberta by the heir to the throne of Great Britain must have led to a flurry of speculation in London. Where exactly was this property? How did one get there? What was it like? What kind of people would now become "royal neighbours"? The aim of this chapter is to answer some of these questions, and to examine the physical and historical setting of the E.P. Ranch. The chapter can be divided into three sections: in the first, the location of the ranch is described and its situation relative to the relief and geology of the region is discussed. The outstanding characteristics of the climate are introduced, and the variability and regional diversity of conditions are stressed. In the second section, the settlement history of the foothills is outlined. The role played by the Canadian government in encouraging the range cattle industry is contrasted with the situation across the border in the United States. Finally, in the last section of the chapter, the Bedingfeld family, from whom the Prince bought the ranch, is introduced. As immigrants from Britain, blessed with advantages in terms of education and imbued with a strong sense of Imperial unity, the Bedingfelds fitted into the social milieu of the foothills without difficulty. Starting from a nucleus of two homestead grants, they gradually increased their deeded land base until they were in a position to offer the Prince a flourishing small ranch of two and a half sections. In this way, the origins of the Prince's new ranch dated back to the beginnings of European settlement in the region.

There are three routes southward from the Bow Valley to the Crow's Nest Pass and the Oldman River (Map 1). The most westerly, Route 40,

---

1 Moira O'Neill, *Songs of the Glens of Antrim* (London, 1910), p. 58.

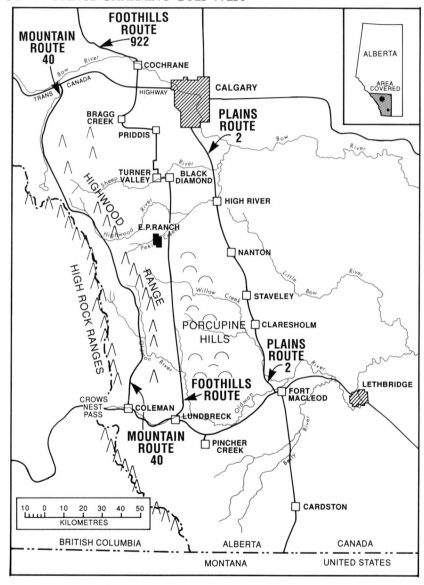

Map 1. The location of the E.P. Ranch, Pekisko, Alberta.

takes one down the Kananaskis Valley into the Upper Highwood Valley. The route lies within the front ranges of the Rocky Mountains, close to the Continental Divide, and follows deep glaciated valleys flanked by shear rock faces and jagged mountain peaks which reach 2,500–3,000 metres. The easterly route, taken by the main highway to Fort Macleod, passes through rolling agricultural countryside. The elevators at Nanton, Staveley, and Claresholm bear witness to the importance of grain farming. The middle route, from Cochrane through Bragg Creek and Priddis to Lundbreck, has been, until recently, a well kept secret. It leads through the heart of the foothills—some of the most appealing country in western Canada.

Scale has much to do with this attraction, for the foothills country does not possess the awe-inspiring magnificence of the mountains, nor the man-dwarfing horizontal extent of the plains. Vision is sometimes limited by forested hillside and tortuous valley, but the switch-back relief allows startling glimpses first of snow-capped mountains and then of rolling plains. "It has openness without the vast monotony of the Prairie country and ruggedness without the impenetrability of the mountains."[2] Each valley and ridge has its own attributes, from the steep, heavily forested slopes around Bragg Creek, to the aspen Parklands rising toward the Porcupine Hills, to the sage-brush grasslands of the upper Oldman River. Together they make up a kaleidoscope of micro-environments captivating to native and visitor alike.

The general trend of the country is from northwest to southeast. The massive horizontally bedded Mesozoic sandstones and shales of the plains have been folded and faulted to form a series of ridges and valleys. Sandstone bedrock is often exposed along the crests of the ridges, and loose debris litters some valley slopes. Here and there streams have cut through superficial glacial deposits to expose dark shales. To the east, the ridges rise less than 100 metres above the high plains, while to the west, they reach 500–800 metres or more above the valley floors. The rounded and forested foothills give way abruptly to the massive grey up-thrust limestones of the front range of the Rocky Mountains (Map 2).

As is the case with so many landscapes in Alberta, it is glaciation which is responsible for the details of the relief. Preglacial river valleys were widened and deepened to form great U-shaped trenches. Immense thicknesses of glacial debris were deposited as the glaciers receded, only to be reworked by meltwater streams. Moraine ridges, outwash plains, the floors of glacial lakes, and river terraces cut into glacial deposits mask the underlying geology and add diversity to the physical landscape.

---

2 Sheilagh S. Jameson, "The Country—Before Settlement," in Lewis G. Thomas (ed.) *Our Foothills* (Calgary: Millarville, Kew, Priddis, and Bragg Creek Historical Society, 1975), p. 7.

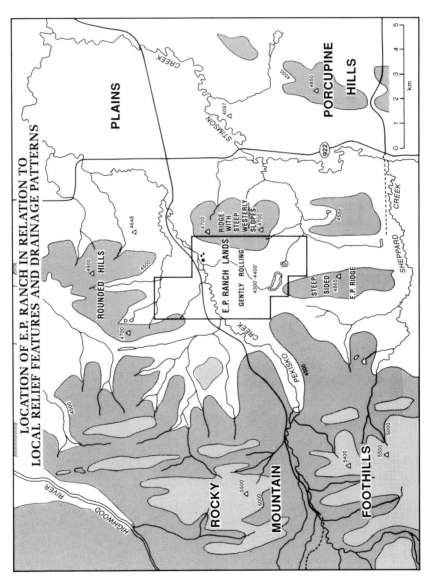

Map 2. The location of the E.P. Ranch, in relation to local relief features and drainage patterns.

The E.P. Ranch lies just within the first low ridge of the foothills (Map 3). From the summit of these rounded hills, one can look north-eastward down Pekisko Creek as it winds out into the plains. The land is for the most part fenced and cropped. Due east across Stimson Creek an outlying forested finger of the Porcupine Hills reaches northward, while to the south the ranch lands stretch almost level for more than two kilometres to a lake. Beyond the lake, a very steep-sided ridge forms a conspicuous landmark which has been named the "E.P. Ridge." West-ward, the foreground is dominated by the heavily wooded flood plain of Pekisko Creek, while across the river, rounded ridges are covered with natural grassland and pockets of scrub. In the middle distance, forested foothills rise to 1,800 metres and form a frieze for the bare grey mass of the Rocky Mountain Front Ranges which rise abruptly above them. The *Times* correspondent described the site of the ranch during a visit in 1923:

> The livestock barns for cattle, sheep, and horses, lie to the east, and with the headquarters building form a crescent-shaped group facing south, all situated at about 3,400 feet above sea level [actually 4,200 feet: 1,280 metres], in a sunny hollow, with a background of sheltering poplars and willows, through which a tributary branch of the High River winds in a gravelly, tortuous and, in some places, beautiful course. The low wooded hills to the east, where the ranch boundary line and the watershed run together, form ideal short grass pasture for sheep, and are fringed at the bases with sheltering bluffs of polar and willow. At a considerable distance to the west, whence come the warm winds of spring, are to be seen the sharply jagged peaks of the Rocky Mountains ranged over rolling grass country.[3]

The climate of the foothills region is the result of the interaction of three major air masses: cold, dry arctic air moving down from the Mac-kenzie Valley; warm, moist tropical air from the Gulf of Mexico, which has been profoundly modified by the time it reaches the Canadian bor-der; and warm, dry air descending from the west as the famed "Chinook" wind. The mountains effectively seal off Alberta from the modifying influence of the Pacific Ocean. The province experiences a continental climate with a high range of temperature between winter and summer. During the winter much of the province is dominated for long periods by very cold arctic air. Bitter cold is made more bearable by long hours of sunshine and low wind speeds associated with anticyclonic conditions. Frontal activity produces severe winter storms when warmer less, dense air is undercut by colder, more dense arctic air. The severity of the winter is broken, especially along the mountain front and in the foothills, by incursions of warmer air from the Pacific. This air loses its

---

3 *Times*, October 13, 1923.

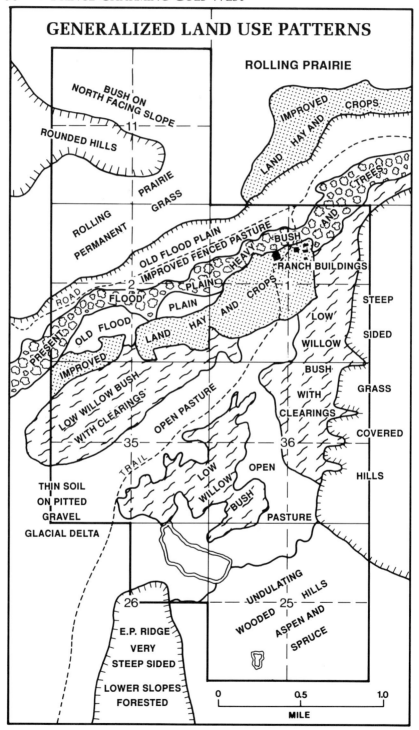

Map 3. E.P. Ranch, generalized land use patterns.

The site of the E.P. Ranch, Pekisko, Alberta.

moisture as it is forced to rise on the windward side of the cordillera, and is warmed as it descends the leeward slopes, and pressure increases.[4]

Moira O'Neill, the Irish-born wife of an Alberta rancher and an accomplished poet, describes the mechanics of the climate in less prosaic language:

> All the months of winter are months of conflict between the north and the west winds. We watch the powers of the air fighting over us. . . . While the northwind blows, every breathing thing shrinks and cowers. The mere holding on to life is a struggle for poor unsheltered animals and the longer it lasts the harder is the struggle, and the less their strength for it. But here comes a change in the air. Some night on looking out we see that the clouds have rolled upwards, as if a curtain were lifted in the west, leaving a well-defined arch of clear sky with stars shining in it. That arch means that the west wind, the preserver, is on his way; and sometimes we hear his voice beforehand in a long, distant roar among the mountains. When next morning breaks, the north wind has fled, overcome. You may go to the house door in a dressing-gown to look out on the snowy prairie, and the Chinook blowing over

---

4 John Stewart Marsh, "The Chinook and its Geographical significance in Southern Alberta," (unpublished M.A. Thesis, University of Calgary, 1975).

you feels like a warm bath. It seems miraculous. All living things are revived and gladdened.[5]

Climatic statistics show that Pekisko experiences five months with average temperatures below zero (Appendix C). Average winter temperatures tend to be slightly higher than for places further east, because of the higher frequency of the Chinook closer to the mountains. The average annual rainfall amounts to seventy centimetres, again considerably more than on the plains to the east. Although nearly half this total falls as snow, there is a marked summer maximum of rainfall, associated with frontal activity and the advance of tropical maritime air from the Gulf of Mexico. Occasionally too, moist, warm Pacific air may be drawn in from the south and west.

Although the general mechanics of climate in southern Alberta are well understood, and the statistics referred to are averages from more than thirty years of careful observations, the reality of the foothills climate is even more complex. Marked seasonal departures from the norm are the rule. Some winters are long, bitter, and accompanied by deep snowfalls. During others the temperature may seldom drop below freezing, and the land remains clear of snow for long periods. Similar variability characterizes the amount and distribution of annual precipitation. Moreover, the relief of the region results in dramatic spatial disparities. One valley may enjoy adequate moisture while another may undergo drought.

Some comparative generalizations can be made about foothills' climates in general and that of the Pekisko valley in particular. Firstly, these are upland climates. The ranch stands at about 1,300 metres, and this means that temperatures are lower and the growing season shorter. Secondly, the cloud cover associated with the mountains tends to reduce summer temperatures and thus the total degree days experienced. This produces a contradictory climate in which stock flourish outside during all but the most severe winters, and yet crops and garden vegetables may be blighted by either a late spring or an early fall frost. One year a hay crop may be burned by drought while in the next it may be threatened with mildew.

The foothills form a narrow southward extension of the aspen parkland vegetation zone. Groves of aspen poplars are interspersed with open grassland, while higher ridges may be dominated by coniferous forest and valley bottoms with a tangled mixture of willows and aspen. This is an ecotone, an area of transition, where the extent of aspen grove and

---

5 Moira O'Neill, "A Lady's Life on a Ranch," *Blackwood's Edinburgh Magazine*, Vol. 163 (January 1898), p. 7. O'Neill was married to Walter Skrine, and the couple owned a ranch west of High River for some years around the turn of the century.

grassland is a reflection of human activity, especially burning and grazing. Recently, cutting and clearing have played a significant role. Since the ranch land was first homesteaded, a constant battle has been waged against encroaching brush, and everything has been done to encourage the growth of grass. There has also been a steady increase in the extent of the ploughed area. During the 1920s a few fields were broken on the low terraces to the west of the ranch house; today almost all of the land southward to the lake is cropped.

The foothills region, in which the E.P. Ranch was located, was the cradle in which large scale cattle ranching in western Canada was nurtured.[6] In 1881, the federal government promulgated regulations under which tracts of the North-West Territories could be leased for grazing purposes. The terms were very attractive, for Prime Minister MacDonald was hopeful that generous terms would attract British and Canadian capital to the Canadian west. He was aware that a flood of capital from Great Britain was underwriting the "beef bonanza" to the south, on the Great Plains of the United States. Therefore, leases of up to 100,000 acres were made available for twenty-one years at a rental of one cent per acre per year.[7]

The response to this new legislation was immediate and overwhelming. In 1882 alone, 154 applications for leases were received and seventy five leases were authorized covering an area of more than four million acres. The estimated number of stock on the range rose from 9,000 head in 1881 to more than 100,000 in 1886. The newly capitalized ranch companies purchased herds from among the best range cattle in Montana and Idaho, and trailed them north to stock their leases.[8] The piece-meal, small scale growth of ranching which had been taking place during the 1870s was overwhelmed and engulfed by these developments.

The early leases formed a compact block of townships reaching from the international border northwards to the Bow River. The line of the Whoop-Up Trail ran through the middle of this block and there was little penetration of the grasslands for more than twenty miles eastward from

---

6 For general descriptions of the establishment and expansion of ranching in the Canadian West see: D.H. Breen, *The Canadian Prairie West and the Ranching Frontier, 1874–1924* (University of Toronto Press, 1983); Edward Brado, *Cattle Kingdom: Early Ranching in Alberta* (Toronto: Douglas and McIntyre, 1984); and Simon M. Evans, "Ranching in the Canadian West, 1882–1912" (unpublished Ph.D. Dissertation, University of Calgary, 1976).

7 For details concerning the legislation and an analysis of the reasons for its proposal, see, Simon M. Evans, "Spatial Aspects of the Cattle Kingdom: The First Decade," in A.W. Rasporich and H.C. Klassen (eds.) *Frontier Calgary: Town City, and Region, 1875–1914,* (Calgary: McClelland and Stewart West, 1975).

8 Simon M. Evans, "Stocking the Canadian Range," *Alberta History,* Vol. 26, No. 3 (Summer 1978), pp. 1–9.

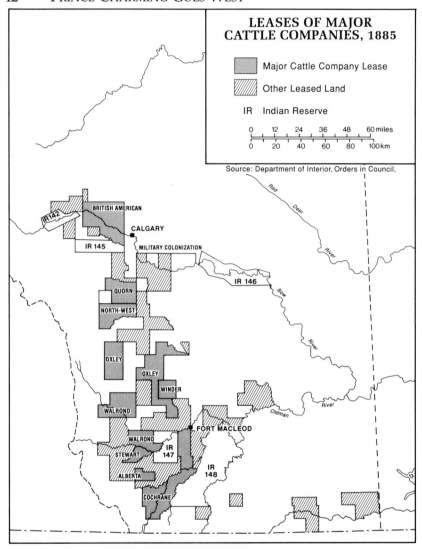

Map 4. Leases of major cattle companies, 1885.

this axis. (Map 4) The area of foothills country so described had certain marked physical advantages for the range cattle industry. It was frequently influenced by Chinook winds, which meant that winter feed was more abundant. Secondly, the varied topography and wooded coulees provided shelter from winter storms on the one hand, and discouraged farming activity on the other. Finally, this area had a higher and more reliable rainfall than did areas further east, and was watered by a number of mountain-fed streams which provided drinking water even in dry years.

These advantages were well understood by those who took out the original leases. Macoun and Begg had eulogized the Bow Valley in their widely circulated book, *Manitoba and the Great North-West.*[9] This publication certainly influenced Senator Cochrane when he came west to select a site for his lease. Duncan McEachran, who was to become the influential manager of the Waldron Ranch, published a glowing report in the eastern press in 1881, while the widespread coverage of the Governor General's western tour stoked the fires of optimism.[10] Ex-Mounted Policemen like Superintendent Winder and Inspector W.F. Shurtliff, who had been ranching in the area for years, advised their eastern friends. Latecomers followed the lead of the knowledgeable and experienced, for many had neither visited the west, nor could distinguish between good range and bad. Some would-be ranchers applied for blocks of lease land "sight-unseen," only to find that their lands were entirely made up of steep forested mountain slopes.

In western Canada, the frenetic growth of the five years from 1881 to 1885 was a response to government initiatives and took place within a well established legal framework. The lessee of grazing land could rely on the support of the North-West Mounted Police to establish his rights against squatters or Indian poachers. At the same time, the Department of Agriculture was actively promoting the sale of cattle in Great Britain, and establishing regulations to insure the health and quality of Canadian cattle exports. This was in marked contrast to the conditions on the Great Plains of the United States.[11] Here, the cattle boom, that explosive surge of men, stock, and capital onto the western rangelands, occurred outside the protection offered by the law. The cattlemen were regarded "as merely an advanced screen ahead of the real conquerors of the land, the pioneer farmers."[12] In this case at least, Canada did not model her land policy on United States precedent; instead she drew on legislation

---

9 John Macoun, *Manitoba and the Great North West* (Guelph: World Publishing, 1882). Author of the chapter titled "Stock raising in the Bow Valley District compared to Montana" was Alexander Begg.

10 F.W. Godsal, "Old Times," *Alberta Historical Review*, Vol. 12 (Autumn 1964), p. 19. Later Lord Lorne was to establish the Alberta Ranch with his equerry, de Winton.

11 Simon M. Evans, "The Origins of Ranching in Western Canada: American Diffusion or Victorian Transplant?" In L.A. Rosenvall and Simon M. Evans (eds.) *Essays on the Historical Geography of the Canadian West* (Geography Department, University of Calgary, 1987).

12 Ernest Staples Osgood, *The Day of the Cattleman* (Chicago: University of Chicago Press, 1929), p. 194.

evolved in Natal and Australia.[13] Thus the ranching frontier in the Canadian west developed in a very different atmosphere from that of the United States.

These deeply significant legal and political contrasts were underwritten by far-reaching social differences. As David Breen concluded:

> What is observed here is not a community of innovators seeking a release from the restraints of traditional ways, but rather a society vigorously attempting, and with general success, to recreate the kind of community in which they had been nurtured and had found congenial.[14]

Even before the lease legislation was passed, the scattered population of small ranchers were hardly typical "frontiersmen." Many were former members of the North-West Mounted Police drawn from eastern middle-class backgrounds, while the presence of Englishmen "of good family" was often mentioned by visitors. On the one hand, ranching required much larger initial investment than did farming; on the other, it allowed a division between owner and his employees which could insure a leisured lifestyle for the former. Under the umbrella of economic success and political power achieved by a handful of major cattle companies a ranch-based society was established. Their ranks were continually added to as contacts in the old country provided introductions and support in the new. The arrivals were drawn into a group which was firmly bound together by common advantages of education, relative affluence, and the pursuit of leisure, especially if it involved horses. Professor Thomas, himself the son of a rancher, observes: "Perhaps no pioneer community ever devoted so much time to amusement. The ranchers had both leisure and exemplary training in its use."[15] Sheilagh Jameson echoes his comments:

> . . . for the most part greater emphasis was placed on living, or on the art of living, one might say, than the process of making a living. . . . In

---

13 During 1903, R.H. Campbell reviewed the situation with reference to grazing leases in western Canada. He compared practices in other parts of the world and observed, "In Australia, from which the lease system which has been followed in Canada is borrowed, the history has been rather similar to our own." PAC RG15, f. 145330, Canada, Department of Interior, "Grazing Regulations," November 6, 1903.

14 D.H. Breen, "The Turner Thesis and the Canadian West: A Closer Look at the Ranching Frontier," in Lewis H. Thomas (ed.), *Essays on Western History* (University of Alberta Press, 1976), p. 153.

15 L.G. Thomas, in Patrick A. Dunae (ed.), *Rancher's Legacy* (Edmonton: University of Alberta Press, 1986), p. 33.

the Foothills life seemed to revolve largely around sport and the church—it would seem in that order.[16]

Horse racing, hunting, and polo, were all pursued with vigour, while cricket, rugby football, hockey and tennis were all enjoyed in their seasons. For those who were drawn to an outdoor life, ranching in western Canada provided an opportunity to preserve a way of life which was fast disappearing at "home." As one rancher's wife explained:

> In England on a narrow income there is no such thing as freedom. You cannot go where you please, or live where you please, or have what you please; you cannot join in amusements that are really amusing, because every form of sport is expensive; you cannot accept pleasant invitations, because you cannot return them. . . . But with the same income in a country like this, you can live on equal terms with your neighbours, and your surroundings will be entirely in your favour; you have only to make the most of them. Shooting, fishing, and hunting, just the things which would bring you to the verge of bankruptcy at home, you can enjoy here for practically nothing. You can have all the horses you want to ride and drive.[17]

Economic and political leadership of the embryo cattle industry was in the hands of a few very large and powerfully backed ranching companies. For the time at least, and to further the purposes of the Dominion, the Canadian government had set aside the ideal image of the homestead settler and the family farm and had created a "big man's frontier." More than 60% of the leased acreage in 1882 was held in units of more than 75,000 acres. By 1885, four leading companies had engrossed a number of speculative leases and together controlled 40% of the leased acreage, and a similar proportion of the stock on the range. Two of these companies were backed by Canadian capital and two by British.[18]

Senator Matthew Cochrane was a very successful businessman from the Eastern Townships of Quebec. He had a passion for stock raising, and his farm at Hillhurst had become an international centre for pedigree shorthorn cattle. With his wide-ranging business contacts in England and the United States, Cochrane watched with interest the growth of the cattle trade between North America and Great Britain. He was quick to see the enormous potential of the virtually unused grasslands of the Canadian

---

16 Sheilagh Jameson, "The Social Elite of the Ranch Community and Calgary," in *Frontier Calgary*, p. 62.

17 O'Neill, "A Lady's Life on a Ranch," p. 13.

18 Simon M. Evans, "Spatial Aspects of the Cattle Kingdom: The First Decade, 1882–92," in A.W. Rasporich and H.C. Klassen (eds.), *Frontier Calgary* (Calgary: McClelland and Stewart West, 1975).

west. It was he who convinced Colonel James S. Dennis of the Department of the Interior, and then Sir John A. MacDonald himself, of the advantages of promoting large scale cattle raising in the North West Territories. Cochrane picked a 100,000 acre lease along the Bow Valley, and, after some early disasters, took out another along the Belly River south of Fort Macleod. During the mid–1800s, when his "empire" was at its height, Senator Cochrane controlled a total of 334,500 acres.

The North West Cattle Company, operator of the Bar U Ranch, also had its origin in the business community of Montreal and the farm enterprises of the Eastern Townships. William Winder had served for eight years with the North-West Mounted Police and, on his return to Quebec, he excited his father-in-law, Charles Stimson, and his brother-in law, Fred Stimson, about the prospects for ranching in the west. They, in turn, interested Sir Hugh and Andrew Allan into putting up the capital for a ranch. The Allans had made a fortune from their steamship company and had diversified into banking, manufacturing, and insurance. Ranching was a natural extension of their interests, for live cattle were becoming a more and more important constituent of their cargoes to Great Britain. Under the energetic and capable management of Fred Stimson, the company's leases were stocked with excellent cattle from Idaho, and the operation flourished from the start. Stimson had a talent for attracting loyal and competent hands, and the outfit avoided many of the management problems which plagued other major ranches.

One of the most famous of the British ranches was the Oxley Ranch. It resulted from the initiative of John Craig, an experienced cattle breeder from Peel County, Ontario. Having made an optimistic assessment of the prospects for large scale ranching in the west, Craig proceeded to England to find backers. He was able to interest Sir Alexander Staveley-Hill, a lawyer and member of the British House of Commons, and Earl Latham, a prominent landowner and cattle breeder, in the project. A limited company was established and grazing leases in the valleys of the Porcupine Hills were acquired from the original lease holders.

The operations of the ranch were continually disrupted by financial crises and by the inability of the resident manager, Craig, and the principal stock holder, Staveley-Hill, to work together. However, in spite of law suits, and the seizure of assets in Montana because the bills had not been paid, the Oxley survived somehow and was reorganized as a public company in 1886.[19]

The last of the "big four" ranches was the Walrond Ranch Company. It was founded in 1883 by Dr. Duncan McEachran. He was able to obtain

---

19 For both sides of this affair see John R. Craig, *Ranching with Lords and Commons* (Toronto: William Briggs, 1912), and Alexander Staveley-Hill, *From Home to Home: Autumn Wanderings in the North West* (New York: Argonaut Press, 1966).

backing from Sir John Walrond and other British interests. A huge block of land was leased on the upper Oldman River, between the Porcupine Hills and the Livingstone Range. Lucrative contracts to supply beef to Indian reserves insured cash flow, and later the ranch pioneered the sale of high grade live stock to the English market. This enterprise was helped by the fact that McEachran was also the Dominion Veterinarian, and had played a major role in facilitating and regulating the cattle trade from Quebec ports during the 1870s.

These four cattle companies were merely the largest and longest lasting enterprises in the ranching country. There were literally hundreds of others. Taken together, the investors in both the great companies and the smaller ranches, along with the men of substance who had moved west to pursue an attractive way of life, formed a group which read like a Who's Who of the Canadian and British establishments. Not surprisingly their combined political power was immense. David Breen has described how the "cattle compact" was capable of manipulating the federal government to look after their interests in terms of leases, import tariffs, quarantine regulations, and stock watering reserves.[20]

The compelling vision of a cattle kingdom in the Canadian west, which had inspired man like Cochrane, McEachran, and Craig, began to fade even as success seemed assured. The lease regulations of 1881 had been framed to focus attention on the potential of the unoccupied grasslands of the North West Territories and to attract risk capital to the region. By the mid–1880s, the Canadian Pacific railway had been completed and the live cattle trade with Britain was established. The pump had been primed and the infrastructure of development put in place. The legislation had involved a departure from the ideal of the family farm and was justified by the belief that the "grazing country" was unsuitable for agriculture. This tenet became less and less easy to accept as farms were developed and homesteaders flourished. As the Deputy Minister of the Interior observed after inspecting the ranching districts:

> . . . there can be no doubt that when the actual settler desires the land for the purposes of making his home on it, it would be impossible, even if it were expedient, to keep him out. It is not meant by this that one or two speculative squatters should be allowed to disturb a whole grazing ranch, but when the wave of settlement reaches the confines of the grazing country, if that country be found fit for the purposes of actual settlement, it will—in my humble opinion—be impossible to maintain it for purely grazing purposes.[21]

---

20 Breen, *Canadian Prairie West*, pp. 68–69.

21 Quoted in Breen, *Canadian Prairie West*, p. 56.

The political costs of supporting the ranchers rose as the conservative government was assailed with increasingly vocal and intense criticism of its range policy. On the one hand, a flourishing industry had been established, which was represented in Ottawa by a powerful lobby; on the other hand, the lease regulations were presented by the Opposition in Parliament, the Territorial Assembly, and by local interests led by C.E.D. Wood, the editor of the *Macleod Gazette*, as an obstacle to settlement.

The government sought to diffuse the opposition by removing the most glaring abuses of the system. Unstocked leases were cancelled, and new leases were to be open to homestead and pre-emption entry. Rental for leased land was doubled, and those who held the original closed leases were urged to accept homesteads and to purchase deeded land at favourable rates. In spite of these changes the dominant position of the "cattle compact" remained unimpaired. Indeed, their position was strengthened by the introduction of stock-watering and shelter reserves from 1886 onwards. Tension between incoming settlers and ranchers along the Bow Valley west of Calgary, and in the south along the Oldman River, threatened to erupt into violence. The situation was brought to the attention of Parliament in 1889, and again in 1891. At this time a start was made on the railway to link Calgary to Fort Macleod. This line ran through the heart of the closed leases and would naturally become the axis for rapid homestead settlement. The government gave notice that the leases would be cancelled at the end of 1896. The terms under which the twenty-one year leases were to be relinquished were negotiated between the Department of the Interior and the cattlemen, and a generous package was arranged. By means of this agreement the major ranches were able to make a smooth transition from a leased to a deeded land base.

While the owners and managers of the foothills ranches were vociferous in their opposition to incoming farm settlers, they welcomed young men and women who had good connections in eastern Canada or Great Britain. Many ranch bunkhouses contained young English public school boys. One much travelled commentator said that he observed:

> ... more scions of the nobility and young Britons of good family, leading free, airy, open, healthy and romantic lives on the ranches of the North West Territories than in any other quarter of Greater Britain.[22]

In many cases, young men would work for a few years on a ranch before taking out a homestead and establishing their own place. They counted their bands of cattle or horses in tens rather than in hundreds or

---

22 James Francis Hogan, Australian-born M.P. and colonial expert, quoted in Patrick A. Dunae, *Gentlemen Immigrants: From British Public Schools to the Canadian Frontier* (Vancouver: Douglas and McIntyre, 1981), p. 92.

thousands, and often their homes were little more than log shacks. However, they had much in common with the larger ranchers. "They tended to be conservative in their politics and Anglican in their religion."[23] They shared common origins and educational advantages. Above all they enjoyed the same pastimes. Because of this "social contiguity" the major ranchers tolerated and even helped the newcomers get established. It was into this kind of society that the Bedingfelds moved in 1884.

Mrs. Agnes Bedingfeld and her son Frank filed homestead claims on adjacent quarter sections in 1886. The holdings were located in section 1, township 17, range 3, west of the fifth principal meridian.[24] The pair had arrived in the foothills country two years before from the United Kingdom, having spent some time in the United States on their way. Fred Ings recorded their arrival in Calgary in his *Tales from the Midway Ranch*.

> The only railway station in Calgary was an old box car. . . . I noticed the Bar U wagon with its four horse team drawn up beside with Herb Miller in charge. Perched on the high wagon seat was an extremely aristocratic, well-bred looking woman and a fair lad of about seventeen, Mrs. Bedingfeld and Frank. It was a cold chilly day with rain not far off and I saw that this lady was not dressed for bad weather. I went up and introduced myself, and got a slicker for her to wear. She was the widow of an English officer who had been stationed in India. While at the Bar U Mrs. Bedingfeld acted as housekeeper while Frank rode as cowboy and learned the cattle game.[25]

During the three decades leading up to the Great War, southern Alberta was described as "the paradise of the younger son."[26] Here, where the climate and the broken relief encouraged ranching rather than cereal agriculture, a way of life which was under increasing pressure in England could continue to flourish. The beauty of the foothills, the excitement of the frontier, and the romance of the west could be enjoyed from the security of a relatively familiar and congenial society.

> For it was the well educated, anglophile immigrants who played a leading role in establishing the ranching industry in the province, and they had a profound impact on the social, cultural, political, and economic life of the region. These privileged immigrants acted as

---

23 Dunae, *Gentlemen Immigrants*, p. 91.

24 Harry A. Tatro, "A Survey of Historic Ranches," Study prepared for Historic Sites and Monuments Board of Canada, 1973, p. 182.

25 F.W. Ings, "Tales from the Midway Ranch," manuscript, 1936, p. 19, quoted in Sheilagh Jameson, "Women in the Southern Alberta Ranch Community," in H.C. Klassen (ed.), *The Canadian West* (Calgary: Comprint, 1977).

26 Dunae, *Rancher's Legacy*, p. 9.

The Bedingfeld Ranch, Pekisko, about the time of its sale to the Prince of Wales.

conduits through which certain old world values were transmitted to the new frontier, including faith in the church, a reverence for monarchy, respect for property and a belief in a conservative type of democracy.[27]

Frank Bedingfeld must have joined with relish the "sort of high-class corps of amateur cowboys."[28] He was part of one of the largest, most stable, and best run outfits in the foothills country. The North West Cattle Company, more familiarly called the Bar U, was often referred to as a school for cowboys because so many well known and successful ranchers had served an apprenticeship there.[29] George Lane was foreman, Herb Miller was senior hand, while famous cowboys like John Ware and Jim Minesinger were on the payroll. The young man from Britain had excellent teachers, and must have received a first-rate grounding in the practical side of ranching.

Things must have been harder for Mrs. Bedingfeld. The headquarters of the Bar U was sheltered, and enjoyed a spectacular panorama of the mountains to the west. However, the ranch buildings were raw and new, and certainly not elaborate. She had to feed a large labour force and to cater to a steady stream of visitors. It must have been a far cry from being a "memsahib" in India. But perhaps her past experience was put to good use in her efforts to create, at least at the main house, some semblances of an English country house. A visitor in 1886 commented that the ranch looked like a home, with comfortable chairs, pictures, and curtains.[30] Mrs. Bedingfeld was typical of a large number of female immigrants from Britain who found employment as "governesses, housekeepers, and companions, and considerably relieved the burden of work which fell to the rancher's wife."[31]

After two years, Frank turned eighteen, and the Bedingfelds were ready to take up the 160 acres promised by the Canadian government to each settler. They built two log cabins, one on each side of the imaginary line dividing the two quarter sections which they had claimed. This was done to establish residence and to prove up their claims. Mrs. Bedingfeld's cabin eventually became incorporated into a much larger structure, while Frank's small cottage survived for many years, serving a variety of functions before it was finally burnt down.

Over the next thirty years the Bedingfelds put down deep roots in Alberta. At first Frank continued to work for the Bar U, but gradually he acquired some cattle of his own, and ran them with the Bar U herd. He

---

27 Dunae, *Rancher's Legacy*, p. xxi.

28 Dunae, *Gentlemen Immigrants*, p. 92.

29 Brado, *Cattle Kingdom*, p. 116.

30 Jamieson, "Women in Southern Alberta," p. 67.

31 Dunae, *Rancher's Legacy*, p. 14.

spent most of his time looking after the horse herd of the larger outfit. Year by year, the original log cabin was transformed into an eight-room loghouse. Mrs. Bedingfeld designed it and managed the building. The original structure became the dining-room, while a large kitchen was constructed on the north side, and a living room with a big fireplace was built to the south. The building was flanked with an attractive verandah. A series of contemporary photographs chart the transformation and show that Mrs. Bedingfeld also turned her attention to clearing and maintaining a lawn and garden. Upstairs was a dormitory-like "bachelor's hall." The Bedingfelds welcomed young men from the neighbourhood every weekend. They would drift in and enjoy the amenities of a civilized home, some good meals off fine china, and music, cards, and good talk about the news from the district and from "home" would follow.

> [The ranch] was noted for the hospitality extended by its former owner Mrs. Bedingfield [sic]. This kindly old lady was known as a sort of godmother to the cowboys of this section, and she is still remembered by them for the Christmas parties to which she invited them from far and wide, and none who sought shelter under her roof were ever turned away.[32]

Mrs. Yule and Elsie Lane went to tea with Mrs. Bedingfeld a year or so before the ranch was sold to the Prince. Mrs. Yule remembered it as being "a very homey, pleasant place."[33]

Frank entered into a partnership with another man who had been working at the Bar U, Joseph Harrison Brown. He homesteaded to the north and east of the Bedingfelds. Gradually the pair acquired more deeded land, until at the time of the sale, the Bedingfelds owned 1,440 acres. In addition, a series of lease agreements assured control over three townships of grazing land south to the Chain Lakes area and westward up into the foothills. Altogether they had more than 40,000 acres at their disposal. Both horses and cattle were run on the ranch, but Frank's particular love was his Clydesdales. He built up a bunch of some 400 extremely well bred horses.

In 1898 Frank Bedingfeld was thirty-one years old. He had worked hard with cattle and horses for fourteen years. He was ready for a change, and like many other young men he was lured to the Yukon in search of gold. He had many adventures, but was unsuccessful in his quest of a fortune.

32　*Calgary Herald*, September 25, 1923.

33　GA M3973 f. 16, Typescript of interview by George Gooderham of Mrs. Helen (Charles) Yule, daughter of Professor W.L. Carlyle.

Ten years later Frank married Josephine Maitland, and his mother returned to England. The outbreak of the First World War disrupted the Bedingfeld family as it did so many others. In spite of the fact that the ranch was providing valuable horses for the army, and that he was forty-seven years old, Frank was determined to enlist. He pulled every string imaginable and was finally accepted as an ambulance driver. He served two years in Belgium and France. In his absence, Mrs. Josephine Bedingfeld ran the ranch with the assistance of Jack Barber. She was already an expert horsewoman, and now proved that she had a good business sense as well.[34]

After the armistice Frank returned to Alberta in poor health. It proved hard to pick up the threads of their former life as though nothing had changed. Moreover, little Josephine was seven years old. Her parents pondered the possibility of returning to England to insure for her the benefits of a first class education. Early in the summer of 1919, Colonel Henderson, who was in charge of planning the details of the Prince's tour, visited the Bar U and met Mrs. Bedingfeld. She, like her mother-in-law before her, had been co-opted by George Lane to help with the preparations for their important guest. In July she wrote to Henderson asking for advice on how she should behave in the royal presence, she explained that:

> My knowledge of English Royalty begins and ends with my presentation to Queen Alexandra. . . . Please tell me how and where to receive H.R.H. now you know the house at the Bar U, and I suppose a bob will do, or is it necessary to fully curtsey? . . . you must remember I have been in these wilds for eight years without a sight of the old country and am sadly rusty.[35]

The Colonel replied:

> You have no reason to be alarmed. Anyone with more savoir faire than yourself would be hard to contemplate, but as you ask for instructions, I will tell you what you should do. On being introduced to H.R.H. you will give your recollection of the curtsey which you gave to Her Majesty Queen Alexandra on the occasion of your presentation . . . I am not going to believe that you are getting "nervy." I should have thought that after years spent at Pekisko your nerves would be hardened to anything.[36]

---

34 High River Pioneers' and Old Timers' Association, *Leaves from the Medicine Tree* (Lethbridge Herald, 1960), p. 72.

35 PAC RG7 G23 Vol. 16, f. 2, No. 14, Bedingfeld to Henderson July 25, 1919.

36 PAC RG7 G23 Vol. 16, f. 2, No. 14, Henderson to Bedingfeld, July 31, 1919.

The Frank Bedingfeld family at Pekisko, 1914.

This exchange of letters illustrates the close feelings which the Bedingfelds still felt for "home," and makes it clear that, when the Prince expressed an interested in acquiring a ranch, both George Lane and Colonel Henderson knew of the Bedingfeld place, and the fact that the family was thinking of returning to England. After the sale of the ranch to the Prince, the Bedingfelds did in fact return to England. They settled in Hertfordshire, but Frank never regained his health and died in July 1920. Josephine eventually returned to Alberta, married a rancher and settled in the foothills.

It is important to finish this chapter which has attempted to describe the physical and historical setting of the E.P. Ranch, with an evaluation of what foothills ranches were like in the period after the First World War when the royal ranch was established. Both the Prince and the eastern commentators who recorded his visits were so much attracted to the colour, vigour and excitement of the ranching activities they observed that they failed to appreciate the degree to which the livestock industry had been transformed during the preceding twenty years. The "Big Four" who had met in Calgary in May, 1912 to plan the "greatest outdoor show on earth," the Calgary Stampede, had hoped to memorialize a way of life and an era in the cattle industry which had disappeared forever. Their collective perception that an epoch had ended must carry much weight.[37]

The open range had ceased to exist by 1919. The "sea of grass" over which stock could move for hundreds of miles in any direction without encountering any man-made obstacles, had been fragmented as a network of railway lines had spread out from the main trunk routes, and had brought more and more land to within ten miles of the nearest elevator.[38] To the ranching industry of the foothills, the rapid expansion of settlement which followed the completion of the railway between Calgary and Fort Macleod was most critical. Superintendent Primrose reported as early as 1903:

> The increase of settlement in this district has been enormous, to the north from Macleod to Nanton, to the east to Kipp, to the south to the boundary, and west to the Crow's Nest Pass, nearly every available section of land has been either taken up or purchased.[39]

Foothills ranchers were cut off from their summer range on both sides of the Bow River by a growing belt of farmland 50–100 miles wide. At the same time, they had to compete with settlers for continued use of winter

37 Guy Weadick, "The Origin of the Calgary Stampede," *Alberta Historical Review*, (Autumn 1966) pp. 20–24.

38 See Donald Kerr, Deryck Holdsworth and Geoffrey J. Matthews (eds.), *Historical Atlas of Canada, Volume III: Addressing the Twentieth Century* (University of Toronto Press, 1990), Plate 18, "Prairie Agriculture"; and Simon M. Evans, "The End of the Open Range in Western Canada," *Prairie Forum*, Vol. 8, No. 1 (Spring 1983), pp. 71–88.

39 Canada, *Sessional Papers*, 1903, XXXVIII, Vol. 12, No. 28, "Report of Superintendent P.C.H. Primrose," p. 51.

range in the Porcupine Hills and the valleys of the eastern slopes of the Rocky Mountains.

Ranchers were faced with two alternatives: either they could intensify production by fencing, winter feeding and growing fodder crops, or they could relocate to the shortgrass prairie to the eastward. Contemporary observers were unanimous in expressing the view that this increase in settlement meant the end of the ranching industry as they had known it in the foothills.

> The farmer and his fences are gradually driving the big ranches further and further back, and it is only a question of years when the real ranch will have ceased to exist and the farm with its small bunch of cattle will have taken its place.[40]

The notorious killing winter of 1906–1907 struck an industry which was already retreating before a flood of farm settlement, and transforming itself through purposive adaption. The most cruel impact of the winter fell on the shortgrass prairie from Sounding Lake southward to the Cypress Hills and the United States borders. Here, cattle losses were estimated at between 60 and 65%. Even leading companies, noted not only for their size but also for the skillful and experienced management, lost more than half their herds. Newcomers who had thrown "Pilgrim" stock from Manitoba onto unfamiliar range in the fall lost almost everything. The exact extent of the losses will never be know, but even the most conservative estimates support the conclusion that about half the working capital invested in the range cattle industry was liquidated. No industry could survive such an ordeal without undergoing profound changes.

> The net effect of the winter of 1906–07 was to make stock farmers out of ranchers. Almost, as suddenly as the disappearance of the buffalo, it changed the way of life of the region.[41]

A process of enclosure which had started in the valleys of the Bow and the Oldman rivers in the 1890s had reached its logical conclusion. Even in the heart of Palliser's Triangle the settled ways of the farmer replaced for a time those of the pastoralist.

The farmers who moved into southern Alberta in the decade before the First World War posed a more formidable threat to the open range than had their predecessors. During the 1890s, the ranchers had had to

---

40 Canada, *Sessional Papers*, 1906, XL, Vol. 13, No. 28, "Report of Superintendent G.E. Sanders," p. 43.

41 Wallace Stegner, *Wolf Willow* (New York: Viking Press, 1955), p. 137.

face the incursions of homesteaders and squatters, most of whom aspired to become small ranchers. They were resented and resisted every step of the way by the larger ranchers, but at least they shared an interest in stock and the range. After the turn of the century, the great influx of settlers was made up of people of a very different ilk. Many of them were experienced cash grain farmers. Some had sold farms in the United States for $15 to $20 an acre and were purchasing land in Canada for $4 or $5. They had capital to invest in machinery and hastened to break up their holdings and to extend the scale of their agricultural operations.[42]

Advancing settlement was spurred by enthusiasm for dry farming which was generated by the work of Hardy Webster Campbell. Incoming farmers were encouraged by his optimistic forecast for the prairies of southern Alberta and Saskatchewan: "I believe of a truth that this region, which is just coming into its own, is destined to be the last and best grain garden of the world."[43] The seventh annual dry farming congress held in Lethbridge in 1912 was a fitting culmination of a promotional campaign which had started five or six years before and had been embraced by small town boosters throughout the region.[44]

The pace of farm settlement increased in the years immediately following the bad winter and continued undiminished until the early 1920s. The activity at Lethbridge and Calgary land offices reached fever pitch. There were some eighteen steam ploughs operating in the Lethbridge area in 1908, while along the Milk River, newly broken land was yielding thirty to forty bushels to the acre.[45] Even around Maple Creek, the service centre for shortgrass ranchers, Superintendent Begin reported:

> Ranching in this part of the province will soon be a thing of the past. Ranchers are going out of business. Most of the land has been opened for homesteaders. Old ranch grounds are gradually being cut up by farmers. Stock cannot anymore roam over the country as hitherto.[46]

Wheat was king and a grid pattern of barbed wire fences and road allowances, which had existed for so long only on the maps of the sur-

42 Karel Denis Bicha, *The American Farmer and the Canadian West, 1896–1914* (Lawrence: Coronado Press, 1968).

43 Mary Wilma M. Hargreaves, *Dry Farming in the Northern Great Plains, 1900–1925* (Cambridge: Harvard University Press, 1957), p. 87.

44 David C. Jones, *Empire of Dust* (Edmonton: University of Alberta Press, 1987); and Paul Voisey, *Vulcan: The Making of a Prairie Community* (Toronto: University of Toronto Press, 1988).

45 Canada, *Sessional Papers*, 1909, XLIII, Vol. 16, No. 28, "Report of Superintendent J.O. Wilson, Lethbridge," p. 89; and *Lethbridge Herald*, 11 December 1947, p. 13.

46 Canada, *Sessional Papers*, 1909, XLVII, Vol. 21, No. 28, "Report of Superintendent J.V. Begin, Maple Creek," p. 98.

veyors, became a finite reality. Few cattlemen were complacent enough to have expected that their hold over the open range would last forever, but the speed of transformation challenged the adaptive capacity of even the most innovative ranchers.

The cattlemen were by no means passive observers of the rising tide of farm settlement which threatened to engulf them. They constantly modified their techniques to respond to changing circumstances. As range became scarce they increased the intensity of their operations. Although U.S. promoters like General Brisbin dazzled potential eastern investors with the spectacular returns which "inevitably" followed by employing the methods of the open range,[47] serious stockmen in both the United States and Canada were quick to see the problems which attended such extensive methods of land use. As more and more risk capital poured onto the western range, and hundreds of new outfits came into being, so the range became overgrazed and competition for scarce grass resulted in illegal fencing and pressure on Indian lands.[48] Careful Canadian entrepreneurs such as Senator Cochrane would not invest a dollar in the Territories until they were assured of land tenure through the lease system. Moreover, they were well aware that only the highest quality steers could earn profits after the long journey to British markets. From the first they stocked their leases with the best available Durham and Shorthorn stock, and started breeding programmes to upgrade their stock by importing first class bulls from the east.[49] Animals like these were very valuable and incapable of adapting immediately to the rigours of an Albertan winter. Hay was put up or purchased from neighbours to feed them. The disastrous winter losses experienced by the Cochrane Ranch on its Bow Valley range in 1881, although a product of inexperienced management, led the company to adopt a policy of putting up large quantities of hay.[50] They were well prepared for the severe winter of 1886–87 and came through relatively unscathed. Their example was widely followed. When the North West Cattle Company sold out to George Lane and Gordon, Ironsides and Fares in 1902, over 1,000 tons of hay

---

47 General James S. Brisbin, *The Beef Bonanza: or, How to Get Rich on the Plains* (Philadelphia: J.P. Lippincott, 1881; republished, Norman: University of Oklahoma Press, 1959); discussion see Ernest Staples Osgood, *The Day of the Cattleman* (Chicago: University of Chicago Press, 1929), pp. 85–90.

48 As early as 1886, T.C. Power's Judith Basin Cattle Company had 5,000 acres enclosed, of which 300 were seeded to timothy, and the remainder devoted to pastures and feeding grounds. See Robert S. Fletcher, "The End of the Open Range in Eastern Montana," *Mississippi Valley Historical Review*, Vol. 16 (September 1929), p. 205.

49 Simon M. Evans, "Stocking the Canadian Range," *Alberta History*, Vol. 26 (Summer 1978).

50 D. Brown, "The Cochrane Ranche," *Alberta Historical Review*, Vol. 4 (Autumn 1956).

were included in the deal.[51] It was stockmen who undertook the first tentative experiments in irrigation, as they diverted creeks to increase the hay crop on bottom lands.[52] The experience of the first few winters demonstrated that losses tended to be concentrated among young heifers with winter calves, and the practice of herding bulls separately from the cows in order to control the calf crop gained wider and wider currency. Once the calving season had been regulated, the next step was to wean the calves in the fall so that their mothers had a chance to recover before facing the rigours of winter.[53] These changes were the first steps to be taken along the road from extensive and wasteful "open range" methods toward more intensive "ranch farming." As major ranches were forced to give up their closed leases and purchase deeded land, so they began to use fences, both to manage their home ranges more effectively, and to protect their improved herds from scrub bulls.[54]

The impact of the killing winter of 1906–1907 accelerated technological change in the livestock industry. There was widespread reaction to the "carrion spring," and a new determination among surviving cattlemen to limit the size of their herds to the number they could safely feed. At the same time, government experimental farms had demonstrated that feeding grain to steers during winter could pay handsome dividends. It meant that cattle could be forwarded to market on a year round basis in response to market demands; moreover, they were more docile and lost less weight in transit. By 1908, wild hay had been replaced by cultivated hay and fodder crops on many ranches, while oats and barley meal were fed in increasing quantities. This practice made great progress during the fall of 1911 because the heavy grain crop was frosted, and much grain was available for feed. George Lane of the Bar U explained:

> From now on I shall feed all my cattle every winter. I began feeding this year simply because feed was cheap, and I have figured out now that it is much more economical and businesslike than the old system of wintering cattle on the range. It was different a few years ago when cattle were cheap and feed was dear. It then paid better to leave cattle on the range and stand the inevitable loss. Even in the most favourable years this amounted to about 5 per cent of the herd. With cattle worth $50.00 a head it pays to feed the whole herd and obviate this loss.

51 *Calgary Herald*, 5 February, 1902.

52 A.A. den Otter, "Irrigation in Southern Alberta, 1882–1901," *Occasional Paper No. 5*, Whoop-Up Country Chapter, Historical Society of Alberta, Lethbridge, 1975.

53 F.W. Godsal, "Old Times," *Alberta Historical Review*, Vol. 12 (Autumn 1964), p. 21; and *Macleod Gazette*, 20 July, 1886.

54 Sherm Ewing, *The Range* (Missoula: Mountain Press, 1990), pp. 41–76.

Besides this you have your beef cattle in shape for market at anytime, and especially at the season when they command the highest price.[55]

Lane was feeding 3,500 beef cattle on frosted wheat for which he had paid only $5 a ton. He was on his way to Idaho to consult a well known authority on the growth of alfalfa. Later in the year 300 head of this batch of cattle were shipped to Chicago and received the highest prices ever paid for beef steers.

The increasing density of farm settlement and enclosure had reduced some of the hazards which had faced pioneer ranchers. For example, the control of wolves had been a major concern of the Western Stock Growers Association in the 1890s and during the early years of the new century, but by 1916 only five wolves were produced to claim the bounty.[56] The widespread epidemic of mange, which had contributed to the devastation of the killing winter of 1906–1907, had been controlled and then eradicated as herds became smaller and more domesticated. Fire on the range remained a nightmare, but ironically it was not flames racing across the prairie which affected the E.P. Ranch, but rather a succession of blazes which swept away barns and the stock they contained.[57]

As the Prince travelled south and west from High River in 1919 on his way to visit the Bar U ranch, he would have passed a great variety of agricultural enterprises, differing from each other in scale, objectives, and methods. Many of the grain farmers in the plain surrounding the town ran some cattle on bottom lands, or wintered-over a bunch of calves for a rancher neighbour. As the royal party approached the foothills they would have seen a number of ranches. Many were modest in size and numbered their herds in hundreds rather than thousands. Typically, the more accessible fields were fenced and land was broken to grow fodder crops, but the Prince, with eyes used to the small fields of lowland Britain with their hedgerows, must have remarked on the extent of open grazing land. Some stockmen were carefully developing purebred herds of cattle or horses, while others specialized in fattening young steers on the last remnants of the open range which still existed in the higher foothills and forest reserves. Representative of these men was "7U" Brown, who is supposed to have said, "If I can live off whisky in the winter, then the cattle can damn well eat snow."[58]

---

55 *Albertan*, 12 January, 1912.

56 For coverage of environmental hazards see W.M. Elofson, "Adapting to the Frontier Environment: The Ranching Industry in Western Canada, 1881–1914," *Canadian Papers in Rural History*, Vol. 8 (Gananoque: Langdale Press, 1992).

57 GA M160 f. 145, Burns to McCormick, 14 December, 1931; and p. 192.

58 Margaret Barry-McGechie, "7U Brown, Alberta Cattle Country, 1881–1883," prepared for Alberta Culture, ca. 1985.

In terms of size, the newly acquired E.P. Ranch was not unlike dozens of other ranches in the foothills. It consisted of nearly 1,500 acres of deeded land, most of which was fenced, and a small portion of which was broken crop land. In addition, there were 20,000 acres of leased land and some 600 head of stock. However, because it belonged to the future monarch, the ranch was unique in three important respects: firstly, it could rely on the immense resources of the Duchy of Cornwall for capital; secondly, it was conceived as a diverse operation which would involve horses, ponies, and sheep, as well as cattle; thirdly, the ranch drew its superb stock directly from the pedigree herds and flocks of Britain. It is to discuss these characteristics, and to trace how they developed, that we must now turn.

III

The Dream Unfolds:
The Development of the E.P. Ranch,
1920–29

The E.P. will be in a very short time probably the most influential factor in improving strains of horses, cattle and sheep in Alberta and in the other western Provinces.[1]

If the purchase of the ranch had been an impetuous whim induced by the euphoria of the moment, the Prince and his advisors quickly developed an unassailable rationale for the enterprise. On his return from Canada, Edward remembered having an interview with his father:

On my return to London, my father questioned me closely about this ranch. Mistaking my motive in purchasing it, he warned that I was setting for myself a dangerous precedent. The Australians would now expect me to buy a sheep station when I visited their country; and, if I failed to acquire at least an ostrich farm when I went to South Africa, its people, he pointed out, might construe my neglect as a deliberate slight.[2]

The Prince replied that he planned to use his small ranch as a means of introducing first class blood stock into the heart of the Canadian ranching country. He pointed out that he possessed prize-winning stock in abundance on his estates in Scotland and Cornwall and such animals would be much more usefully deployed in the Dominion than at home.

Professor W.L. Carlyle, the newly appointed manager of the ranch, was already obligated to take a consignment of Percheron horses to England for George Lane. The shipment included a number of mares and fillies which had won distinction at various Canadian exhibitions, and four stallions, Paragon, Perfection, Pershing, and Orlando. They were to

---

1 *Calgary Herald*, September 28, 1923.

2 Duke of Windsor, *A King's Story; The Memoirs of the Duke of Windsor* (New York: G.P. Putnam, 1951), p. 152.

be delivered to well-known stockmen in Britain, including Lord Minto, Sir Alexander Parker, and Sir Henry Hoare.[3]

Carlyle was instructed to make contact with the Prince's household while he was in England so that he could bring back the foundation stock for the new ranch. He toured the royal estates with Walter Peacock, the secretary to the Duchy of Cornwall, and they decided to ship thirty head of shorthorn cattle; six or eight thoroughbred fillies and a stallion; twenty head of selected Dartmoor ponies; and twenty-five head of purebred Shropshire sheep. The ponies and the shorthorns were from the Prince's own farms, while the Shropshire sheep were provided by the Duke of Westminster, who owned the championship flock and generously offered the entire lamb crop of 1919 to the Prince for his new venture.[4]

It was felt that Dartmoor ponies, used to the damp uplands of Dartmoor, would do very well on the ranch. The expectation was that judicious breeding with Dartmoor-Arab half-breds would produce a rather larger animal which would make a good polo pony, as well as excellent children's ponies for isolated farm youngsters to ride to school. Carlyle used the Dartmoor stallion for hacking round the ranch and was favourably impressed with its staying power.[5]

There were some delays in shipping the stock to the ranch because of an outbreak of foot and mouth disease in England. Eventually, however, the animals arrived in good condition. Some sheep were exhibited at the fall show in Calgary, and one ram carried off the all round championship honours, and brought in the highest revenue of the show with a purchase price of $225.[6] Thus the tangible advantages of establishing a gene-pool of pedigree stock were immediately demonstrated. While a select group of cattlemen in Canada were already in the habit of exchanging fine animals with their counterparts in the United Kingdom, the hope was that the E.P. could make first rate stock available more easily to a broader clientele.

Canadian commentators were quick to see that the purchase and development of the E.P. Ranch was likely to have indirect results which far transcended the significance of the importation of a few hundred head of stock, however fine they were. The visits of the Prince to his Alberta ranch focused immense media attention on that province, and indeed on Canada in general. The editor of the *Calgary Herald* stated baldly, "The E.P. Ranch is the most famous property in western Canada. Thousands

3 *High River Times*, October 16, 1919.

4 *Farm and Ranch Review*, January 20, 1920.

5 *The Nor'West Farmer*, February 5, 1920.

6 *Strathmore Standard*, January 19, 1921.

of travellers pass through Calgary, and invariably their first question is the location of the Alberta home of the Prince of Wales."[7]

John Lamont, writing in the *Farm and Ranch Review*, contrasted the revered status of stock rearing in Britain with its more lowly status in Canada. He stressed that the interest and involvement of the heir to the throne could gradually change this.[8] The former Minister of Agriculture, Dr. S.F. Tolmie, made a similar point after visiting the ranch:

> I consider that Alberta is particularly fortunate in having the E.P. Ranch located within its borders. The royal family of England has for many generations taken an interest in improving the livestock of that country. And many of our Kings, in addition to operating large breeding establishments have been first class judges of livestock. The royal family, in making fashionable the breeding of pure-bred stock have been followed by many others with the result that Great Britain has today a most enviable reputation of having created and maintained a high state of perfection in more breeds of horses, cattle, sheep and swine than all the rest of the world combined.[9]

The degree to which Prince Edward was personally involved in decisions concerning the E.P. at this vital stage of its evolution is difficult to gauge. It is obvious that he was a very busy young man. There is no evidence that he had the time or inclination to develop a critical eye with regard to bloodstock, but he was always interested and enthusiastic when he visited his estates in Great Britain. As one biographer comments:

> . . . he will give as much serious attention to an application for a new pigsty or a new roof, or a new barn, farmer or estate hand, as he will to an important ambassadorial duty for the government. At a Duchy meeting he will delve into drainage questions, estate disputes with County Councils, contributions to local institutions, with all the interest of a conscientious country squire who has little else to occupy his mind and life.[10]

However, he did not spend long in the country side and left most decision making to his advisors. It was much the same with the E.P. Ranch.

The opportunity for riding which the ranch provided was one of the lures which drew the Prince to Alberta, for during the 1920s he became

---

7 *Calgary Herald*, October 3, 1923.

8 *Farm and Ranch Review*, June 5, 1923.

9 *Albertan*, November 13, 1923; see also an editorial in the *Washington Post*, August 19, 1927.

10 Frank E. Verney, *H.R.H.: A Character Study of the Prince of Wales* (London: Hodder and Stoughton, 1926), p. 165.

The first of the new barns, the E.P. Ranch, 1923, with growing network of corrals in the foreground.

a passionate horseman. This love had developed slowly; when he was up at Oxford, the Prince had complained that riding was very dull and was only to be endured to "please papa." Soon, however, Major Cadogan, his patient riding instructor, had captured his interest and Edward was enjoying hunting with the South Oxfordshire Hounds. After his Canadian tour he hunted regularly with the Pytchley and the Quorn, and an acknowledged commentator on hunting wrote, "he was a real sportsman, taking the rough with the smooth, scorning all privileges, and ever ready to take his turn at the chores of the hunting field . . . he was as brave as a lion and bore pain without a sign."[11] As his skill grew he started to ride in point to point races with considerable success. While in India he distinguished himself in a series of gymkhana races, including the prestigious Kadir Cup meeting. Polo became a useful way of breaking down barriers between the royal visitor and his Indian subjects, and his enthusiasm for the sport was one reason for his popularity.

It was on this tour that Prince Edward met the man who was to become his closest man friend, Captain Edward Dudley Metcalfe, known to his friends as "Fruity." Born in Ireland, Metcalfe was a graduate of Trinity College, Dublin. He joined the Indian Army and served with distinction in Mesopotamia and France with the Third Bengal Cavalry. When the Prince visited India, Captain Metcalfe was commissioned to arrange some recreational riding and polo for him. He was a handsome, easygoing, and charming young man, and managed to combine deference and respect for the royal person in public with an ability to treat Edward as an equal, and say exactly what he thought, in private. Edward wrote of him:

> Of all my friends it was he alone, with his informal and expansive Irish nature who behaved toward me, not as though I were a Prince, but, as though I were an ordinary human being like himself . . . he always referred to me as "the little man." People were sometimes shocked by the familiarity of his attitude toward me.[12]

The older members of the household were not at all sure that the Prince needed any encouragement in the pursuit of irresponsible pranks and ill-considered fun. Halsey thought Metcalfe was "not at all a good thing for H.R.H., an excellent fellow, always cheerful and full of fun, but far, far, too weak and hopelessly irresponsible. He is a wild, wild, Irishman."[13]

---

11 Guy Paget, quoted in Philip Ziegler, *Edward VIII: The Official Biography* (London: Colins, 1990), p. 176.

12 Duke of Windsor, *A Family Album* (London: Cassell, 1960), p. 143.

13 Duff Hart-Davis (ed.), *In Royal Service: The Letters and Journals of Sir Alan Lascellees, 1920–1936*, Vol. 2 (London: Hamish Hamilton, 1989), p. 4.

The E.P. ranch house from the east, 1920. Notice the hops growing around the verandah.

On his return to England, Prince Edward took a house in the centre of hunting country and, with Fruity's help, built up a string of good steeplechasers and hunters. His success in this field was immensely important to him because it presented him with an opportunity to compete with the rest of the world on equal terms. Moreover, it provided an opportunity to exorcise those demons which built up inside him due to family pressures and the tedium of formal functions. He wrote to Freda Dudley Ward, "Thank God I've got two races tomorrow as I must do something desperate, which is just what race-riding gives one."[14] There is no doubt that he was a first-rate horseman. However, he pushed hard and took risks, and this inevitably led to falls. The press made the most of these incidents and the Prince's supposed inability to stay on a horse became, most unfairly, something of a music hall joke.[15] In 1924, the Prince took a particularly nasty toss, and from then on he was under pressure from the King and politicians to forego the hazards of steeplechasing. At the time of his father's illness in 1928, he finally acceded to his mother's request and gave up racing. He sold all his horses and surrendered his rooms at Craven Lodge, Melton Mowbray.

The Prince of Wales did not develop the abiding interest in horse racing which has become such a hallmark of Queen Elizabeth II's court. Of course he attended Ascot and the other major race meetings, but mainly because they were important social functions, not because of the racing itself. His interest in horses was as a rider, a participator, rather than as an observer. During the vital build-up phase of the E.P. Ranch the Prince was very much involved with horses. Indeed, Lord Wigram observed, "All his thoughts and passions seem centred on the horse."[16] It is likely that he took a direct interest in the establishment of a thoroughbred stable in Canada, and that he was intrigued with the idea of developing his own polo ponies based on a Dartmoor-Arab cross. He left the cattle breeding and sheep rearing strictly to his estate managers, although he expected that his ranch would be a show piece which would bring him credit, and he thoroughly enjoyed the numerous successes of his show animals.

For more than twenty years, through the heady years of expansion in the 1920s, and the struggle for survival in the 1930s, the day-to-day management of the E.P. Ranch was in the hands of Professor William Levi Carlyle, M.Sc. A kinsman of Thomas Carlyle, the famous Victorian

---

14 Ziegler, *Edward VIII*, p. 176.

15 "The Prince's falls are becoming a joke all over the world, particularly in America . . . the Prince of Wales is getting everywhere a sort of pantomime association." Hart-Davis, *In Royal Service*, pp. 11–13.

16 Ziegler, *Edward VIII*, p. 175.

historian and "Prophet,"[17] William Carlyle was born at Chesterville, Ontario, on September 22, 1870. He was educated in the Ontario school system and then went to agricultural college at Guelph, which was a branch of the University of Toronto. Having earned both a B.Sc. and a Master's degree, he was hired as an instructor at the age of twenty-two.[18]

In 1893, he obtained a position as an extension lecturer at the University of Minnesota. He was there five years, and married Inez Mary Fairbanks. He then moved to the University of Wisconsin as a Professor of Animal Husbandry. Ten years of successful experience earned him an appointment as Dean of Agriculture at Colorado Agricultural College, 1903–1909. While at Colorado he worked for the U.S. Government, Department of Agriculture, and even went to Europe on their behalf. It was during a visit to Seattle to judge the livestock exhibits at the Pacific Exposition that he first met George Lane. Carlyle's daughter remembered riding through Seattle in Lane's wagon drawn by a team of Percherons. Next, the Carlyles moved to Idaho for five years, and then to a position as Dean and Director of Oklahoma Agricultural and Mechanical College, 1914–17. Finally, Lane persuaded Carlyle to come to Alberta to manage his ranching interests.

Thus, the man who became manager of the E.P. Ranch was a distinguished livestock authority. For almost thirty years he had played an important role in University agricultural education in the United States and had been instrumental in building up a number of experimental farms. He was well known wherever first-rate stock were exhibited, and was often asked to judge top-rated competitions. He was forty-nine when he took over management of the E.P.

One must wonder why he came back to Canada and gave up his quite distinguished career in the U.S. university system. Was his health giving cause for concern? Was he in search of a less stressful way to make a living? We don't know. Obviously, however, the opportunity of helping the Prince of Wales develop a centre of breeding excellence must have been a dream come true. Carlyle could continue to make his annual visits to the various stock shows in Chicago and the Pacific Northwest, but now he would have the added cachet of being "by appointment to His Majesty," and also have the satisfaction of showing some first-rate stock which was directly under his charge.

The Prince could have absolute confidence that the management of his stock was in good hands. It is difficult to believe that there were

---

17 Thomas Carlyle, 1795–1881, Scottish essayist and historian. His most famous work was his history of the French Revolution.

18 Information on Carlyle comes from an obituary published in the *Calgary Herald*, August 5, 1955; and from an interview with his daughter, Mrs. H. Yule. GA M3973, f. 16.

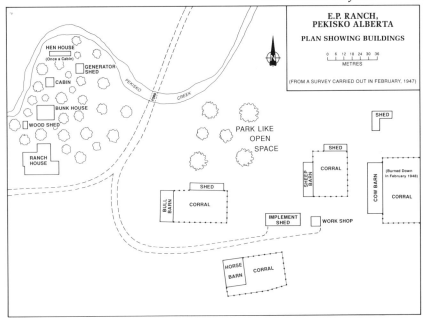

Map 5. E.P. Ranch, plan showing location of buildings.

many men available who had so much broad-based experience with all manner of breeds and species of stock. Moreover, it is clear that Mr. and Mrs. Carlyle and their family became comfortable in the social role which was thrust upon them. As the ranch developed into a show place, so they had to contend with a continual flow of visitors from all kinds of backgrounds. No published account of a visit to the ranch fails to mention the warm hospitality which was provided and the excellent meals which were enjoyed.

Carlyle's first priority at the ranch was to provide shelter for the prize-winning stock from England, which could not be expected to withstand the rigours of an Alberta winter. A large new barn was constructed capable of accommodating seventy-two animals. It fitted in well with its surroundings, being built of logs set on a concrete foundation. Inside, all the fittings were hand hewn from local wood (Map 5).[19]

It was not until plans for a visit from the owner were announced that any changes were made in the ranch house itself. Over their period of occupancy the Bedingfeld family had gradually transformed the original log cabin into a comfortable residence. A kitchen had been added to the

---

19 *Farm and Ranch Review*, June 5, 1923; and *Calgary Herald*, September 15, 1923.

The E.P. Ranch after the first remodeling, 1923.

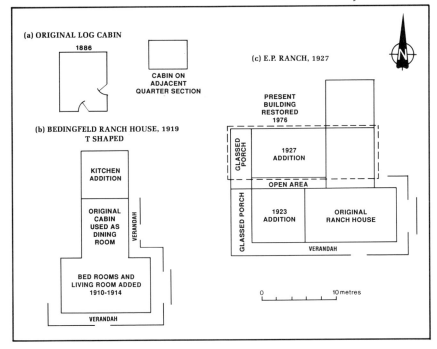

Map 6. E.P. Ranch, plans showing the evolution of the ranch house.

north, and a longer addition enclosing a sitting room and bedrooms was constructed on the south side. The building the Prince bought was therefore "T"-shaped. Its most striking characteristic was the attractive open porch or verandah which surrounded the building. (Map 6) The photograph of the ranch taken during the winter of 1914 looks rather stark, but a summer close-up taken a year or two later from the east shows a path leading to the porch and into the original cabin which was used as a dining room. On the left is the gable end of the bedroom wing, and on the right the kitchen (see photographs on pp. 50 and 68).

In anticipation of a fall visit by the Prince of Wales, things moved quickly during the summer of 1923. "Within recent weeks painters and carpenters have transformed the old red ranchhouse into a bright modern house containing every comfort and convenience."[20] Actually, every effort was made to preserve the character of the original building. An annex of three bedrooms was added on the west side of the house, elongating one side of the "T." It was surrounded by a wide enclosed porch which caught a lot of sunshine. Indeed, the roof line and attic windows of the new extension matched the older structure so perfectly

---

20 *Calgary Herald*, September 25, 1923.

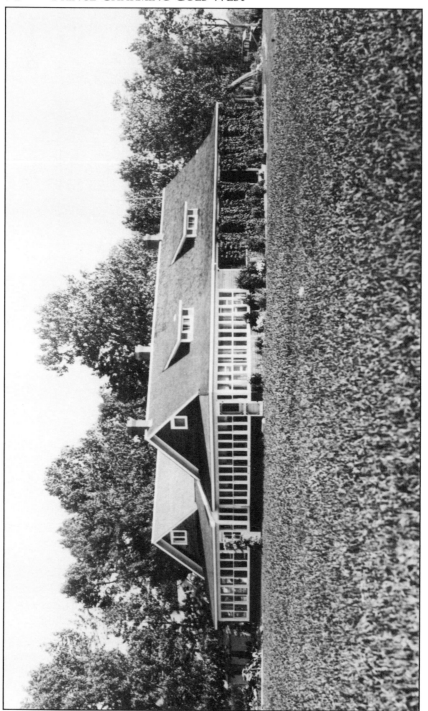

The ranch house after renovations, 1927.

that it was only the glassed-in porch which distinguished the new wing in the contemporary photographs. The plumbing was modernized, prompting the *Calgary Herald* to boast, "Even York House, the London residence of the Prince, can boast nothing more attractive than the white tiled baths and shower."[21] The small reception room was very similar to those found in ranch houses up and down the foothills country:

> In the sitting room, the simplest informality marks the room. A couch, half a dozen wicker easy chairs, a cushioned window seat, and a table or two. Half a dozen ash trays scattered about, a newspaper, a magazine; on the polished floor a couple of antelope skins; on the walls, one or two pictures, King George, Pat Burns, Lord Renfrew himself, and a couple of steel engravings of Persimmon and Minoru, the race horses which belonged to King Edward.[22]

The renovations were completed with time to spare, but the reception committee had forgotten one thing: each member of the Prince's staff would be accompanied by a valet. Where were these extra bodies to be accommodated? The extensive "bachelor's hall" of the Bedingfeld homestead was pressed into service, and an S.O.S. went out to Calgary to send several wash stands for these upstairs bedrooms (Map 7).[23]

Final and substantial enlargements were made to the ranch house during the summer of 1927, again in anticipation of a fall visit from the Prince. A new wing was added parallel to the 1923 addition on the west side of the house. This structure was free standing, and its peaked roof gave the house the appearance of a double dwelling. A number of old outbuildings and the water tower were cleared away. The objective of this renovation was to provide space for a new reception room in which a royal house party could gather in comfort. The character and decoration of this new room were described in a contemporary journal:

> This has hardwood floors and a ceiling beamed in dark oak. It is lighted by seven large windows and double French doors which open into a sun porch running the entire length of the west side of the house. The walls, papered with buff grained paper, are adorned with sporting and various outdoor pictures. The floor is covered with three oriental rugs and the room is furnished throughout in mission oak. On the south side of the room is a huge fire place made of stone taken from the ranch and having the initials E.P. worked into the masonry above the firebox. The most original and interesting note in the furnishing is discovered in the two floor lamps. The bases of these lamps are made from two 250 pound

---

21 *Calgary Herald*, September 25, 1923.

22 *Calgary Herald*, September 15, 1923.

23 GA M3973, f. 16, Yule Transcript.

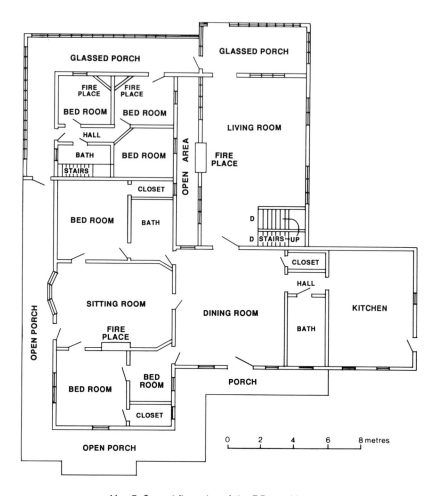

Map 7. Ground floor plan of the E.P. ranchhouse.

German shells. A maple leaf design, in colour, is worked into the stem.[24]

The addition of this new reception room meant that H.R.H. could use the modest old sitting room as a private retreat. Two additional bedrooms were completed above the new room. About fifty metres from the main house, sheltered in the trees, a new bunk house was constructed. It had eight bedrooms, and a modern kitchen and bathroom. Taken together the

24 *Literary Review*, August 27, 1927.

The new drawing room. Big stone fireplace on the right,
with German shell in front of it.

renovations were valued at $11,400. Construction was delayed by an
unusually wet spring. For nine days Pekisko Creek was over its banks
and the ford was impassable; the schedule fell dangerously behind. It
took twenty-two men working furiously for six weeks to get everything
ready for the owner's inspection.

During the first visit to the ranch in 1923, the Prince turned his
attention to the possibility of creating a garden around the house. Mrs.
Bedingfeld had planted trees and flowers immediately adjacent to the
house and had introduced hops to grow up and over the porch. H.R.H.
talked over several possible ways of building on this foundation with
William Reader, who was Superintendent of Parks in Calgary.[25] Reader
drafted a somewhat elaborate looking plan for five acres of flower and
vegetable gardens, separated by hedges and flowering shrubs (Map 8).
By 1924, the first steps to implementing these plans were taken, a
perennial border was laid out and hedges were planted to mask the
fences. Some 500 trees had been planted toward the creek, and the
beginning of a "woodland walk" had been cut out. Three years later it
was clear that running a complex ranching operation and gardening were

---

25 *Calgary Herald*, June 7, 1924.

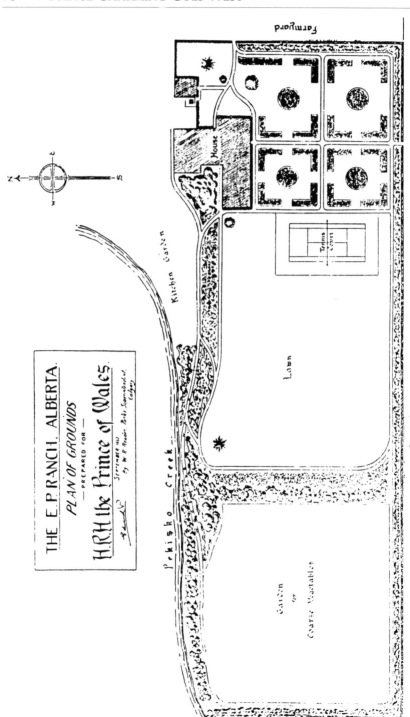

Map 8. William Reader's plan for the E.P. Ranch grounds.

not always compatible! Reader's dreams had only been partially realized. The sweep of the lawn in front of the house was bordered with old fashioned flowers like phlox, candy tuft, forget-me-not, petunias and Canterbury bells. Flourishing hedges of carragana provided some shelter to the beds and kept out stock, but the projected tennis court and the formal pattern of flower beds were thought to be an unnecessary extravagance and were shelved.

Professor Carlyle had put together an experienced staff to look after the newly arrived stock. William Elliott was foreman, and he was destined to serve on the ranch for nearly thirty years. Jimmy Watson looked after the shorthorns, and Jock Stevens the sheep. They were Scots who had travelled to Canada with their animal charges and had been persuaded to stay at least until the stock had settled down in their new surroundings. An important Canadian member of the household was James Shimbashi. He had immigrated to Canada from southern Japan in 1906, when he was only sixteen. After some time in the logging camps of British Columbia he moved to Raymond, Alberta, and worked in a restaurant and in the sugar beet fields.[26] In 1915 he saw a moving appeal from King George V for recruits for the great struggle in Europe, and the next day he enlisted in the 50th (Calgary) Battalion. After serving two years overseas, he was discharged in 1919, and an officer recommended him to Carlyle. He joined the E.P. as cook. During the winter of 1922 he returned to Japan and married Teru Nishida. The couple returned to the E.P. in time to prepare for the first visit of the Prince to his ranch. Over the next few years "Jimmy" and his wife became the mainstay of the establishment.[27] Apart from the routine of feeding the ranch hands, the Shimbashis did all the cooking for the royal parties, as well as looking after a productive garden, and showing guests the best fishing holes along Pekisko Creek.[28] The Shimbashi's eldest son was born on the ranch and, not surprisingly, they named him Edward. Their eldest daughter was also born there and named Helen after the Carlyles' daughter. In 1926, the family moved to Welling, Alberta, to start what was to become a distinguished career as pioneers of irrigated potato farming. The letters, cards, and photographs sent by the Prince remained treasured possessions of the family as did the fine gold watch presented to "Jimmy" when he left royal service.[29]

Professor Carlyle worked persistently during the 1920s to increase the deeded land base of the E.P. Ranch, and to insure that critical sections of

---

26 *Western Producer*, May 5, 1966; and *The New Canadian*, June 2, 1972.

27 GA M3973, f. 16, Yule Transcript.

28 *Calgary Herald*, September 17, 1923.

29 Interview with Albert Shimbashi, Calgary, June 1990.

The Prince with James Shimbashi, his wife, and son Edward, 1923.

The original "sitting room" at the E.P. which became "the office" after renovations of 1927.

land remained under the long-term control of his royal master. When the Prince of Wales purchased the "Bedingfeld place" in the fall of 1919, he bought two blocks of freehold land and a half share in extensive grazing leases. Some of these leased sections were crucial to the viability of the ranch, as they linked the deeded acreage (Map 9). Although the leases to these strategically placed lands were assigned to H.R.H. from George Lane during 1921, they were due to lapse in 1926.[30] Carlyle wrote to W.W. Cory, Deputy Minister of the Interior, asking that the newly assigned leases be changed to ten year leases, renewable at the end of the first ten years. The lands in question were inspected during June 1922 by the Senior Appraiser of Grazing Lands, who reported that they were unsuited to agriculture, and stocked according to the lease regulations. In due time the paper work was completed, and, for the payment of the princely sum of $25.80, the ranch acquired the use of 1,280 acres of pasture for the next twenty years.[31] But Carlyle was not satisfied, he arranged the purchase of 160 acres under the favourable terms of the

---

30 PAC RG15, Vol. 1285, fl. 606254, Assignment from George Lane to H.R.H., November 5, 1921. These leases had been issued to Frank Bedingfeld and his partners in 1905. As they were good for twenty-one years, they were due to lapse in 1926.

31 PAC RG15, Vol. 1285, fl. 606254, York to Carlyle, September 30, 1922.

Glassed in verandah, a real sun trap, at the E.P. ranch house.

Irrigation Act, and sought to take over the lease on another quarter section from Lane.[32] These exchanges with the various government departments responsible for administering western lands were concluded to the benefit of the E.P. Ranch and its royal owner. They proved to be but an overture to a flurry of bureaucratic activity in 1929 and 1930, which would double the deeded acreage of the ranch and secure for the Prince the mineral rights under his property.

Carlyle was in England during the summer of 1929, and met with the Prince and his council. He expressed his concern that the privacy, and indeed the integrity, of the ranch was threatened by exploration for oil and natural gas. Already some petroleum leases had been issued for land close to the ranch house. He explained that drilling involved the construction of wooden derricks, and these, along with roads, pipes, and storage facilities, seriously impinged upon the landscape. H.R.H. empowered Carlyle to make every effort to gain control over the mineral rights underlying his property.

On his return to Alberta, Carlyle wasted no time in raising his concerns with the government. C.W. Martin, Commissioner of Dominion Lands, collected information about the ranch, and had his staff prepare

---

32 PAC RG15, Vol. 1285, fl. 606254, Internal memo. Timber and Grazing file, January 31, 1922; and fl.608935, Carlyle to York, October 14, 1922.

a map of the ranch lands.[33] In a letter to the Deputy Minister of the Interior, he put the particular case of the E.P. into a general context:

> The ranchers' associations in western Canada, supported by the Provinces, are most anxious that all grazing leases of Crown lands be protected by permitting them to secure by purchase portions of their leaseholds in order to protect their improvements, and, as the Prince has very extensive improvements, he is, like all others, no doubt, most anxious to have his holdings absolutely protected during the period of operations, and for this reason, desires to become actual owner of both surface and underrights so that he may remain entirely undisturbed.
>
> It is the consensus of opinion that the establishing of a ranch in the west by H.R.H. is a great asset to the country, and it is my opinion that there would be no objection from any quarter to the Prince securing what he desires in this connection.[34]

Having established that the authorities would look favourably on H.R.H.'s request, Carlyle made formal application to purchase the lands which were currently under lease, "together with the mineral rights underlying the same." He included a rider that the mineral rights should revert to the Crown should the Prince dispose of the surface rights.[35] In his reply, Charles Stewart, Minister of the Interior, concluded with this sentence:

> The patent will contain the reversion clause discussed and at the same time make it clear that the underrights are conveyed with the surface in order that such underrights may be held for the protection of the surface, so that there can be no development of oil and gas rights or any other mineral rights.[36]

At this stage mineral rights were to be held only as a precautionary measure to prevent unwanted or unsightly development. Further discussion took place when Carlyle met the minister in Calgary during the latter's western tour. In December, Carlyle wrote again to Stewart and reported that an oil exploration company was prepared to exchange the petroleum rights on sensitive land near the house for similar rights in section 11, which was masked from the ranch by a hill. "If any drilling is to be done on the ranch either of these quarter sections would be most desirable from our standpoint since it could not interfere with the

---

33 PAC RG15, Vol. 1285, fl. 606254, Martin to Pereira, August 12, 1929.

34 PAC RG15, Vol. 1285, fl. 606254, Martin to Gibson, August 19, 1929.

35 PAC RG15, Vol. 1285, fl. 606254, Carlyle to Dominion Lands, September 24, 1929.

36 GA M2398, f. 161, Stewart to Carlyle, October 2, 1929.

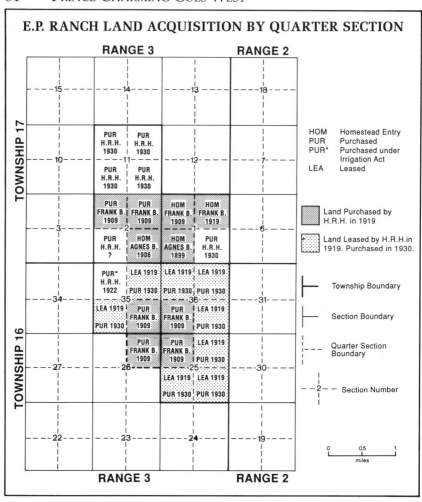

Map 9. E.P. Ranch, land acquisition by quarter section.

operation of the ranch."[37] Stewart replied that he was delighted that an accommodation had been reached which would "remove as far as possible from the buildings of the E.P. those rather unsightly derricks which do not add very much to the beauty of the landscape, and preserve this territory as a typical foothills ranch." He went onto say that he would recommend the sale of both surface and underrights, "on the distinct understanding that the underrights are not to be developed and that they

---

37 GA M2398, f. 161, Carlyle to Stewart, December 9, 1929.

are to revert to the Crown in the event of H.R.H. discontinuing his ranch operations."[38]

The sale price of $3.00 per acre was based on the recommendations of Albert Helmer, Supervisor of Grazing. He knew the E.P. lands quite well, having made an inspection of the ranch when Bedingfeld purchased four of five sections in 1909. He describes almost all the lands in question as "only fit for grazing purposes," and goes on to explain how he reached his evaluation. He argued that the land could only support one head of stock per twenty acres, and at current rental charges this meant forty cents per head per annum. Even if the land were purchased at the relatively low capital cost of $3.00 per acre, at current interest rates this would mean a cost of $4.80 per head per annum. He went on to point out that the department would receive twelve cents per acre per year instead of two cents. With regard to the underrights, "my understanding is that the underrights are being disposed of for the sole purpose of preventing the mutilation of this ranch for oil development works"; therefore, as the underrights are "simply being held by him (H.R.H.) in trust for the people, he can derive no monetary profit from their control," and therefore should not be charged for such rights.[39]

It is clear, however, that at this stage the Prince and his advisors started to shift their position. They did not want to preclude the possibility of exploring for oil and gas at some future date. A letter from Lionel Halsey to Carlyle in January 1930 refers to a geological survey of the possibilities of oil development on the ranch,[40] while a letter to Premier Brownlee of Alberta from Carlyle sums up the Prince's new position:

> In brief what we want is to reserve the ranch as a stock ranch for the breeding and dissemination of high class pure bred stock for the farmers of western Canada. We wish control of the oil development on the ranch so that the value of the place may not be completely destroyed as a stock ranch by having oil companies exploit the place by putting up derricks everywhere and practically throwing the place open to the public at all times. We would like the right, should it at some time later be desired to develop the mineral oil rights under certain small and obscure portions of the ranch under the regular legal provisions governing such developments.[41]

Brownlee made it clear to the federal government that the ranch was an asset which "does create an unusual and peculiar interest in the province

---

38 GA M2398, f. 161, Stewart to Carlyle, December 27, 1929.

39 PAC RG15, Vol. 1285, fl. 606254, Helmer to Martin, October 25, 1929.

40 GA M2398, f. 161, Halsey to Carlyle, January 6, 1930.

41 PAC RG15, Vol. 1285, fl. 606254, Carlyle to Brownlee, January 9, 1930.

and we are, therefore, anxious to meet his wishes as far as possible."[42] He advocated that a lease be issued under the normal regulations. This proposal was discussed at a meeting with the Deputy Minister of Justice in Ottawa. Carlyle and members of the staff of the Ministry of the Interior were present. Orders in council were prepared and approved,[43] and by June 23, 1930, J.W. Martin was writing to ask that the 2,000 acres purchased should be paid for so that patent for them could be issued. This was done on August 11.[44]

As one reads through this maze of letters between various government departments and Carlyle, one feels rather sorry for the bureaucrats involved. Probably they had to hire extra staff to handle the steady flow of requests and inquiries from the ranch manager. It is clear that the driving force behind the development was Carlyle. The Prince was content to leave all negotiating in his manager's hands, and was even prepared to grant him power of attorney. For his part, Carlyle wielded his royal connections like a weapon to bludgeon prompt attention from relevant government departments. He developed personal relationships with Stewart, the Minister of the Interior, and Martin, Commissioner of Dominion Lands. He had also entertained Premier Brownlee of Alberta at the ranch. The memoranda and letters are peppered with phrases like "at the very earliest opportunity"; "with the least possible delay"; and "as quickly as possible." A telegram from Brownlee concludes with the sentence, "I understand these terms are acceptable to Carlyle," and the Minister sent the Order in Council for provincial approval with the following words: "As Professor Carlyle is anxious to have this matter finally settled with the least possible delay, I would appreciate word from you by wire." It is clear that the "Professor" was a formidable and determined negotiator and that he pushed hard to secure concessions which were, in his opinion, in the best interests of the E.P. Ranch.

Matters were complicated by the fact that the federal government was finally going to relinquish control over land and resources to the provincial governments of the prairie provinces. This is why Premier Bronwlee was kept informed about the negotiations and was asked to approve the terms of the mineral lease. Moreover, the transfer of responsibility was due to take place in October 1930, and this may account for some of the urgency with which the matter was treated.

During the 1920s a remarkable transformation had been achieved at the E.P. Ranch. Under the competent leadership of Carlyle and with the generous support of the Duchy of Cornwall, it had become the most

---

42 PAC RG15, Vol. 1285, fl. 606254, Brownlee to Stewart, March 25, 1930.

43 PAC RG15, Vol. 1285, fl. 60625, Daly to Cory, April 16, 1930.

44 PAC RG15, Vol. 1285, fl. 60625, Martin to Carlyle, June 23, 1930.

famous ranch in Canada, and an acknowledged centre of breeding excellence. The Prince made three visits to his ranch during the decade. To those who excitedly prepared for his arrival, basked in his presence, and discussed every incident after his departure, each visit was a memorable occasion to be savoured, and the Prince was always "Prince Charming." To his staff, who were responsible for making arrangements, and "managing" their royal charge, Edward displayed very different characteristics. He was in turn depressed and moody or wildly irresponsible. The discharge of his formal public duties became more and more of a burden to him as each year passed. In the next chapter the three visits to the ranch are described, and an attempt is made to illustrate the way in which Edward's personality was changing under the twin pressures of adulation, and the hedonistic lifestyle of the rich during the "roaring twenties." The Prince's attitude toward his ranch changed markedly during the decade.

IV

The Prince Visits his Ranch

The Prince is a vivid figure in the imaginations of millions who have never heard of Napoleon or Mr. Lloyd George.[1]

The heir apparent in his unbridled pursuit of wine, women, and song . . . will soon become no fit wearer of the British Crown.[2]

For a few weeks during the late summer and fall of 1923, it seemed that the Prince of Wales' dream of using his ranch as a get-away from his princely duties had come true. He packed his working calendar during the summer, first with a visit to the west country, and then with a tour of the industrial north of Britain.[3] When he sailed for Canada on September 6, on the Canadian Pacific liner Empress of France, he had done more than enough to deserve a holiday.[4] An editorial in the *Calgary Herald* observed:

> The Prince needs a rest. He wants a change. He wants fresh air, and sunshine, and some riding and fishing and shooting. He does not want official events. That is what he is escaping from, and Albertans will show him no truer hospitality than just to leave him alone and let him enjoy himself in his own way while in this province. Above all the people of Calgary and southern Alberta have a responsibility in this connection. It is the responsibility of a host to see that the privacy of a guest is not intruded upon.[5]

1 Frank E. Verney, *H.R.H.* (New York: George C. Doran Co., 1926), p. 13.

2 Duff Hart-Davis (ed.), *In Royal Service: The Letters and Journals of Sir Alan Lascelles, 1920–1936*, Vol. 2 (London: Hamish Hamilton, 1989), p. 50.

3 Basil Maine, *The King's First Ambassador* (London: Hutchinson & Co., 1935), p. 161.

4 *Daily Mail*, September 6, 1923.

5 *Calgary Herald*, September 6, 1923.

Prince Edward travelled under the name of Lord Renfrew, the same alias used by his grandfather, Edward, Prince of Wales, when he visited the United States in 1860. A special train conveyed the royal party across the continent. They arrived in Calgary on September 16, and were able to drive to the ranch with a minimum of formality. A plea had been made to the press for a complete release from publicity, and this was scrupulously respected.[6] For this reason the day to day activities during the next three weeks are hard to piece together. It was harvest time and the royal party, undoubtedly led and encouraged by the ever energetic "Lord Renfrew," helped with stooking oats, chopping sunflowers, and filling the silo. "I've even helped muck out the cow house," boasted H.R.H. in a letter to his father, "and I chop and saw up wood and I can assure you that it is very hard work indeed."[7] Trees were planted, and the ravages of a spring flood were repaired. Each day offered opportunities for riding as the fall colours touched the trees along Pekisko Creek and the snow caps on the distant mountains became more extensive and obvious. "Our conversation is largely of sheep-dips, shorthorns, and stallions," reported the sophisticated Thomas with some disgust.[8] One biographer, from a city background, displayed considerable awe for "country life":

> Here was a rare chance of leading what was mistakenly called the simple life. Eagerly he took it, lending a hand at everything from the common round of hay making to the not so trivial task of rounding up cattle. The simple life! Not a few items comprising that kind of existence in Canada represent acts of the greatest skill and tests of humanity's utmost wit. The bronco's one obsession is to make man's life anything but simple.[9]

The Prince insisted on being treated like a normal human being. "I want to live just like they all live," he is reported to have said to Carlyle. "I want to eat the same way," he persisted. "That's the way it will be," answered the manager, "you will have the same cook . . . who looks after the rest of the boys. You'll get spuds and carrots, and lettuce and beets and all the rest of the truck out of your own garden. Your own hens will supply the eggs. Maybe we will kill a lamb or so and nice baby beef, and the occasional spring chicken."[10] This did indeed prove to be the case; for example the prince enjoyed breakfast of flapjacks, known to Alberta

---

6 *Calgary Herald*, September 13, 1923.

7 Philip Ziegler, *King Edward VIII: The Official Biography* (London: Collins, 1990), p. 149.

8 Ziegler, *Edward VIII*, p. 149.

9 Maine, *King's First Ambassador*, p. 99.

10 *Calgary Herald*, September 15, 1923.

farm hands as "stack of wheats," and brook trout, and lunch of corn on the cob.

One of the most accomplished fishermen among the royal party was Brigadier-General G.F. Trotter. Known to his friends as "G," General Trotter had lost an arm in the Boer War and was considerably older than H.R.H. In spite of his disability "G" was an expert fly-fisherman, and delighted in providing trout for the table from Pekisko Creek. His official post was that of assistant comptroller, and he was for several years the Prince's constant companion. "I learned from 'G' Trotter that life should be lived to the full,"[11] wrote the Duke of Windsor some years later. "G" was the epitome of the man about town, the boulevardier, "an amiable roué whose function was to facilitate the Prince's pursuit of pleasure." He always knew where the best parties were, and was affectionately described by a colleague as "a right old rip. "[12] His role is illustrated in a couple of chance remarks which a fellow aide wrote in a letter to his wife. "There is a vast ballroom where H.R.H. dances himself into a sweat every night, but is generally reduced to pulp fairly early, when I am released from my role of guarding his table in the 'Palm Court' while he and 'G' foot it with the damsels." That these dances were energetic is evidenced by a later entry: ". . . old 'G' being very lame as result of a violent hack on the ankle from a fellow dancer on the ship."[13] It must have been both physically and mentally exhausting trying to keep pace with the Prince's frenetic energy, but it is clear that "G" became devoted to the young man who he referred to as "my master." A year later Alan Lascelles wrote:

> I have got very fond of old "G," he is such a gallant old thing, and so cheerful and unruffled. But I really do believe that trying to live at the Prince's place, as he has now been doing for over a year, will kill him before long. He looks perfectly ghastly some mornings, after a night's dancing, though he is too game to admit it or even allow himself to be bad tempered. I notice that he keeps himself going with large quantities of the strongest black coffee he can get, which is a bad sign. After all he is fifty three and there are few men of any age who can compete with the Prince's inexhaustible vitality. I shall be really relieved on his account when we get safely home, and he can disappear to the Tweed for a bit.[14]

---

11 H.R.H., *Edward, Duke of Windsor, A King's Story* (Toronto: Thomas Allen Ltd., 1951), p. 190.

12 Ziegler, *Edward VIII*, p. 149.

13 Hart-Davis, *In Royal Service*, pp. 20 and 22.

14 Hart-Davis, *In Royal Service*, p. 38.

IN THE WILD AND WOOLLY
Will II. R. II. succumb to environment?

Cartoon which appeared in the British press on the occasion of the Prince's
first visit to his ranch. *Literary Digest*, October 6, 1923.

Shooting party at the E.P., September 1924. "G" Trotter, H.R.H., Professor Carlyle,
Sir Walter Peacock, "Fruity" Metcalfe, and Tommy Lascelles.

This was something of a prophetic utterance; four years later while accompanying the Prince on a safari in east Africa, "G" had a heart attack. He recovered and remained in the royal household until 1931.[15]

Although the Prince was eager to avoid formality, he did not ignore his neighbourly duty. He gave a luncheon for "the ranching aristocracy" from Calgary, and a picnic tea-party for his neighbours. He addressed his visitors as "My fellow Albertans," and went on, "you are welcome and I hope you enjoy your outing, my ranch is open to you today."[16] Although the press and city folks were excluded from the ranch, local people on horseback could usually find their way in, and might find the Prince, dressed in rather disreputable clothes, pitching hay, or painting a barn. H.R.H. likewise felt free to drop in on his neighbours. One of the ranches which he visited was that of an old Royal Naval Officer turned rancher, William C. Gardner, who was living to the south of the E.P.

---

15 The Prince broke with Trotter in 1931, when "G" refused to drop Lady Furness. J. Bryan III and Charles J.V. Murphy, *The Windsor Story* (New York: Morrow Co. Ltd., 1979), p. 183.

16 *Calgary Herald*, September 15, 1923.

Ranch in the shadow of Mount Sentinel. It was there one Sunday morning that the Gardner family awoke to find the Prince eating breakfast with their ranch hands along with Quon York, their Chinese cook. Apparently, H.R.H. had "escaped" for an early morning ride.[17] Rather more formally, the royal party rode over to Lord Minto's ranch near Nanton for a day's shooting. They returned with "a large bag of prairie chicken, Hungarian Partridges, ducks, and one rabbit."[18] On one of his last days at the ranch the Prince went coyote hunting. Six wolf hounds stirred up plenty of action as fourteen coyotes were sighted and three were bagged.[19]

The most elaborate semi-public event mounted during this first visit to the ranch was a picnic for shorthorn breeders. It was most successful and is described by the editor of the *Farm and Ranch Review*:

> It was a great day. One of the warmest, brightest and loveliest of our beautiful autumn season. The shorthorn breeders and their wives and families were out in force to do justice to the hospitality of the royal "boss," who, disguised as Lord Renfrew, mixed among the guests in a thoroughly western and democratic manner, ably assisted by his manager Professor Carlyle, who was everywhere and making everybody feel at home. A substantial lunch was served under the trees near the ranch headquarters, which all did ample justice to. Afterwards the serious part of the program commenced. All the four-legged "top-notchers" on the ranch, which have received commendation in these columns from time to time were brought out into the open one by one and in a few words Mr. Carlyle introduced them to the admiring crowd. There was much snapping of cameras and asking of questions and it is safe to say that our shorthorn men are beginning to look to the E.P. Ranch for leadership in the contest of breeds in Alberta.[20]

The stock show was followed by a rodeo, organized by Guy Weadick, the irrepressible American who had done so much to initiate the Calgary Stampede. He rode over from his ranch with some of his "outlaws," and put on a show which was very much enjoyed by the royal party. The Prince took lots of photographs of the stunts, and afterwards presented the Prince of Wales' Trophy to Peter Vandermeer, the overall winner at the Calgary Stampede.

On Sunday, September 30, the party left for Calgary. Basil Maine commented, "No holiday in the Prince's career has been more necessary than that interval on his ranch, and by none had he been so well and

17 *Calgary Herald*, September 6, 1980.
18 *Calgary Herald*, September 20, 1923.
19 *Calgary Herald*, October 1, 1923.
20 *Farm and Ranch Review*, October 20, 1923.

immediately restored."[21] The evidence is overwhelming that H.R.H. really enjoyed his time on the ranch. Indeed he is supposed to have said to Carlyle, "This has been the happiest day of my life!" Carlyle was inclined to be sceptical. "I mean it," the Prince insisted, "this is the first time in my life that I've felt like a real man. I've met my neighbours and I like them. What's more, I think they like me, not because I'm a Prince, but because I'm one of the gang."[22] This may have been true, but the Prince would not have been content with an unrelieved diet of ranch chores and rural pursuits. He wrote, "Its a fine healthy life and a real rest for the brain . . . but of course one couldn't stick it for very long."[23] On his first visit, he had only been on his ranch for three days when he took off for a four day weekend at the Banff Springs Hotel. There he played several rounds of golf each day and danced at night. As will be seen, the same pattern held true for his later visits. Much as Albertans and their media cast him in the role of "ordinary rancher," he was actually a "holidaying Prince" and arranged his days exactly as he wished.

The Princely day-dream of 1919 had become the enchanting reality of 1923, and those who had met briefly with H.R.H. on his first tour must have felt that they had got to know him a little better during his more leisurely residence at his ranch. It must have been extremely hard for his new friends in Alberta to comprehend the whirlwind of events which had been carrying Edward along during the four intervening years, and the way in which his personality had developed during that time.

The immense success of his Canadian tour had been followed, in the spring of 1920, by an arduous tour of New Zealand and Australia. Once again he had dazzled and charmed the people of the Dominions. He had shaken hundreds of thousands of hands and had been touched and prodded by enthusiastic crowds from Auckland, New Zealand, to Perth, Australia. As Lady Donaldson has observed: "the manners and the personality of this young Prince were in tune with a philosophy they cherished deeply and were marvellously reassuring to the sense of uncertainty and insecurity inevitably felt by the citizens of these aggressively young countries."[24]

After a year's respite at home, the Prince once more embarked on H.M.S. Renown to tour India and the Far East. This was the most politically sensitive of the tours for it took place in the aftermath of the massacre at Amritsar and at a high point in Gandhi's movement of passive resistance and non-cooperation with the government. The Prince

---

21 Maine, *King's First Ambassador*, pp. 161–62.

22 *Calgary Herald*, September 13, 1924.

23 Ziegler, *Edward VIII*, p. 149.

24 Frances Donaldson, *Edward VIII* (London: Weidenfeld and Nicolson, 1974), p. 80.

displayed conspicuous bravery and determination to press ahead with planned events even when difficulties were anticipated. Triumph followed triumph, from his arrival at Bombay; his wildly enthusiastic reception at Poona; to his less formal and friendly visits with the immensely rich Indian Princes. "In my most sanguine moments," the Viceroy wrote to King George, "I never expected such a complete success as has happened and this is due to the Prince himself."[25]

These tours made Edward the best known personality of his time. He became "the first star of . . . public media through which millions of people all over the world watched (and listened to) his progress round it."[26] One contemporary biographer reported:

> Every word that the Prince utters in public is eagerly read by thousands of people both at home and abroad, and since the popularization of radio broadcasting, the Prince has been brought even more into touch with the peoples of the Empire through his speeches. His speech at the annual banquet of the Company of Master Mariners was distinctly heard in Cape Town, and fully reported the next day in the newspapers there.[27]

One ardent biographer discussed the Prince's global profile in terms of which Rudyard Kipling would have approved:

> It is a fact that he is a vivid figure in the imaginations of millions who have never heard of Napoleon or Mr. Lloyd George. . . . On the North-West Frontier of India, I have seen the eyes of a wild Afghan gleam with interest at the mention of his name. A group of naked Barotse hunters round a camp fire in the basin of the Zambesi invited me to applaud a legend of his hunting prowess. I saw his photographs hanging in the mud hut of a Dinka chief in the Soudan. I have bought picture post-cards of him in most of the bazaars of Egypt. I once heard some river Arabs discussing him fantastically on a Tigris mahalla.[28]

The hyperbole may be florid and dated, but it would be hard to exaggerate the interest in and knowledge of the Prince of Wales. Never had a royal personality established himself so firmly in the hearts of people all over the world. The tragedy was that this outpouring of adulation constituted an irresistible pressure which was to change Edward's personality. As Walter Bagshot shrewdly observed, "Whatever is most

---

25 Donaldson, *Edward VIII*, p. 94.

26 Lord Kinross, *The Windsor Years* (New York: Viking Press, 1967), p. 89.

27 W. and L. Townsend, *The Biography of H.R.H. The Prince of Wales* (London: E. Marritt & Son, 1929), p. 271.

28 Verney, *H.R.H.*, p. 13.

attractive, whatever is most seductive, has always been offered to the Prince of Wales of the day, and always will be. It is not rational to expect the best virtue where temptation is applied in the most trying form at the frailest time of human life."[29]

Relationships between the Prince and his staff were becoming more strained. "The golden-hearted charmer 'full of fun and rags with everyone,' as one of them described the Prince, whose abundant vitality had enchanted them all in the early 1920s, was turning into a difficult, obstinate charge whose impulses they could not control and whose lapses they had to struggle to conceal."[30] At the height of the Indian tour the Prince wrote to Freda that his staff was "the finest ground possible for foul and bloody gossip and scandal!! They do their utmost to make life hell for me instead of helping me."[31]

It was not only the heady worship of the public which contributed to the deterioration in Edward's character. "He was a genuine product of his period, in which large sections of society spent their time in the pursuit of pleasure with a single mindedness which marks this generation off from almost every other in history."[32] During the brief period between the cessation of hostilities and his departure on his Canadian tour the Prince of Wales had sampled briefly the joys of the London season. He had begun to develop an appetite for parties which remained unsatiated throughout his life. Whenever he was in London, particularly between the conclusion of his Australian tour and his departure for India, his formal engagements would be completed and then, "Fruity and I would go out and have a good time."[33] In the 1920s, as the Duke of Windsor was to recall nostalgically, "the party round was almost continuous. One might receive invitations for as many as four parties the same evening . . . if the first failed to please, one could always move on to another."[34] If all failed to amuse, or when the last was over, there were the fashionable night clubs: The Cafe de Paris, The Kit Kat, or, his particular favourite, The Embassy. Here the atmosphere was bright and noisy, and the dancing was energetic, above all, the small party that accompanied H.R.H. were chosen friends and there was no hint of duty.

---

29 Ziegler, *Edward VIII*, p. 107.

30 Sarah Bradford, *The Reluctant King: The Life and Reign of George VI, 1895–1952* (New York: St. Martin's Press, 1989), p. 126.

31 Ziegler, *Edward VIII*, p. 142.

32 Donaldson, *Edward VIII*, p. 103.

33 Brian Inglis, *Abdication* (New York: Macmillan, 1966), p. 21. Inglis discusses the atmosphere of the 1920s as a whole.

34 H.R.H., *King's Story*, p. 193.

Stuffy protocol and the norms of the establishment were boring and were to be swept away by the chic new post-war generation.[35]

What were the results of these twin pressures of fame and adulation on the one hand, and a pleasure-seeking hedonistic society on the other, on a man who had been starved of affection as a child and who had come of age in the trenches? To those who came to know him well, or had occasion to observe him critically, it seemed that he never really matured beyond adolescence. "He was subject to a tension too unique, too subtle, too varied and too continuous for his character to ripen and strengthen."[36] Stanley Baldwin framed the same idea more precisely, "He is an abnormal being, half child, half genius . . . it is almost as though two or three cells in his brain remained entirely undeveloped while the rest of him is a mature man."[37] His private secretary, Alan Lascelles, echoed this thought: "For some hereditary or physiological reason his mental and spiritual growth stopped dead in his adolescence thereby affecting his whole consequent behaviour."[38]

Edward developed a number of coping mechanisms which cast him in an increasingly unfavourable light. State pageants and court functions left him cold, and whenever he was involved in formal parts of his program he became less and less successful in hiding his boredom and indifference. As early as 1923, the veteran newspaperman Frederick Griffin remarked that the Prince was not out to please the populace and "made very little pretence at trying." By 1927, Griffin noticed that the Prince made no attempt to hide his ennui with the formal reception, and "in Montreal he changed the announced route and slipped away in a taxi to play golf thus disappointing thousands of people who had waited in the heat for hours."[39] H.R.H. became increasingly unpunctual in spite of the meticulous planning of his staff. This resulted partly from his ability to become totally involved in a part of his schedule which did interest him, but also from a growing lack of concern and sensitivity, which some interpreted as spoilt arrogance. He also became ruthlessly selective in choosing which "unofficial" private functions he would or would not attend. Sometimes he would accept invitations only to disappoint his hosts with transparent excuses.

---

35 Donaldson, *Edward VIII*, pp. 103–104.

36 Robert Sencourt, *The Reign of Edward VIII* (London: Gibbs and Phillips, 1962), p. 33.

37 Ziegler, *Edward VIII*, p. 163.

38 Ziegler, *Edward VIII*, p. 163.

39 Frederick Griffin, *Variety Show: Twenty Years of Watching the News Parade* (Toronto: MacMillan, 1936), p. 205.

The pressures of his position also resulted in less observable but none the less fundamental changes in personality and behaviour. In some ways the Prince was the epitome of the extrovert who:

> . . . is sociable, likes parties, has many friends, needs to have people to talk to, and does not like reading or studying by himself; he craves excitement, takes chances, acts on the spur of the moment and is generally an impulsive individual. He is fond of practical jokes, always has a ready answer and generally likes change; he is carefree, easy going and likes to "laugh and be merry." He prefers to keep moving and doing things: tends to be aggressive and loses his temper quickly; his feelings are not kept under tight control and he is not always a reliable person.[40]

But these characteristics only describe one facet of a complex psyche. Those closest to him during the 1920s noticed that the Prince's periods of depression and melancholia, always a part of his personality, became more frequent under the immense pressure of his tours. Lord Mountbatten recalled years later:

> On this journey [to Australia] I got to know my cousin very well indeed. I soon realized that under that delightful smile which charmed people everywhere, and despite all the fun that we managed to have, he was a lonely and sad person, always liable to deep depressions.[41]

When these depressions were on him the Prince would sometimes pass whole days by himself in his cabin in the Renown, seeing no one except his cousin and hardly eating. A year later on the Indian tour Mountbatten wrote, "I am having a great time, but it is very difficult to keep David cheerful. At times he gets so depressed and says he would give anything to change places with me."[42] Sometimes his bouts of depression were so pervasive as to be incapacitating. The Prince wrote to Freda Dudley-Ward apologizing for his behaviour on the previous evening, "I just couldn't help it; the black, mist came down and enveloped me irrevocably . . . and it wasn't any good making an effort to cheer up."[43] On another occasion he wrote, "I feel fit enough but mentally I'm absolutely worn out. Thank God its all over bar the shouting now as I really don't think that I could carry on much longer without the top of my head cracking like an

---

40 Inglis, *Abdication*, p. 28.

41 Donaldson, *Edward VIII*, p. 81; and Christopher Warwick, *Abdication* (London: Sidewick & Jackson, 1986), p. 54.

42 Donaldson, *Edward VIII*, p. 81.

43 Ziegler, *Edward VIII*, p. 164.

egg."[44] His doctor stressed that he was pushing himself too hard. "H.R.H.'s present method of life is such as may involve a complete breakdown of his whole nervous system."[45]

Another facet of Edward's character that became more obvious during the 1920s was his tendency to form opinions on matters, often on very shallow evidence, and then hold onto those opinions stubbornly. His lawyer and confidant Walter Monckton commented, "Once his mind was made up one felt that he was like the deaf adder, 'that stoppeth her ears and refuseth to hear the voice of the charmer'."[46] His mother felt that he was the most obstinate of her sons, and recognized that to oppose him over anything was a sure way to make him more determined to do it.[47] After the Great War H.R.H. became convinced that he alone, rather than courtiers or parliamentarians, could understand and interpret the feelings of his generation, because he had suffered in the trenches with them. On his tours of the Dominions he was most successful when he threw over protocol and made direct contact with the people. Surely, he felt, the same direct, straightforward, person to person approach would be successful in the diplomatic arena. His success in India confirmed this view and led to his personal intervention in Turkey, with the Balkans, and eventually with various peace groups and the Nazis. Unlike his brother, the Duke of York, Edward had no sense of history and absolutely no grasp of the way constitutional monarchy had evolved. Sir Anthony Eden formed the impression of "an impetuous and often opinionated man who did not understand the limits imposed on a modern monarch and lacked his father's intimate knowledge of foreign affairs." Whereas his father knew much and interfered little, he knew little and interfered much.[48] There was much truth in Baldwin's comment to the editor of the *Times*, Geoffrey Dawson, "You know, Geoffrey, the little man hasn't the least idea of how this country is governed."[49] As he became increasingly conceited over his popularity, he had no ability to place his real success into a constitutional context. "Every incident of fifteen years of his life had contributed to the weakness of self-centredness, and his

44 Ziegler, *Edward VIII*, p. 130.

45 Ziegler, *Edward VIII*, p. 140.

46 Lord Birkenhead, *Walter Monckton: The Life of Viscount Monckton of Brenchley* (London: Weidenfeld and Nicholson, 1969), p. 126.

47 Michael Thornton, *Royal Feud* (New York: Simon and Schuster, 1985), p. 87.

48 Inglis, *Abdication*, p. 124.

49 Pierre Berton, *Macleans*, April 1, 1953.

fantastic vanity over his own capacity . . . led him to believe he could 'get away with' almost anything."[50]

It is against the background of his fast paced and rather raffish social life, and significant shifts in his character, that the Prince's visits to his ranch in Alberta must be placed. Clearly the E.P. was a wonderful place to set aside the burdens of princedom. It really was isolated, and the press were prepared to respect his privacy. But for all its country charm and the warmth of the welcome he got from his neighbours, one wonders how long the Prince would have been content to stay away from the sophisticated pleasures of London night life, and the stimulation of his set. During the late summer of 1924 it seems that the Prince—consciously or unconsciously—was forced to choose between the fast life of the very rich on Long Island and the bucolic pleasures of his Alberta ranch.

In 1924, the Prince of Wales again determined to spend his holidays in the New World. The international polo matches between Great Britain and the United States were to be held outside New York, and H.R.H. planned to enjoy watching the matches before travelling to the E.P. Ranch. Having lunched with President and Mrs. Coolidge in Washington, the Prince took up residence in Syosset, Long Island, where he had been lent a house. As the Duke of Windsor described it years later:

> All around were fine houses and well kept lawns and swimming pools. Compared to the creature comforts the Americans took for granted, the luxury to which I was accustomed in Europe seemed almost primitive. . . . Everything seemed to go well amid a gay round of sport and entertainment.[51]

The Prince threw himself with enthusiasm into the round of amusements which the very rich had arranged for him. He played polo, roared around Long Island Sound in a special boat, swam, and went racing at Belmont Park. At night he attended a succession of balls, each more elaborate than the last. His visit became an endurance contest, "with the bank balances of the refulgent chieftains of the Long Island set pitted against H.R.H.'s health . . . never in the history of metropolitan society has any visitor to these shores been so persistently and extravagantly fêted."[52]

H.R.H. was enjoying himself so much that, when poor weather forced postponement of the polo matches, he was delighted to stay on. Originally, he had planned to leave for Canada on September 7, but departure was put off again and again.

---

50 Hector Bolitho, *King Edward VIII: An Intimate Biography* (New York: Literary Guild of America Inc., 1937), p. 253.

51 H.R.H., *King's Story*, p. 199.

52 Ziegler, *Edward VIII*, p. 151.

Such was the interest of the public in the royal holiday maker that most U.S. newspapers devoted a front page column to his activities, and included pages of further coverage inside. The Long Island swells tried with some success to keep the press at bay, and reporters dubbed the stand-off "the battle of Long Island." "These Yank pressmen are b...s," the Prince wrote to Thomas, "one does resent their damn spying so and they get so tight! It seems a mean shame having them around when one is on holiday."[53] The extensive and unrestrained coverage conveyed a picture of the Prince as a frivolous playboy. The *New York World* commented disapprovingly:

> He managed by his choice of friends and diversions, to provoke an exhibition of social climbing on the part of a few Americans which has done nothing to add to his prestige nor to the prestige of royalty in general . . . civilization would survive if the King business were wound up.[54]

The Prince's staff were faced with the unenviable task of trying to contain the damage. This was a major challenge for Captain Alan Lascelles, who was responsible for writing the royal speeches and for handling the press. "Tommy" Lascelles, as he was known to all his friends, was a brilliant and cultivated young man. A nephew of the fifth Earl of Harewood, Lascelles was born into the heart of the old landed aristocracy. He had joined the royal household two years before, but this was the first time that he had been on a tour. His letters home to his wife provided fascinating glimpses of H.R.H. and the people who surrounded him. Lascelles tried valiantly to mute the critical press commentary which the Prince's "Playboy" activities were earning him. He arranged a tea-party at which some key editors would be able to meet the Prince. Later, Lascelles recalled that it was a successful ruse:

> They all came, and it was amusing to see how every one of them, even the two Hearst editors, who have been anti-British for years, succumbed to him completely after five minutes' talk. It did a lot of good, that little party, and since it happened there's hardly been an unkind word written, even in the Sunday rags, which are notoriously filthy and scandalous.[55]

It is clear that Edward was apprehensive about the impact which all this publicity would have on his father, King George V. In a letter from

---

53 Ziegler, *Edward VIII*, p. 150.

54 Bolitho, *King Edward VIII*, p. 242.

55 Hart-Davis, *In Royal Service*, p. 32.

the E.P. Ranch posted immediately after his arrival there, the Prince stressed his more prosaic activities and went on to comment on the character of the press in the United States:

> I have learnt a great deal about the U.S. press . . . you can't compare it in any way with the British press because it is a far bigger industry than ours. . . . It indulges in queer and extravagant headlines daily which means that they are forgotten the next day. Sometimes they don't look so good . . . but being a daily habit their bark or their look is worse than their bite.[56]

However, his letter and Lascelles' efforts failed to turn away the King's wrath, he replied to his son:

> I was glad to get your letter of the 4th and to hear that you were enjoying yourself at Long Island. But according to the daily telegrams in the papers you must be having a pretty strenuous time, as besides playing polo and various other things in the day at most of which you are mobbed, you dance until 6 o'clock every morning, including Sundays. It is a pity the press can't be induced to leave you alone, when you are supposed to be on a holiday.[57]

On his return to England the Prince had to review with the King headlines like "Prince gets in with Milkman"; or "Here he is girls—the most eligible bachelor yet uncaught." The British press was restrained in its reporting of the Royal Family and abstained completely from commenting on their private doings, so the King reacted strongly against this unfamiliar effrontery. "If this vulgarity represents the American attitude toward people in our position, little purpose would be served in your exposing yourself again to this kind of treatment."[58] Indeed for the remainder of his life the King was able to frustrate the efforts of his sons to make any other visits to the United States. Perhaps the Prince's growing tendency to seek out American friends in London reflected his admiration for the U.S. and the fact that he was denied access to that stimulating country. "America, with all its unchained enthusiasm and love of show, was nearer to his sympathies than the prejudice ridden countries of Europe."[59]

The Prince finally left Syosset on September 28, and the whole town turned out to see him off. For the next three days the special train sped

---

56 H.R.H., *King's Story*, p. 202.

57 H.R.H., *King's Story*, p. 202.

58 H.R.H., *King's Story*, p. 203.

59 Bolitho, *King Edward VIII*, p. 102.

H.R.H. chatting with Prime Minister Mackenzie King at Ottawa station en route to the ranch from his holiday in the northeastern United States, 1924.

westward on the C.N. line. The trees in northern Ontario had begun to turn, and several times moose were seen close to the track. American hunters asked the Prince to spend a day hunting with them, and provided a quarter of meat for him to enjoy when he had to refuse.[60]

A few days later, Sir Walter Peacock described the Prince's first weekend "at home" in idyllic terms:

> The Prince's life for the first two or three days after his arrival at his ranch was very quiet. There was absolutely nothing arranged for at present, and he did just as he pleased. His life is so mapped out for him that he will be glad of at least a few days of absolute peace and quiet. He will do just as the spirit moves him, and after all, this is the only place for that. He has been rather much in the limelight at Long Island, and now he'll have a chance to have a real rest.[61]

However, in a letter from the ranch to his wife, Tommy Lascelles gives a more down-to-earth picture of the royal party's arrival at the ranch:

> My darling, nothing could have been more melancholy than our arrival here; H.R.H with a roaring cold and very depressed, leaden skies and bitter sleet storms. The drive out from High River, was the chilliest I've ever had, and we got here to find all the fires smoking and the one living-room practically uninhabitable. It seemed a very depressing place, and I began to wonder how we could endure five days of it. But, three hours after we got here, the sky cleared and since then we have had the most flawless, golden weather, with blazing sun and air like wine.
>
> The ranch consists of the homestead--a large wooden bungalow in which we all live—and three or four barns and cattle-sheds, all thrown down by the side of the little Pekisko river, which winds through a narrow belt of trees and scrub from the Rockies, bounding the whole horizon some thirty miles to the west. There are two low ranges of hills on each side of the river, and between them lies a vast undulating plain, broken only by occasional bluffs, set with stunted trees. It is not really beautiful country, save for the wonderful line of the mountains, but the space and the cleanness of it make one love it.[62]

Saturday was a beautiful fall day and, as usual, it was packed with activity. H.R.H. had a cold; he wrote to Thomas, "I had the flu and fever the whole time," but he did not let it slow him down.[63] He spent the early

---

60 *Family Herald and Weekly Star*, October 1, 1924.

61 *Family Herald and Weekly Star*, October 1, 1924.

62 Hart-Davis, *In Royal Service*, p. 39.

63 Ziegler, *Edward VIII*, p. 154.

H.R.H. and Calgary's "Big Four" cattlemen, at the E.P. Ranch, 1924. Pat Burns, George Lane, H.R.H., A.J. McLean, and A.E. Cross.

part of the morning hay-making, and hiked to the top of the hills to the east of the ranch house to get a view of the whole valley. After lunch the party rode over to Rod MacLean's ranch for some duck shooting. One would think that this was enough activity to pack into a day, but one observer noted "On every occasion that he has a few minutes to spare the Prince seizes a fishing rod and makes a sally after trout in the stream on his ranch. His efforts along this line have proved very successful and he brought in a good string of trout on Saturday evening."[64] The next two days were spent in the same kind of ranch based activity. The lawn, repaired after a wash out the previous year, had recovered well and the trees he had planted were flourishing. A new barn had been constructed on much the same plan as the first.

The Prince always enjoyed talking with "old timers" about the pioneering days, and their adventures as cowboys. He had a splendid opportunity to hear a mix of yarns when he invited a number of distinguished ranchers and business men to lunch. Pat Burns, George Lane, and A.E. Cross were there along with Archie MacLean, W.R. Hull, W.R. Pierce, and Dan Riley, each man a contributor to the story of the settlement of Alberta. The Honourable R.B. Bennett was also present and introduced the guest of honour, the Canadian High Commissioner to London, the Honourable P.C. Larkin.

On the last day of his visit, the *Calgary Herald* trumpeted: "Prince's Ranch open to the world: Cameras click and reporters hob-nob with Royal Rancher." The occasion was the annual picnic of the Alberta Shorthorn Breeder's Association. In spite of a blustery day with overcast skies, 500–600 people had arrived by noon. "Visitors were present from far and near. Livestock men, government officials, newspapermen, and just plain curiosity seekers, but all had a good time."[65] The Prince mingled with the crowd and posed for photographs. Edythe Smith, one of the Calgary ladies who had volunteered to prepare an outdoor lunch for the crowd, was introduced to the Prince of Wales in the midst of her sandwich making. "Shake," chuckled the Prince, "I've shaken a lot more hammy hands in my time!"[66]

In the afternoon the first sale of stock from the ranch took place. Before any animals were auctioned the undefeated grand champion bull, the King of the Fairies, was paraded round the ring. Duncan Marshall, President of the Dominion Shorthorn Breeders' Association, stressed the benefits of having access to some of the best purebred cattle in the world, and referred to the long association between the Royal Family and

---

64 *Calgary Herald*, September 29, 1924.

65 *Calgary Herald*, October 2, 1924; and *Farm and Ranch Review*, October 25, 1924.

66 *Calgary Herald*, September 6, 1980.

shorthorn breeding, which he said went back to the days of Queen
Victoria. At the end of the afternoon twenty-one head of shorthorns had
been sold for a total of $6,400. Purchasers included local ranchers like Pat
Burns, A.E. Cross, and John Brown of Lineham, but the top price was
paid by Colonel G.W. Lilley, of Parnee, Oklahoma, for a young bull
which had been undefeated as a junior calf at the six leading western
Canada shows during the 1923–24 show year. Lascelles reported:

> Yesterday there was a sale of cattle and sheep, which all the countryside
> attended; in spite of having previously consumed liberal supplies of
> whisky in the house, they showed no enthusiasm in the ring. Prices were
> disappointing, not, I gather because the stock wasn't all that it should be,
> but because there is very little spare cash in these parts.[67]

PROBABLY BILL DURNO

The auctioneer was John Durno of Calgary, and a well publicized
story suggests that his rhythmic chanting of prices was rudely interrupted by uninhibited argument and laughter from behind the stand. Durno
suddenly whirled round and bellowed behind him, "Stop that racket!"
There was muffled giggling, then silence as all eyes turned on the guilty
parties. Instead of paying attention to the sales, the Prince of Wales was
enjoying a noisy series of cutthroat noughts and crosses games with a
couple of local youngsters, using builder's chalk on the boards of the
auctioneer's platform. Durno later confessed to considerable embarrassment upon finding that he had snapped at the future monarch.[68]

As the sale closed a cold rain began to fall and the crowd started to
melt away. The Prince found time to make his way down to George
Lane's car because his friend was in poor health and could not get out to
enjoy the festivities.[69] In his parting remarks the "Royal Rancher" made
it clear that he would be unable to visit next year, as he was bound for
South Africa; however, he said that he hoped to return in 1926.

On this occasion then, H.R.H. spent only five days on the ranch
rather than the planned three weeks. He made no attempt to curtail his
visits to Vancouver and Victoria, prompting his mother to comment
sardonically, "So after all you are only spending a week on your ranch,
what a pity when I thought that was the raison d'être for your going
out."[70] One must conclude, as she obviously did, that the ranch was in
no way the focus of the trip, rather it was an interlude between the more
sophisticated pleasures offered by Long Island and British Columbia.

---

67 Hart-Davis, *In Royal Service*, p. 24.

68 *Calgary Herald*, September 6, 1980.

69 *Farm and Ranch Review*, October 25, 1924. Lane died on September 24, 1925.

70 Ziegler, *Edward VIII*, p. 153.

The next royal visit to Canada and the ranch was much more formal than the two previous ones. In 1927, the Prince of Wales was invited to help celebrate the Diamond Jubilee of Canadian Confederation. The aim of the visit was to cement relations between "the Dominion and the motherland." The organizer went on:

> The spread of mutual enlightenment, mutual sympathy, and the closer knitting of our family ties, the value of the personal touch and personal communication, make up a total of factors making for Empire unity and Empire amity. As such they are incalculable in their value and ineffaceable in their lasting effect.[71]

The Prince of Wales was accompanied by his brother, Prince George. This was a real pleasure for both men, as they were close friends and shared a number of interests.[72] Prince Edward enjoyed introducing the younger man to the various techniques which he had learned over the years for surviving, and even enjoying life, on a hectic public tour. He also encouraged Prince George to step forward into the limelight occasionally, and to make his first public speeches, for example at Edmonton and Vancouver.

The royal party was accompanied by the Prime Minister of Great Britain, Stanley Baldwin, and his family. Baldwin masked the well-honed skills of a master politician behind a facade of an old-fashioned and somewhat ineffectual country squire. One dismissive aristocrat wrote:

> I have never met a man in a big position with less inspiration in him. Lloyd George has more electricity in one finger than Stanley Baldwin has in his whole system. In the analogy game his dish is unquestionably cold mutton, without mint sauce. I like cold mutton, as you know, and often eat it from choice, but all the same it is cold mutton.[73]

The Prime Minister's decision to go to Canada at this time aroused much discussion and some criticism. The Geneva Conference, which had been called to discuss the naval arms race between the great powers, had ended inconclusively. Relationships between Great Britain and the United States were strained, and foreign policy was in turmoil. After the abdication crisis it was suggested that Baldwin undertook the tour to get

---

71 *Financial Times*, August 25, 1927; and *Times*, August 2, 1927.

72 When he left the Navy Prince George went to live with the Prince of Wales at York House. When the younger man got involved with drugs in 1928 and 1929, Edward personally intervened to help him, and was successful in breaking the addiction. Later George had a room of his own at Fort Belvedere. See Ziegler, *Edward VIII*, p. 200; Bradford, *Reluctant King*, pp. 50 and 140; and Donaldson, *Edward VIII*, p. 157.

73 Hart-Davis, *In Royal Service*, p. 52.

Prince Edward and Prince George with Mr. Stanley Baldwin, Prime Minister of Great Britain, and his wife, being welcomed to Calgary, 1927.

to know the Prince of Wales better, so that he could exert a beneficial influence. In fact, the Prince and the Prime Minister were already well acquainted. H.R.H.'s letters to Baldwin prior to the tour showed affection, and at times almost veneration. There was no need to make an unprecedented journey merely in order to ingratiate himself with the heir apparent. However, the tour did enable them to deepen their already cordial relationship. The Prince commented that the Baldwins were "most charming travelling companions . . . a very nice family indeed and I am glad to have got to know them." The Prime Minister reciprocated, "The Prince of Wales was at his best and it was a real pleasure to be with him."[74] The real reason that Baldwin accepted the invitation of the Canadian government was because he saw an opportunity to "take the pulse of the Empire," and to interpret post-war Britain to the Canadians. As he argued in many of his more than twenty major speeches across Canada, ". . . there has been too long an idea uncontradicted that we are played out, idle, hopeless, and so on, and I went for that with all the energy I could command. The reception I got was amazing."[75] Baldwin was accompanied by his wife, daughter, and son-in-law. As the tour

74 Ziegler, *Edward VIII*, p. 188.

75 Keith Middlemas and John Barnes, *Baldwin: A Biography* (London: MacMillan, 1969), p. 377.

proceeded it became clear that it was turning into something of a triumph for the homely Prime Minister:

> We [the press] were all inclined to agree that Baldwin, middle aged, unpretentious, grinning puckishly at the least excuse, stole the honours of the visit from the Prince of Wales. H.R.H. played the part of the bored elder; the PM carried himself like a youngster having a jolly good time.[76]

As for Prince Edward, "he had long since ceased to be the sunshine Prince, the smiling Prince, Prince charming, or any of the other creatures ballyhooed on the 1919 tour."[77] On some occasions his boredom was so obvious as to be offensive. When Baldwin and his family arrived punctually to dine at Government House in Ottawa, they saw the two Princes in sports clothes heading for the squash court. Dinner had to wait until the game was over and the royal pair had changed. In Montreal, Brockville, and Calgary, golf came before the demands of the waiting crowds. Perhaps most serious of all was the Prince's cavalier omission of crucial political material from his key speeches, because he felt it was pompous or tedious. This occurred at a time when an editorial in the *Times* was suggesting that his speeches were of greater significance than ever.[78] His private secretary was driven to the point of despair. He arranged an interview with Prime Minister Baldwin, and told him directly:

> In my considered opinion, the heir apparent, in his unbridled pursuit of wine, women, and whatever selfish whim occupies him at the moment, is rapidly going to the devil, and unless he mends his ways, he will soon become no fit wearer of the British crown.[79]

Admiral Halsey, whose organizational skills had smoothed the Prince's path on so many tours, went home from this one halfway through, feeling like "the fifth wheel of a coach" because his advice was constantly ignored. The Prince refused to acknowledge that his right to personal privacy and "some life of his own" had to be balanced by a responsible attitude toward his state role. Lascelles complained:

> It is the impossibility of making him realize this side of his position that defeats me. All the work his private secretaries have to do centres round

---

76 Griffin, *Variety Show*, p. 203.

77 Griffin, *Variety Show*, p. 216.

78 *Time*, August 10, 1927.

79 Hart-Davis, *In Royal Service*, p. 50.

that—the fact that he is the future king—and not round his individual personality; and as he makes no effort except in the direction of expressing that personality, in one form or another and usually at the expense of the other thing, one is continually trying to carry water in a sieve. In fact, one is like a jockey trying to induce a horse to race, whose only idea is to stop in the middle of the course and perform circus tricks; or an actor manager, whose Hamlet persists in interrupting the play by balancing the furniture on the end of this nose.[80]

It was against this background that the tour unfolded. A week of ponderous ceremony in crushing heat and humidity culminated in the opening of the "Peace Bridge" between Canada and the United States at Niagara. The Prince described it as "a frightful week of Princing, and burning the candle etc., and I'm getting too old to make it now." He went on to explain to his father the relish with which Canadian politicians seemed to approach speech making "a speech to them is like a good day's shooting to you."[81] It was with some relief that the party finally headed westward, the Baldwins to Banff and Lake Louise, and the Princes to the ranch.

The royal party drove to the E.P. from Calgary, and by-passed the crowd which was waiting patiently in High River Station. The next morning the Princes explored the ranch together and went for a long ride to "beat the bounds." However, the following day they drove back to Calgary, to attend a huge gathering at which Baldwin was to speak. Some 6,000 Calgarians gave the speech a tumultuous reception. In it, the British Prime Minister paid tribute to the role played by pioneer farmers and ranchers, and noted that improvements in transportation and communications were doing much to make rural life less isolated. He committed himself to encouraging those without employment in the old country to seek the enormous opportunities available in the new. "I want to bring the open spaces and the willing hands together." When Baldwin returned to his favourite theme and said that Great Britain was not down and out and that "we shall come through, and are coming through slowly, steadily, and surely," he was interrupted by cheers for several minutes.[82]

On Friday, August 12, the newspapers announced a last minute change of plan. The Princes were to visit Edmonton next day, and Prince George would unveil two memorial tablets at the government building. While loyal Edmontonians prepared to receive their royal visitors, and authorities in the provincial capital congratulated each other on their successful propaganda campaign to lure the royal party northwards, a

---

80 Hart-Davis, *In Royal Service*, p. 65.

81 Ziegler, *Edward VIII*, p. 187.

82 *Times*, August 13 and 14, 1927.

member of the Prince's staff interpreted the decision in a rather different way:

> I had a bad jolt when we detrained at Calgary yesterday, for the Lieutenant Governor of Alberta got hold of the Prince and induced him to say that he would go off to Edmonton, another one-horse town one hundred miles off, to do stunts there the day after tomorrow. I had already, on his instructions, told the Major and everybody else connected with the place that he couldn't possibly fit in a visit there, but he is so utterly bored here that he clutched even at that extremely unattractive straw to get him away from it into the whirl of crowds and cities again, and I'm damned if he didn't say he would do it.[83]

On his return from Edmonton, H.R.H. redeemed himself in the eyes of the locals by meeting veterans on the platform at High River:

> It was a beautiful morning and the crowd greeted vigorously the unassuming approach of the Prince and his brother as they came forward to meet the men. Young and old had a close-up view that created a sense of intimacy and the click of cameras was constant.[84]

Tommy Lascelles was relieved to be left behind at the E.P. Ranch while the main party went to Edmonton. He wrote a vivid description of an early morning fishing expedition along Pekisko Creek:

> I was walking straight for the Rockies, forty miles away, with the red sun just rising over the foothills at my back, through the clearest possible dawn to a really fine day. Early August is still high summer in Alberta, and the Prairie for miles was ablaze with a mass of flowers, clusters of trailing dog-roses, great clumps of Golden Rod and Michaelmas daisies, and golden acres of great yellow Marguerite with a velvety brown centre, which they call Brown-eyed Susan, and a dozen varieties all new to me. Kites overhead and little birds still busy with their broods scolding me from the bushes, and a drenching dew under foot.[85]

Monday, August 15, was the last day at the ranch, and the royal brothers spent the morning hay-making, and left in the afternoon for Calgary and the Drag Hunt Ball that night. During this visit the Prince of Wales had spent only one full day and two half days at his ranch.

Thus, the Prince paid three visits to his ranch during the 1920s. The first lasted almost three weeks and was wholeheartedly enjoyed; the

---

83 Hart-Davis, *In Royal Service*, p. 56.

84 *High River Times*, August 18, 1927.

85 Hart-Davis, *In Royal Service*, p. 57.

second was marred by sickness and depression and lasted only five days; and the final visit, during which H.R.H. seemed bored with the ranch, was pared down to a mere two days. This sequence suggests that, as Edward became more and more caught up in the sophisticated pleasures which his position and the times put in his way, so the appeal of the ranch waned. Why then did not the Prince empower his advisers to dispose of the E.P. as quickly and tactfully as possible? Although this possibility was discussed again and again over the years, the fact remains that H.R.H. hung on to the ranch tenaciously and was still reluctant to part with it in 1960. It seems likely that the ranch had a strong symbolic significance to him which far transcended the pleasure given by the few days he spent there. For him it remained a possible "escape hatch" from the official side of his life which he was finding increasingly difficult to stomach. The fact that it was hopelessly impractical, and that he would not have enjoyed ranch life for long anyway, was irrelevant. He could dream that there was an alternative to the unpalatable present. Perhaps too, the ranch remained a nostalgic memento of some of his finest hours, and an enduring symbol of his hopes for pursuing new ways of "Princing" and forging new links within the Empire. In spite of these ties of sentiment and psyche, the Prince did make several attempts to divest himself of the ranch, both during the bleak days of the Great Depression, and during his brief reign. There were a number of reasons why the sale was not pushed to a conclusion, and these will be discussed in the next chapter.

V

Depression and Abdication, 1930–38

Those were the years Canada went belly-up. "Ten lost years" one man called them.[1]

To throw away the love of the Empire . . . for the soiled affections of a social climber. . . . History holds no tragedy more wasteful, more pitiful.[2]

The fate of the E.P. Ranch during the 1930s was inextricably linked to two significant historical events: the great depression and the abdication crisis. The former touched ordinary people's lives all round the world. Attitudes and perceptions were cast during those years of economic disruption and environmental disaster which affected the behaviour of a whole generation. Nowhere was this more true than in western Canada, where a combination of drought and chronically low prices resulted in wholesale migrations comparable to some of those which were to take place during the Second World War.[3] Indeed, the depression left deeper and longer lasting scars on the people of the Prairies than did the global conflict which followed it.[4] The decision of King Edward VIII to renounce his throne so that he could marry "the woman he loved" only affected the lives of a few hundred people directly. Millions, however, were titillated by the apparent romance of the story, and it became the media event of the decade. Many felt passionately either that "an American adventuress had stolen Prince Charming," or "the stuffy British

1 Barry Broadfoot, *Ten Lost Years* (Toronto: Doubleday, 1973), p. vii.

2 Beverley Baxter, "Why Edward Quit," *Macleans*, June 20, 1964.

3 James Gray, *Men Against the Desert* (Saskatoon: Western Producer, 1967); and *The Winter Years: The Depression on the Prairies* (Toronto: Macmillan, 1966).

4 Barry Broadfoot, *Ten Lost Years*; and Pierre Berton, *The Great Depression, 1929–1939* (Toronto: McClelland and Stewart, 1990).

Establishment would not let King Edward marry his gal!" But when the farewell speech had rung out over the airwaves from Windsor Castle on December 11, 1936, the people got on with their Christmas shopping and promptly forgot the so-called "crisis." The change in status of the absentee landlord had a more profound and long lasting effect on the fortunes of the E.P. Ranch.

Both these crucial events, the depression and the abdication, have been described and analyzed in great detail.[5] No attempt is made in the pages that follow to discuss either theme in its entirety. Rather, an attempt has been made to block in the major events in as much as they affected the management and operation of the ranch. It will be argued that the onset of the depression led to a period of belt-tightening in all the royal households, and this was reflected in attempts to make the management of the ranch more accountable. Economies in some areas were made even more vital because of the Prince's enthusiastic outpouring of energy and resources to restore and remodel Fort Belvedere as his private retreat. Evidence suggests that the E.P. was well managed through the depression and survived intact to reap the benefits of better prices in 1936 and 1938. However, Edward's growing obsession with Wallis Simpson meant that he evaluated all decisions from the perspective of that relationship. The ranch belonged to a former stage of his life, and was redundant to this vision of domestic bliss at the Fort with Wallis. This is the background against which the attempts to dispose of the ranch in the mid-1930s must be set.

The onset of the depression in the United Kingdom introduced a period of strict economy at the Duchy of Cornwall, and indeed throughout the royal estates. Increasingly, the E.P. Ranch was regarded as an unjustifiable expense by the Prince's advisors. At first, every attempt was made to make the management of the ranch accountable and the annual deficit smaller, but when it became clear that the E.P. could not break even, efforts were made to dispose of it.

As the world economy slowed down and then plummeted into depression, even royal households were forced to make cutbacks. King George V pledged to cut £50,000 from his expenses.[6] He disposed of his

---

5 Gerald Friesen, *The Canadian Prairies: A History* (University of Toronto Press, 1984); David C. Jones, *Empire of Dust* (Edmonton: University of Alberta Press, 1987); and Michiel Horn (ed.), *The Dirty Thirties: Canadians in the Great Depression* (Toronto: Copp Clark, 1972). On the abdication, see Frances Donaldson, *Edward VIII* (London: Weidenfeld and Nicolson, 1974); Christopher Warwick, *Abdication* (London: Sidewick and Jackson, 1986); J. Bryan III and Charles J.V. Murphy, *The Windsor Story* (New York: William Morrow, 1979); Sarah Bradford, *The Reluctant King* (New York: St. Martin's Press, 1989); and Philip Ziegler, *King Edward VIII: The Official Biography* (London: Collins, 1990).

6 Bradford, *Reluctant King*, p. 130.

purebred Hereford herd on the Flemish Farm at Windsor. The Duke of York was forced to sell his hunters, while the Prince of Wales disposed of Grove Farm at Lenton in Nottinghamshire, and his shorthorn dairy herd.[7] It was clearly time to review critically the manner in which H.R.H.'s Canadian ranch was being run. For more than ten years, since its acquisition, Professor Carlyle had managed things with only very loose supervision from the staff at the Duchy of Cornwall. The secretary of the Duchy, Sir Walter Peacock, had played a role in the purchase and stocking of the E.P. and was a personal friend of Carlyle's. This meant that the resident manager got both the cash and the stock he needed to build the ranch into a show place. During the 1920s about $120,000 in cash was transferred to the ranch accounts, while an additional $110,000 worth of stock moved across the Atlantic from the royal estates.[8] During 1930 Peacock retired and was replaced by Major Hilgrove McCormick. McCormick brought to his duties the eye and mind of an accountant rather than that of a country squire or estate manager. Although he and his wife had stayed in Calgary with Senator Pat Burns and had visited the E.P. and made the acquaintance of Professor Carlyle, he came to view the ranch as an expensive royal toy which absorbed funds over which he had little or no control. He was deeply suspicious of Carlyle's management ability. At his urging H.R.H. invited some of his ranching friends to form an advisory committee to help to look after the E.P. The committee was chaired by Senator Patrick Burns, and included A.E. Cross and Alick Newton. Together, they made a formidable team. Burns, an almost legendary "cattle king," was seventy-five years old when he undertook this new responsibility, but he brought a lifetime of experience to the task.[9] A.E. Cross, too, had retained his passion for ranching in spite of his varied and successful business ventures. He knew and loved fine horses and cattle. Unfortunately he was to serve for only one year before his death. The workhorse of the committee was Alick Newton. He was forty-five years old and a director of Burns and Co. Ltd. He remained a close advisor to the Duke of Windsor on his Canadian interests until his death in 1954.

By the early spring of 1931, Burns was able to report that the committee had met several times, and that he and Cross had inspected the ranch with Carlyle.[10] They liked what they saw, and felt that the basic concept of maintaining pedigree animals for sale to Canadian stockmen was sound. However, they suggested that only a few additional

7 *High River Times*, August 10, 1933.

8 GA M4843 f.58, Halsey to Newton, November 12, 1936.

9 Grant McEwan, *Pat Burns: Cattle King* (Saskatoon: Western Producer, 1979).

10 GA M160 f.145, Burns to McCormick, February 25, 1931.

bulls and rams would be required from England in the immediate future, and that these could be picked out by a competent judge in the United Kingdom, thus reducing travel costs. They also found the financial records of the ranch to be in disarray, as Burns explained to McCormick:

> We are gradually getting the books into better order. They were in the past quite inadequate, consisting only of a cash book which was written up from time to time from counter-foils of cheques, the fact of the matter being that there were no books, such as there were being of little use. . . . Professor Carlyle was very slipshod in his methods, but is beginning to appreciate the changes we are marking.[11]

The books were transferred to Burns' office in Calgary and looked after by an accountant. A year later the Prince presumed even further on his friend's goodwill. He wrote:

> As you have kindly offered me help from the staff in your office, I would like to avail myself of these facilities by having all letters as far as possible, written and filed in your office.[12]

There was so much ranch business to deal with that the committee took to meeting regularly on the first Tuesday of each month.

Although it is clear that Professor Carlyle was unprofessional in the manner in which he kept the books, there is no evidence of lavish or irresponsible expenditures. Indeed, neither Carlyle nor his foreman, James McMillan, had been paid at all during 1930, and Carlyle himself suggested a reduction in his salary from $2,400 to $2,000 or $1,800 in December 1931.[13] The committee adopted the lower figure, "because we consider that in view of present conditions, $1,800 is as much as the ranch will stand."[14] It seems a somewhat paltry reward for the man who by his determined advocacy had doubled the deeded acreage of the ranch and obtained the underrights for the Prince. The snide implications of McCormick that Carlyle was gadding about the country visiting too many stock shows seem petty and misplaced.[15]

In 1932 the Prince of Wales asked Sir Douglas Newton, Alick's brother, who was in Canada as part of the United Kingdom delegation to the Imperial Economic Conference, to travel west to the ranch so that

---

11 GA M160 f. 145, Burns to McCormick, December 14, 1931.

12 GA M160 f. 145, H.R.H. to Burns, March 16, 1933.

13 GA M160 f. 145, H.R.H. to Burns, March 16, 1933.

14 GA M160 f. 145, Burns to McCormick, December 14, 1931.

15 GA M160 f. 145, McCormick to Burns, October 13, 1931; and February 2, 1932.

he could bring back a confidential report.[16] In it he criticized Carlyle for his preoccupation with the U.S. market, and for his absences from the ranch. He also drew attention to the growing gap between the inventory values of stock on the books, and the real prices they were likely to bring on the auction block. This was also a concern of McCormick.[17] It was almost impossible to estimate fairly the value of pedigree livestock held at the ranch. The value of any beast—however blue-blooded it might be—depended entirely on how much stockmen were prepared to pay for it. Thus the actual figure would reflect the state of the economy, the price of beef, competition from other breeders, and other intangibles like snobbery, fashion, and reputation.[18] The value of a bull on a royal estate in England was difficult to translate realistically into a western Canadian context. Moreover, the value of a bull on the E.P. would fluctuate wildly according to local stockmen's perception of the current situation and their reading of the future. It is not surprising that pedigree livestock on the ranch were overvalued in the inventory. During a period of generally falling prices and expectations the gap between the "book price" and the actual selling price tended to widen.[19] For example, the proceeds from the sale of twenty-six cattle in November 1931 amounted to $4,535, a most successful day. However, the inventory value of the stock sold was $8,850. There was therefore a loss of $4,315 on the books.[20] Thus, the greater was the sale, the greater the book loss. McCormick remarked to Burns that "I think H.R.H. would feel happier if in future the stock were shown at the price arrived at having due regard to the economic conditions in western Canada."[21] But such an evaluation was easier to write about than it was to assess.

After the death of A.E. Cross, the advisory committee was enlarged by the recruitment of lawyer E.D. Adams and, to provide closer liaison with H.R.H., the Honourable William Dudley-Ward, a Liberal member of

---

16 GA M7005, Douglas Newton to Alick Newton, August 12, 1932.

17 GA M160 f. 145, McCormick to Burns, March 13, 1931.

18 See for example S.G. Porter, Calgary Manager of Canadian Pacific, Department of Natural Resources to Sir Edward Beatty, Chairman and President. Porter comments on the sale of pedigree shorthorns from the E.P., ". . . a considerable amount of the returns on the sales during the last two months have been because of the sentimental value attached to the stock as being the King's property and the personal interest taken in the sale by a group of buyers who are willing, because of the special circumstances, to pay a substantial premium over and above the actual value of the stock." GA M2269 f. 1357, Porter to Beatty, November 4, 1936.

19 This was the classic problem during the "Beef Bonanza," 1881–1886; see Ernest Staples Osgood, *The Day of the Cattleman* (Chicago: University of Chicago Press, 1929).

20 GA M2398 f. 86, Profit and Loss Account for the year ending December 31, 1931; and Schedule 1, "Sales of Livestock and Cattle Burned."

21 GA M160 f. 145, McCormick to Burns, March 13, 1931.

parliament, and the ex-husband of Freda Dudley-Ward, who had been the Prince's close friend since 1919. The latter spent some time in Calgary and at the ranch during the summer and early fall of 1933, and submitted a thorough report on his return to London.[22] He felt that even greater economies might be affected, especially with regard to the Clydesdale horses, which were expensive to maintain. He also passed on gossip which threw some doubt on Carlyle's competence.

During the early 1930s, the Prince's English advisors, particularly McCormick, but also Sir Douglas Newton and Dudley-Ward, were critical of the ranch manager, and pessimistic concerning the ability of the management committee to turn things around and stop the drain on funds. When H.R.H. wrote to Burns in March 1933 he admitted:

> I have had some doubts as to the advisability of retaining the services of Mr. W.L. Carlyle as manager, but I gather from your replies to my enquiries on the subject, that it would be best to retain his services, at any rate for the present.[23]

As the grip of the depression tightened and new interests and enthusiasms entered the Prince's life, he began to talk over with his advisors ways to dispose of the E.P.

The early 1930s were a pivotal period for the Prince Edward. He was thirty-six years old and his round of travelling the Empire was completed. Having given up hunting and his pied-a-terre at Melton Mowbray, he was looking for a country retreat. He found his ideal in Fort Belvedere, which was within an hour's drive of London and very close to his favourite golf course at Sunningdale. Situated on the margin of Windsor Great Park, the miniature fortress was dominated by a castellated tower built in the 1730s, but the house had been enlarged during the 1820s by Wyatville, the architect of Windsor Castle.[24] It had originally been used for picnics and excursions from the main castle, and for lodging favourites and dignitaries. Indeed, the young Prince had visited it frequently from Frogmoor with his tutor.[25] Not surprisingly it had caught his imagination, for Lady Diana Cooper described it as "a child's idea of a fort . . . it had battlements and cannon and cannon balls and all the little furnishings of war. It stood high on a hill, and the sentries, one thought, must be of tin."[26] For twenty years the house had

---

22 Minutes, Duchy of Cornwall, January 23, 1934. Relevant minutes read aloud to the author by the Duchy Archivist, Dr. G. Haslam, May and June 1989.

23 GA M160 f. 145, H.R.H. to Burns, March 16, 1933.

24 Michael Bloch, *The Secret File of the Duke of Windsor* (London: Corgi Books, 1988), p. 126.

25 Bryan and Murphy, *Windsor Story*, p. 83.

26 Donaldson, *Edward VIII*, p. 139.

been occupied at the King's "grace and favour" by Sir Malcolm Murray. When he died, in 1929, the Prince asked his father for the use of it. King George granted it to him, reputedly with the words, "What do you want that queer old place for? Those damn weekends I suppose?"[27]

H.R.H. threw himself wholeheartedly into remodelling the house and gardens. There was much to do. Sir John Aird recalled accompanying the Prince on a tour of inspection:

> "A unstately ruin" is the only proper term for its condition. The dust was inches deep. Splintered floors, sagging doors, no more than two or three W.C.s in the whole establishment. The servant's quarters would have disgraced a prison ship. . . . A vision of what could be made of it seized his imagination. One afternoon's look convinced him.[28]

With the help of both Freda Dudley-Ward and, later, Thelma Furness, "the castellated conglomeration," or "pseudo-gothic hodge podge," as the Prince was wont to describe it, was gradually transformed. Modern plumbing was installed and bathrooms added to each bedroom. The light, high-ceilinged rooms were furnished with comfortable good taste. The heart of the house was "the magnificent octagonal drawing room panelled in natural pine. In this wide and spacious room, with its Chippendale furniture, Canalettos from the Royal Collection were hung on the panelled walls and yellow velvet curtains dressed the tall gothic windows."[29] Those who visited the Fort, however, remember the warm, relaxed and unpretentious atmosphere rather than any grand objets d'art. In his memoirs the Duke of Windsor remembered:

> The Fort laid hold of me in many ways. Soon I came to love it as I loved no other material thing, perhaps because it was so much my own creation. More and more it became for me a peaceful, almost enchanted anchorage, where I found refuge from the cares and turmoil of life.[30]

The Prince was particularly proud of his transformation of the grounds. While contractors dug out an old lily pond to create a swimming pool, H.R.H. worked tirelessly to cut and clear dank, dark laurel and undergrowth. Often friends and acquaintances were pressed into reluctant service. "A weekend at the Fort meant blisters and a sore back," remem-

---

27 Bloch, *Secret File*, p. 127.

28 Bryan and Murphy, *Windsor Story*, p. 84.

29 Warwick, *Abdication*, p. 71.

30 H.R.H. Edward, Duke of Windsor, *A King's Story* (New York: Putnam's and Sons, 1951), p. 239.

bered one recruit.[31] Edward's enthusiasm and passion ring through phrases written twenty years later, "I found a new contentment in working about the Fort with my own hands, I begrudged as lost a daylight hour that did not see the work progressing."[32] Both his old-fashioned English border full of phlox, sweet william, nasturtiums, and delphiniums, and his fine collection of rare rhododendrons bore witness to his careful planning. He was to throw himself into building the garden at the Mill outside Paris with the same enthusiasm.[33]

The Fort became the physical embodiment of the Prince's determination to have a private life separated from his public duties. Above the tower flew the standard of the Duchy of Cornwall to signify that this was not a formal royal residence, but rather a private retreat, a resting place for a "rolling stone," as the Prince once put it. Here he could put aside ceremony and relax in old clothes with a few close friends. After a week spent "stunting" (as he called the discharge of his public duties), and enjoying the pleasures of the London season he could retreat to the Fort. There he created a home life for himself which he had never before had the opportunity to enjoy. Thelma Furness recalled, "Our life was quiet, even domestic, he pottered in the garden, pruned his trees, and blew his bagpipes."[34] Even when there was a house party there was still needle-point, giant jig-saw puzzles, and reading aloud, as well as jazz and dancing.

As he contemplated the possibility of having to set aside the throne, the thought of leaving the Fort weighed heavily on him. He wrote:

> The Fort had been more than a home, it had been a way of life for me. I had created The Fort just as my grandfather had created Sandringham; I loved it in the same way; it was there that I had passed the happiest days of my life.[35]

The Duchess of Windsor echoed these sentiments as she talked to a reporter about her efforts to refurbish Government House in the Bahamas. "Don't you see, I must make a house for him, the only one he ever had, he made for himself at Fort Belvedere. He had to leave it—you don't know what that meant to him."[36] During the last few days of his

---

31 Bryant and Murphy, *Windsor Story*, p. 84.

32 Duke of Windsor, *King's Story*, p. 239.

33 Suzy Menkes, *The Windsor Style* (London: Grafton Books, 1987), p. 53; see also photographs, pp. 54 and 55.

34 Gloria Vanderbilt and Thelma Lady Furness, *Double Exposure: A Twin Autobiography* (New York: McCay, 1958), p. 282.

35 Duke of Windsor, *King's Story*, p. 410.

36 Russel Page, *Life Magazine*, July 1956.

reign, Edward VIII secured a promise from his brother and successor that the Fort would be made available to him when he returned to England.[37] This never happened, but the Duke of Windsor was able to satisfy his nostalgia, at least in part, by recreating some of the ambience of his old home in the various houses which he occupied. He christened his own quarters at La Cröe, the villa he rented in the south of France, "Fort Belvedere." Furniture brought from the original was also used in his bedroom in the house on the Boulevard Suchet in Paris, and later at the Mill. One professional decorator was to recall, "the only thing about the Mill that was ravishing was one great room which had been taken almost verbatim from Fort Belvedere."[38]

The acquisition of Fort Belvedere by the Prince of Wales had clear implications for the E.P. Ranch. The Fort provided most of the advantages which he had hoped to get from owning the ranch, and it could be used all the year round. He could get away from both the public and the court and be his own man there. Moreover, the ranch had fitted into a phase of his life when global journeys round the Empire were commonplace; those days were now past. H.R.H. was pouring out his resources to refurbish his new home; he spent £21,000 on the Fort in 1931 alone. His advisors thought that it was time to stop funding an enthusiasm of which the Prince had clearly tired. At best they hoped to recoup some of the capital which had been invested in what they felt was a highly dubious venture.[39] Their hopes of achieving this goal were constrained by the economic nightmare of the depression.

No region of western Canada escaped the pervasive impact of the depression. However, conditions in the foothills of southern Alberta differed markedly from the stereotypical images of rolling dust clouds, outmigration, and abandonment, associated with the semi-arid and recently settled short grass prairie of Palliser's Triangle. The ranchers of the Upper Highwood were spared the worst of the catastrophic droughts which devastated the plains to the east. Even in dry years some rain fell, and snow melt from the Rockies fed the eastward flowing streams. This was a well established region of comfortable homes, good farm buildings,

---

37 Bloch, *Secret File*, p. 126.

38 Menkes, *Windsor Style*, p. 63.

39 There is always a certain air of unreality in discussing the financial affairs of the very rich. The ranch had to be sustained during its build-up phase by regular transfers of money from London. It never quite broke even. The Prince's comptroller concluded that "a sum in the neighbourhood of £60,000 has been found from this side for the purchase of land, cattle and working capital for the ranch since 1919." This sum has to be set against the fact that the Prince of Wales saved about $1 million from his income from the Duchy of Cornwall during his period as heir to the throne. It is also relevant to remember his extravagant purchases of jewellery for Mrs. Simpson. GA M4843 f. 58, Halsey to Newton, November 12, 1936.

adequate equipment and productive fields. The output of gardens could be augmented by picking wild berries and by hunting and fishing. Churches, schools, and sports clubs provided social supports.[40] Moreover, the development of the Turner Valley gas field pumped hundreds of thousands of dollars into the region and provided a variety of short term construction jobs.[41] The contrast in physical fortunes between central and eastern Alberta on the one hand, and the foothills on the other, is illustrated by the report of the Livestock Commissioner for 1929. Already the short grass prairies had suffered two years of shattering drought, he wrote:

> Owing to the drought over the central eastern part of the Province, surplus stock in these districts was rushed to market in the early part of the fall, but in the ranching districts where most of our cattle are raised, there has been an abundance of grass and feed. Cattle from these districts went to market in good condition.[42]

However, the farmers and ranchers of the High River region did not escape unscathed. During the "Dirty Thirties" the unpredictable foothills climate became even more capricious. For example, in 1933, a snowstorm in mid-April was followed by a period of heavy rain which prevented the farmers getting onto their land. "Spring work delayed: Sets new late record," was the headline in May.[43] By mid-July it was drought that was causing concern for both hay and grain crops. On July 27, the editorial in the *High River Times* was captioned "Unfathomable Nature," and it explained:

> There has been something cruelly disheartening in wheat developments over the past week. On top of the season's drought came the frost, an unusual and unanticipated blow in this part of the world. True, in 1918, a year very similar to this, there was a July frost . . . but the calamity of frost has come in 1933, after 3 years of poverty prices, when farmers have been drained to the limit of their resources putting in the present crop. This has been the black week of a black year. It has laid the heavy hand of the depression on all of us.[44]

At the E.P. Ranch, stock could not be turned out into the pastures until the third week of May, and crops yielded less than a third of normal

---

40 Lewis G. Thomas (ed.), *Our Foothills* (Calgary: Millarville Historical Society, 1975), p. 26.

41 See below, Chapter 6.

42 Alberta, *Department of Agriculture*, Annual Report, 1929, p. 15.

43 *High River Times*, May 11, 1933.

44 *High River Times*, July 27, 1933.

amounts of fodder. The severe July frosts "destroyed practically all our garden crops and most of the flowers and many of the shrubs about the residence."[45] At year's end the Livestock Commissioner reported:

> Due to the extreme drought in the foothills district, and also from Hanna to Medicine Hat, there is a great shortage of feed, and large numbers of cattle were placed on the market during the fall months, for which there was practically no sale. All markets were congested and all cattle raisers, especially the ranchers, have taken a very heavy loss on their operations.[46]

Carlyle had cut hay on the rougher and less accessible parts of the ranch, and had put up sixteen large stacks. He increased his purchases of feed to augment the hay, which was of indifferent quality, and held back his stock from market, hoping that prices would improve.[47]

The following year was a complete contrast and something of a reprieve, Carlyle wrote to Halsey from the ranch:

> We have had a delightful autumn until the present week. I do not remember any year in the past twenty in Alberta where we have had as favourable an autumn season, mild and bright with an abundance of sunshine. Stock have done remarkably well. This means very much to the stockman as feed supplies in many sections are very low. Fortunately, we had a fair crop and will, I think, have plenty of feed to carry us through the winter.[48]

In contrast, once again, the winter of 1935–36 was considered to be the hardest since 1907 in the High River district.[49] For more than six weeks the Chinook failed to blow. Rivers froze, wells dried up, feed supplies dwindled and cattle shrunk and shrunk.[50] In May a dust storm thundered into High River from the north. The high wind "sweeping cultivated soil before it, the air was thick with dust and visibility was obscured."[51] In June the temperatures ranged from several degrees below freezing to more than 100°F in the shade. "Farmers in the district with 30 years experience say they have never seen a drought until this

---

45 GA M2398 f. 1, Carlyle to Burns, August 28, 1933.

46 Alberta, *Department of Agriculture*, Annual Report, 1933, p. 16.

47 GA M2398 f. 1, Carlyle to Burns, August 28, 1933.

48 GA M2398 f. 42, Carlyle to Halsey, November 22, 1934.

49 *High River Times*, February 13, 1936.

50 *High River Times*, February 27, 1936.

51 *High River Times*, May 7, 1936.

time."[52] In mid-August the editor remarked, "About the only things we will remember this year for is that it has been the coldest, the hottest, the driest, and so on in the history of settlement."[53] Pekisko Creek ceased to flow round the Bar U buildings for the first time since 1881. And yet, in spite of these climate vagaries, seedtime was followed by harvest, hay was put up, and calves and lambs were born in their appointed seasons. There was no wholesale retreat of the farming and ranching frontier in the foothills.

If stockmen escaped the worst ravages of natural calamity, they bore the full brunt of economic dislocation and the disruption of world trade. After the phenomenal demand and exceptional prices of the late 1920s, the bottom fell out of livestock prices in 1931.[54] Pat Burns could not remember a time when prices were lower,[55] and the Livestock Commissioner wrote:

> The year 1931 will go down in history in Alberta as recording the lowest prices of livestock and livestock products for the past 30 years.[56]

In 1932 prices continued to drop, and they reached new lows in 1933. It was prices rather than drought which was uppermost in the minds of people attending stock shows and association meetings. "If prices were stabilized to some extent at least, it would do more than anything else to make Alberta the great livestock province for which by nature she is well adapted," surmised the Livestock Commissioner (Appendix B).[57]

In 1929 the Hawley-Smoot Tariff between Canada and the United States had once more shut Canadian cattle out of the vast Chicago market. The British market acted as something of a safety valve, but only the prime quality stock could earn high enough prices to pay their transport costs.

> It was unfortunate for the cattle men of Alberta that the depression started just at this time, and between the tariff and the depression the result has been a large surplus of cattle, with ruinously low prices, which put the cattle business in a deplorable condition. Ranchers and

---

52 *High River Times*, July 9, 1936.

53 *High River Times*, August 13, 1936.

54 See, for example, the remarks of the Livestock Commissioner, "The Price for well finished cattle in the spring of 1928 looks exceptionally good and farmers and ranchers are looking forward to good prices for the next few years." Alberta, *Department of Agriculture*, Annual Report, 1927, p. 16.

55 GA M160 f. 145, Burns to McCormick, December 14, 1931.

56 Alberta, *Department of Agriculture*, Annual Report, 1931, p. 15.

57 Alberta, *Department of Agriculture*, Annual Report, 1933, p. 15.

farmers have been producing at below the cost of production, and unless something is done to remedy the situation, whereby higher prices will be obtained, the largest and best cattlemen in the Province will be out of business.[58]

Ranchers were in no position to pay premium prices for pedigree bulls from the E.P. Ranch. Carlyle reported, "We have quite an increase in livestock over previous years, which owing to the very unfavourable economic conditions prevailing in Alberta and Western Canada this year, we may not be able to sell to full advantage."[59] The only strategy was to hold stock back for as long as was possible in the hope that things would improve. McCormick and Halsey in London had no idea of the seriousness of the situation and found it hard to understand why more stock was not being marketed regularly.[60]

Throughout the 1930s, even in the worst years of the depression, stock from the E.P. Ranch continued to win prizes in stock shows throughout Canada and the Pacific Northwest. Showing cattle and horses at agricultural fairs was the only effective way to advertise. The shows brought together breeders from widely separated areas who would never have the opportunity of visiting one another. As Carlyle commented, "our exhibitions offer almost the only means whereby they may learn where they may secure the class of animals they desire to maintain and improve their herds."[61] Moreover, the shows were often the best place to complete sales and to maintain and extend contacts with likely customers. Every prize won added to the reputation of the ranch and enhanced the value of the stock. Carlyle adopted an innovative policy of sending young pedigree stock to shows while his best sires were kept at the ranch for breeding purposes. For example, twelve head of young cattle toured Calgary, Edmonton, Regina, Saskatoon, Vancouver and Victoria. They left the ranch on July 7, and did not return until September 20. During this period they were fed at the expense of the various shows which they attended. The ranch earned $1,367 from prize money in

---

58 Alberta, *Department of Agriculture*, Annual Report, 1934, p. 14.

59 GA M2398 f. 1, Carlyle to Burns, August 28, 1933.

60 For example, McCormick comments, "this quarter the sales apparently amount to no more than $400 out of a inventory of over $48,000. Probably the stock is being held over for some reason, but the sales for the whole of last year certainly seemed rather poor, particularly the cattle sales." Obviously he had no idea that agriculture in western Canada was locked in a battle for survival which was to last for the rest of the decade. GA M160 f. 145, McCormick to Burns, June 8, 1933.

61 GA M398 f. 12, Carlyle to Burns, December 21, 1933.

1933.[62] The following year Carlyle received a congratulatory letter from the Alberta Minister of Agriculture, which is worth quoting in full:

> We have recently received the awards from the Royal Winter Fair at Toronto, and the Grain and Hay show at Chicago, and we were pleased to note that many prizes were won by the ranch.
>
> It is a real accomplishment to have succeeded in winning prizes in classes where the competition is so keen as that encountered at Toronto, and we wish to congratulate you on the singular honour you have achieved on your own behalf, and for the credit you have brought to the Province.[63]

Professor Carlyle had built up an enviable reputation for the ranch and had assumed a place of honour in the cattle business. It was to him that the influential John Clay and Company of Chicago wrote when they saw good prospects for increasing Canadian beef imports.[64] In another instance, a prize winning shorthorn bull, Princeton Lomond, was sent from the ranch to New Zealand in 1935, to play a key role in building up the beef industry there. This deal was achieved in the face of stiff competition from Great Britain.[65] Unlike the correspondence from the Prince's advisors in London, which tended to be suspicious and critical, letters and reports from other breeders and stock associations create an impression of an efficiently run business with a growing reputation, and far-flung contacts.

The financial records of the ranch suggest that Carlyle was able to steer a remarkably circumspect course through the economic storms of the 1930s. Expenses were cut from some $20,000 per annum in the late 1920s to less than $15,000 in the 1930s (Appendix A).[66] Regular cash payments from the United Kingdom virtually stopped after 1931, and amounted to only $7,500, paid in 1935, over the next seven years. Above all, the pedigree shorthorn herd, which had been held back from market when prices were low, was sold to great advantage in 1936. Forty head of registered shorthorns were sold at T.A. Russell's Bonnie Brae Farm,

---

62 GA M2398 f. 101, Profit and loss account for year ending December 31, 1933.

63 GA M2398 f. 6, Grisdale to Carlyle, December 22, 1934; see also letter from the secretary, Chicago International Livestock Exhibition, May 7, 1935; and minutes of the E.P. Ranch Committee, December 21, 1935, reporting sixteen first prizes won at an exhibition in Great Falls, Montana.

64 GA M2398 f. 14, Clay to Carlyle, January 26, 1935.

65 The bull, Princeton Lomond, took some time to settle down in New Zealand, and there was an anxious exchange of letters worrying lest he should prove to be a "non-breeder." GA M2398 f. 14, Exchange of letters between Clark and Carlyle, January 14, 1935 to November 9, 1935.

66 GA M2398 ff. 101–104, "Financial Statements."

Downsview, Ontario, as prices were better in eastern Canada. A show herd of fourteen head were sold as a lot, and earned a premium price just before the Toronto Show.[67] In addition, seven head of Clydesdales and two hunters from the E.P. were shipped to California.[68] Total sales for that year amounted to $17,678. The experiment of auctioning cattle in Ontario was repeated in 1937, when five young bulls and nine young females were sold for $3,630. The final disposal sale of pedigree shorthorns was held at the E.P. Ranch on September 30, 1938, and earned more than $11,000.[69] Thus stock held back during the early 1930s realized more than $30,000 when prices ameliorated: a vindication of Carlyle's policy and patience. Alick Newton wrote a fitting epitaph for this phase of the ranch's existence in a letter to the Prince: "I feel sure, Sir, that you are please to know that your object has been abundantly achieved, and that the people of Canada are indeed grateful to your Royal Highness for the generous assistance you have given the livestock industry."[70]

For almost a decade the E.P. Ranch, along with farmers and ranchers throughout the Canadian west, had been locked in a grim battle for survival. It was "perhaps the most significant ten years in our history, a watershed era which scarred and transformed the nation."[71] Yet the royal owner was largely indifferent to the fate of his Alberta property, for his own life was rushing toward its climax. Edward's growing obsession with Wallis Simpson, the twice-divorced woman from Baltimore, was to precipitate a constitutional crisis of shattering importance. The course of these events, which had far reaching consequences for the E.P. Ranch, will be reviewed in the following pages.

The happiness which the Duke of Windsor nostalgically associated with Fort Belvedere was not derived solely from his sense of creative achievement in resurrecting a ruin, but also from the fact that it was there that his acquaintance with Wallis Simpson deepened into an obsessional love. She visited the Fort for the first time with her husband in January 1933, and the couple were occasional weekend guests during the following year. Early in 1934, Thelma Furness returned from the United States to find that her place as the Prince's hostess and confidante had been usurped by her friend Wallis.[72] Thereafter Edward's social life began to

---

67 *High River Times*, October 29, 1936; and November 5, 1936.

68 *High River Times*, August 27, 1936.

69 GRI M2398 f. 103, Memoranda on "Sale of Purebred Shorthorn Cattle," September 30, 1938; and *Western Producer*, August 18, 1938.

70 GA M843 f. 58, Newton to H.R.H., April 3, 1939.

71 Berton, *Great Depression*, p. 9.

72 Vanderbilt and Furness, *Double Exposure*, pp. 297–98.

Edward and Wallis, the Duke and Duchess of Windsor at the Château de Candé
during the days before their wedding, June 1937. Photographed
by Cecil Beaton, postcard from the National Gallery, Ottawa.

revolve round Bryanston Court, the Simpsons' London apartment, and his weekends at the Fort accompanied by an emerging new "set" of friends chosen by Wallis. Gradually Mrs. Simpson assumed control of the household, and servants who would not accept her were replaced.

As the Prince's slavish devotion to her grew, so too, she took control over his life. His favourite brother George said of Edward, "He is besotted with infatuation."[73] If it was indeed infatuation, it was deep and long-lasting; for the rest of his life his greatest happiness was to carry out her slightest wish. He evaluated everything according to her reaction to it: whether it was a jewel, a plan, or a person, if it or they did not enhance her pleasure or bring a smile to her lips, it was without interest or worth. Edward's need for a dependent relationship, which had been latent during his long association with Freda Dudley-Ward, was now consummated. Frances Donaldson remarked, "he was made for domination, while she was made to dominate. He and Wallis Simpson were quite unusually suited to each other, two parts of a whole."[74] King Edward VIII had no firmer or more faithful friend than Walter Monckton, and no more shrewd servant. In Monckton's opinion the key to understanding the events of 1936 lay in "the intensity and depth of the King's devotion to Mrs. Simpson. To him she was the perfect woman. . . . It is a great mistake to assume that he was merely in love with her in the ordinary physical sense of the term. There was an intellectual companionship, and there is no doubt that his lonely nature found in her spiritual comradeship."[75]

The course of the affair, which was to lead to abdication, exile, and finally to marriage, was marked by a series of holidays on the continent of Europe. These excursions exposed the couple to more and more worldwide media attention. The first trip, in August 1934, was to Biarritz, and was followed by a cruise to the Balearic Islands and Cannes. For the most part the Prince behaved well in public, apart from his tendency to appear in shorts and sandals not only on the yacht and beaches, but also when playing the tourist among large crowds. His behaviour in private was described as "awful and most embarrassing for others, the Prince has lost all confidence in himself and follows Wallis around like a dog."[76] The following February, Edward again travelled to the continent with Wallis in his party. This time the destination was Kitzbühel, Austria, and the object was to ski. Once again the holiday proved so enjoyable that it was extended so that Vienna and Budapest could be visited. The European

73 Alistair Cook, *Six Men* (New York: Alfred Knopf, 1977), p. 70.

74 Donaldson, *Edward VIII*, p. 169.

75 Birkenhead, *Monckton*, p. 125.

76 Ziegler, *Edward VIII*, p. 230.

press followed the party's progress with interest, and Admiral Halsey observed, "people will not remain silent for ever."[77]

Even during the heady days of the Prince of Wales' great tours of the Empire, his staff had had great difficulty in persuading him to face his public duties responsibly. We have noted that some of those close to him were seriously concerned about the way in which he would respond to the demands of kingship. As his infatuation for Wallis deepened, so he became increasing unwilling to bestir himself to carry out even the minimum of duties associated with his role as Prince of Wales. Godfrey Thomas, his friend of twenty years, was, for once, bitter enough to speak out:

> I've wasted hours and hours sitting here till late at night in the hope of seeing you. I don't mind a bit working out of office hours if there's any certainty of catching you, however late, but I can't go on like this. You come up [to London from the Fort] nowadays on such rare occasions which means it's always such a rush.[78]

The problem centred round Edward's insistence that he be allowed to live a private life apart from his official role. In his desperate need to spend every minute with Wallis, and to consult her on every detail, his private life had really become his only life. His principal private secretary was to reflect later:

> It was scarcely realized at this early stage how overwhelming and inexorable was the influence exerted on the King by the lady of the moment. As time went on it became clearer and clearer that every decision, big or small, was subordinated to her will. It was she who filled his thoughts at all times, she alone who mattered, before her affairs of state sank into insignificance.[79]

When George V died in January 1936, and Edward VIII acceded to the throne, it seemed that past uncertainties could be set aside. No previous monarch had had such far-reaching knowledge and first-hand experience of the Empire, nor more enthusiastic support from his people at home and abroad. Even those closest to him, whose doubts and fears were greatest, hoped against hope that new responsibilities would call forth a new sense of duty in King Edward. He carried off his first engagements with aplomb and, at first, he showed unwonted enthusiasm for the dispatch boxes which contained the affairs of state. Within a few

---

77 Ziegler, *Edward VIII*, p. 231.

78 Ziegler, *Edward VIII*, p. 220.

79 Donaldson, *Edward VIII*, p. 184.

weeks, however, papers were being returned without even the most cursory look. Indeed, concern was expressed about the security of confidential memoranda while they were in the King's charge. Attempts by his staff to get his attention to deal with the most vital outstanding business were met with irritation or even anger. Instead of evading his "handlers" with humour, as if it were a game, as had often been the case when he was Prince, the King now seemed to regard his closest advisors as potential enemies whose loyalty was questionable. Those who dared voice any criticism of Mrs. Simpson faced instant dismissal. After it was over an aide wrote, "nobody will ever know what we have had to endure during the last year. The King refused to have regular hours and would escape from Thursday to Tuesday to Belvedere where none of us was allowed to go."[80]

In contrast, the King, with Mrs. Simpson's help, was only too glad to concern himself with the minutiae of his campaign to affect sweeping economies in the management of the royal household and estates. His official biographer has emphasized for the first time the tremendous impact that his father's will had on Edward.[81] George V had bequeathed some three-quarters of a million pounds to each of his children, but had left out Edward, the new King, on the grounds that he would receive a large income from the Privy Purse and the Civil List, as well as continuing to enjoy the revenue of the Duchy of Cornwall. Edward reacted with bewildered anger which masked a deep hurt. He felt that his father had found one last way to display his disapproval of his eldest son. By cutting expenses ruthlessly, and selling off assets, he sought to redress what he regarded as a slight. It is significant that he slashed the upkeep of his father's favourite residence, Sandringham, and even planned to sell off a number of adjacent farms. The wages of royal staff were reduced and many traditional "perks" were eliminated. For those close to the royal household of higher or of lower degree, the petty meanness of some of these economy measures contrasted shockingly with the blatant extravagances with which the King surrounded Wallis. "Thus there was understanding for the servants at Buckingham Palace, who resented having their beer money cut down at a time when they were often employed loading cases of champagne, or furniture, or plate, destined for Mrs. Simpson's flat."[82]

During the summer of 1936, the cruise of the Nahlin moved the royal drama inevitably towards its climax. Edward chartered the large yacht for a cruise through the waters off Yugoslavia, around Greece, and up to

80 Bradford, *Reluctant King*, p. 161.

81 Ziegler, *Edward VIII*, p. 247.

82 Donaldson, *Edward VIII*, p. 301.

Istanbul. Philip Ziegler warns that the image of "the King, his mistress and a group of disreputable hangers-on carousing around the eastern Mediterranean" is far from the truth.[83] He points out that the royal progress yielded valuable political dividends, and behaviour on the yacht was at least as decorous as that experienced during a weekend at an English country house. However, the key fact that the King of England was travelling with a married woman who was assumed to be his mistress was bandied about by the international press. The King seemed to be going out his way to "feed the world press with gossip and scandal."[84] It was not the behaviour itself which was so shocking as the vapid frivolity and hedonistic values system which it implied. "If this was to be the pattern of his future conduct then the outlook was infinitely depressing. For dedication above all was needed on the part of the sovereign."[85] While the British press maintained its conspiracy of silence, the colourful outpourings of the American papers gave Mrs. Simpson cause for reflection as she lay sick in Paris after the cruise. If the rest of the world knew of Edward's affair with a married woman, how long could the secret be hidden from the British people?

In October, the Prime Minister of Canada, Mackenzie King, was visiting Britain. He was told that King Edward had regularly visited this woman's suite at Claridge's, had bought her a house in Hyde Park, and had missed official engagements to be with her.[86] Stanley Baldwin expressed to the Dominion's leader his fears that the monarch was bent on marriage. Both Baldwin, and the King's private secretary Hardinge, attempted to cajole Mackenzie King into confronting Edward, and explaining in forthright terms that the people of Canada would not countenance his marriage to a twice divorced woman. But Mackenzie King was too cagey a politician to risk having anything to do with such a delicate matter. During his audience he merely conveyed to Edward the exalted place which he held in the hearts of Canadians, and stressed the role of the Crown as the linchpin of the Empire.

Baldwin was forced to handle the disagreeable task himself. He met with the King at Fort Belvedere on October 20. He explained that in his view, Victorian moral standards had been swept away by the war and its aftermath, but that in a curious way this led people to expect an even higher standard from their King. "People are talking about you and this American woman, Mrs. Simpson. I have had many nasty letters written

83 Ziegler, *Edward VIII*, p. 282.

84 Donaldson, *Edward VIII*, p. 301.

85 Helen Hardinge, *Loyal to Three Kings* (London: William Kimber, 1967), p. 114.

86 H. Blair Neatby, *William Lyon Mackenzie King* (Toronto: University of Toronto Press, 1976), p. 178.

by people who respected your father but don't like the way you are going on."[87] He went on to speak of the impact of American press coverage on Canada. The Governor General, Lord Tweedsmuir, had reported that Canadians were reluctantly coming to believe what they read, and were resentful and hurt by the gossip.

> Canada is the most puritanical part of the Empire and cherishes very much the Victorian standards of private life . . . she has a special affection and loyalty for the King. This is strongly felt particularly by the younger people, and they are alarmed at anything which may take the gilt off their idol. Canada's pride has been deeply wounded by the tattle in the American Press.[88]

Baldwin pointed out that if Canada, "the oldest child of the Commonwealth," wavered in its loyalty, then the edifice of Empire was indeed in danger.

Toward the end of October Mrs. Simpson's plea for a divorce was heard at Ipswich. Coverage of the event by the British press was minimal, and it is doubtful if, even at this late stage in the drama, the "man in the street" even knew who Mrs. Simpson was. However, the reality of the divorce forced a further wedge between the monarch and his government, and between Edward and his staff. The King withdrew more and more to the make-believe world of the Fort. There, in isolation and propped up by the woman on whom he had become emotionally dependent, he could continue to believe that his popularity with the people was such that he would be able to "get away with it" and have both the Crown and marriage to Wallis.

The cabinet had reached the conclusion that they could not accept the King's marriage to a woman with two husbands still alive, even if it was a morganatic marriage which did not confer the title of Queen on Wallis Simpson. Baldwin telegraphed the Dominions to solicit their views on the impending constitutional crisis. Mackenzie King stated that Canadians would not accept Mrs. Simpson as either Queen or consort, but he urged caution because he felt that if abdication were thought to have been forced on the popular King, it would provoke an upsurge of affection which would be even more divisive. Prime Minister King was careful not

---

87 Keith Middlemas and John Barnes, *Baldwin: A Biography* (London: MacMillan, 1969), p. 984.

88 Brian Inglis, *Abdication* (New York: MacMillan, 1966), p. 266.

to do or say anything which might have cast Canada with a major part in the crisis.[89]

Finally, the silence of the British press was broken. The people of the United Kingdom suddenly found themselves in the midst of a well developed constitutional crisis, about which the rest of the world had been speculating for months.[90] At first there was a feeling that the popular King should be allowed to marry whoever he wanted. However, after a few days a feeling of revulsion set in. Many found it hard to believe that Edward was prepared to abrogate his duty in order to pursue his selfish pleasures, and had thus jeopardized the monarchy. "Isn't it dreadful," read a letter in the *Daily Express*, "that Edward VIII, the son of our beloved King George, should bring Hollywood ideals to Britain."[91] "The King had been guilty of vulgarity: he had betrayed the standards which in the eyes of his people it was his duty to protect."[92] Labour politician Ernest Bevin, speaking for the Welsh miners he knew so well, said simply, "Our People won't 'ave it!"[93] Harold Nicholson wrote in his diary, "He imagines that the country, the great warm heart of the people, are with him. I do not think so. The upper classes mind her being an American more than they mind her being divorced. The lower class do not mind her being American but loath the idea that she has two husbands already."[94]

In Canada, the press had respected the privacy of the sovereign in spite of the extravagant coverage that the crisis was receiving south of the border. During November, the papers were full not of gossip about Edward's private life, but rather with speculation concerning the possibility of a royal visit after the coronation. In Alberta the *Calgary Herald* ran a headline "King's visit hint cheered by Dominion," and went on to explain that "Canada has always had a particularly warm spot in

---

89 Neatby, *Mackenzie King*, p. 183. Mackenzie King was so anxious to avoid being blamed for ousting the popular monarch that he made a press release to distance himself from any backlash. In it he stated that "no proceeding or course of action in Great Britain has been at the instance or upon the insistence of the Dominions, and of Canada in particular," Neatby, *Mackenzie King*, p. 184.

90 Both Alistair Cooke and Beverley Baxter, who were influential commentators on the abdication in later years, felt that the "conspiracy of silence" on the part of the British press had been a grave disservice to the people. They found themselves in the middle of a constitutional crisis without any preparatory time to weigh the issues and make up their minds. Cooke, *Six Men*, p. 72; and Beverley Baxter, "Why Edward Quit," *Macleans*, June 20, 1964.

91 Philip Ziegler, *Crown and People* (London: Collins, 1978), p. 35.

92 Ziegler, *Crown and People*, p. 35.

93 Ziegler, *Edward VIII*, p. 304.

94 Harold Nicolson, *Diaries and Letters, 1930–39* (London: Collins, 1966), p. 280.

her heart for the man who now is sovereign of the Empire."[95] The *High River Times* claimed that "Canada is pleased to believe it has a special link with the King in the E.P. Ranch and it would be a memorable occasion if he were to include a visit to his Alberta property in the Canadian tour."[96] On December 1, the *Calgary Herald* referred indirectly to the crisis:

> In recent months there has been much malicious gossip in American papers . . . the result has been detrimental to the prestige and popularity of the monarch. However, the strong Empire note sounded, and the strict sense of personal duty voiced in the King's recent speech from the throne did much to reverse this unfavourable opinion.[97]

Next day, however, the paper reported: "Bishop's reproof to King startles public in Britain," the column went on to reveal "what no English newspaper had dared to publish so far . . . the King's friendship with Mrs. Simpson."[98] The *High River Times* hoped that "the King's advisors bear constantly in mind the great service he has rendered the Empire. Possibly he has done more to create goodwill for England, among other people of the world, than all the clergy and statesmen of England."[99]

In London, the final scenes of the drama succeeded each other with shocking rapidity. On December 3, Wallis left the Fort for the south of France. By December 8, the inescapable fact of abdication was accepted by both the King and his government. The following day Baldwin recounted the details of the story to a hushed but sympathetic House of Commons. Finally, on December 10, the article of abdication was signed, in the octagonal drawing room at the Fort, by the King and his three brothers. In the evening he made his goodbye speech on the BBC from Windsor, and departed into exile.

Edward's decision to abdicate was accepted with respectful regret in Canada, and the manner of his going was widely admired. There was also a smug feeling that a trial had been survived which would have overcome a lesser breed. Under the headline "God Save The King," the editor of the *High River Times* went on:

> The British Empire has just passed through one of the most tense weeks of its history. Rarely have the hearts and minds of the people been so distressed, so divided in conviction. The particular qualities possessed

---

95 *Calgary Herald*, November 6, 1936.

96 *High River Times*, November 12, 1936.

97 *Calgary Herald*, December 1, 1936.

98 *Calgary Herald*, December 2, 1936.

99 *High River Times*, December 3, 1936.

by the former King Edward VIII brought to him admiration and affection that was no automatic tribute to the crown, but a personal vital sentiment. To those somewhat removed from the monarchical tradition he was the visible interpretation of kingly qualities, such qualities as sportsmanship, courage, human compassion and understanding. His people loved him and their grief at the thought of his abdication was an experience that will not soon be erased from memory. But it is a remarkable commentary on the British people that once Edward made his final decision, there were no unruly demonstrations, no embarrassing protests.[100]

The abdication had provoked passionate opinions and might have been expected to leave a wake of controversy. It did not. The scheduled soccer matches were played, and people returned to their Christmas shopping. Diarist Chips Channon remembered listening to the farewell speech while he was out to dinner: "I wept, I murmured a payer for he who had once been King Edward VIII. Then we played bridge."[101] Alistair Cooke wrote an epitaph for Edward's brief reign with the benefit of hindsight and his ironic wit:

All in all, few disasters in the history of English Kings were more fortunate for the British people than the appearance in the Prince's social set of the divorcee from Baltimore. When the war came . . . Britain found herself with a modest and dutiful King, a devoted Queen and two bright children, a microcosm of middle class dependability that saw the country through when the going was bad.[102]

The rejection of the throne by the royal owner had profound implications for the E.P. Ranch. From being an important link in the fabric of Empire and a focus of intense interest both within Canada and abroad, the ranch, at the stroke of a pen, found itself in the shadows, its owner officially a "non-person," an embarrassment to the British government and the monarchy alike. Edward would not have been welcome to take up residence in Alberta even if it had crossed his mind to do so. Even three years later the Canadian government was unwilling to allow the Duke and Dutchess of Windsor to visit the Dominion. No longer was the ranch a place of pilgrimage for visitors, and the link with the royal estates, which had provided a steady stream of purebred stock, was severed. As the duke came to terms with his new life, the fear of penury loomed as a pervasive nightmare, and the importance of money management assumed an even greater importance in his mind. He resolved to

---

100 *High River Times*, December 17, 1936.

101 Ziegler, *Edward VIII*, p. 333.

102 Cooke, *Six Men*, p. 81.

divest himself of the ranch along with other unprofitable investments and unnecessary expenditures.

The future of the ranch had been the subject of continuous review even before Edward's accession to the throne. The suggestion that it be sold was tabled at a meeting of the Duchy of Cornwall in January 1935. The ranch management committee had been in place for some time, but Dudley-Ward's report had suggested that it was ineffective, and that its directives were not being carried out by the manager. The ranch looked likely to be a liability for the foreseeable future. However, the popularity of the Prince and the success of the E.P. Ranch made the question of disposing of it a very sensitive one. Apart from its undoubted value as a conduit for purebred stock, the ranch had caught the imagination of Canadians and seemed to epitomize the imperial links between the Dominion and the mother country. Several years later H.R.H. recalled:

> The annual accounts of the ranch have always been in the red and on more than one occasion I considered disposing of this liability but refrained from doing so because, until I abdicated in December, 1936, I was consistently assured by the Canadian government that my owning this western property was a valuable asset in the relation between the Dominion and Great Britain.[103]

To avoid these difficulties, the idea of presenting the E.P. as a gift to the Canadian nation was discussed in general terms. Later that summer, the future of the ranch was the focus of meetings at Canada House. Three alternatives emerged. The first was to lease the ranch on the open market for the best possible price. This was rejected as being unacceptable in Canada, and not practically possible in the economic climate of the times. The second idea was to lease the ranch for a relatively long term (twenty-one years) at a nominal rent to an institution like a university or agricultural college. This would be a popular solution in the Dominion, and would build upon the cordial contacts already developed between Carlyle and the University of Alberta. The third possibility involved using the E.P. as a training farm for immigrants from the United Kingdom, rather as the Military Ranch and the Bradfield Ranch had been used to train upper class immigrants a generation or so earlier.[104]

Sir Edward Peacock, the Receiver General for the Duchy of Cornwall, was able to visit the ranch briefly in the fall of 1935. A meeting called after his return brought matters to a head. He expressed the opinion that recent dealings with the ranch had been very unsatisfactory, and that

---

103 H.R.H. to C.G. Heward, September 1941, quoted in Michael Block, *The Duke of Windsor's War* (New York: Coward McCann, 1983), p. 212.

104 Minutes, Duchy of Cornwall, July 30, 1935.

nobody at the Duchy should be asked to continue to pay out money over which they had no control whatsoever. The ranch should be disposed of as swiftly as possible. A clear-cut gift to the Dominion seemed the best course of action, and Walter Monckton was suggested as the man to negotiate the transfer.[105]

The death of King George V and the accession of Edward VIII interrupted the negotiations, but in May the King told Newton that he was still in touch with the Canadian government through the High Commissioner with reference to the ranch, and that he was not interested in selling it on the open market.[106] A rumour that the E.P. was to be given to Fairbridge Farm School of Vancouver Island was discounted by the *High River Times* on the grounds that "the King's ranch in Alberta is a strengthening tie with a sentimental value much greater than any material consideration."[107] Interestingly enough, this was just the kind of solution that had been under consideration for some time.

In the fall of 1936, as his brief reign moved toward its dramatic conclusion, Edward decided to sell the ranch on the open market to the highest bidder. He enlisted the help of E.W. Beatty, the President of Canadian Pacific. A flurry of telegrams passed between Beatty and his agent in Calgary, S.G. Porter. The position concerning the mineral rights was clarified, and attempts were made to establish the value of the property.[108] Admiral Halsey reviewed the account books in London and reported to Newton that "It would appear that a sum in the neighbourhood of £60,000 ($300,000) had been found from this side for the purchase of land, cattle and working capital for the ranch since 1919."[109] In Alberta, Porter enlisted the help of J.W. Durno, an executive with the Canadian Shorthorn Association, to value the livestock, and Mr. Jones, of Toole, Peet and Company, to value land and improvements. They concluded that the livestock still on the ranch would bring $22,000, while the land and improvements were worth $18,000, for a total value of $40,000.[110] On December 4, when Edward had only a week to reign, the *High River Times* reported that Lionel Ellsworth, the American polar explorer, had denied purchasing the E.P. Ranch. He had dismissed the rumour as nonsense; he had indeed seen the King, but only because of

---

105 Minutes, Duchy of Cornwall, October 12, 1935.

106 GA M4843 f. 58, Halsey to Newton, May 29, 1936.

107 *High River Times*, July 30, 1936.

108 See GA M2269 f. 1357.

109 GA M4843 f. 58, Halsey to Newton, November 12, 1936.

110 GA M2269 f. 357, Porter to Beatty, November 4, and November 11, 1936.

the latter's interest in exploration.[111] However, it is interesting to note that Ellsworth was to appear as a possible buyer several times over the next five years. After the abdication, letters continued to pass between Newton, Beatty, and Porter, identifying possible purchasers, and updating evaluations in the light of changing market conditions, but H.R.H., the Duke of Windsor, had many other claims for his attention and no negotiations reached a critical stage.[112] It was not until after his marriage in 1937, and the establishment of the first home of his long exile at La Cröe, in the south of France, that Edward thought seriously about the future of the ranch. By that time, war seemed imminent, and the prospects of an oil strike on the property were improving. In the next chapter, the development of the Turner Valley oilfield is discussed, and its impact on the attitude of the Duke of Windsor toward the ranch is evaluated.

---

111 *High River Times*, December 4, 1936. This was the day after the abdication crisis became public knowledge in Britain and Canada.

112 See, for example, GA M2269 f. 371, Porter to Beatty, December 20, 1937.

VI

War and the Mirage of Oil

It is believed by many that the crude oil pool . . . on the western flank
of Turner Valley extends in a southerly direction into the ranch.[1]

The E.P. Ranch was located close to Turner Valley, the most important oil
and natural gas field in Canada until the late 1940s. This factor had, as
we have already seen, led Carlyle to obtain subsurface rights for his royal
master, both to insure that no unsightly development spoil the Prince's
rural retreat, and to enable H.R.H. to profit from oil related development
at a later date. During the 1930s the mineral lease became a "wild card"
in the various negotiations which took place to sell the ranch. Finally, as
wartime shortages drove the price of oil upward, the Duke of Windsor
visited the ranch and made the fateful decision to prospect for oil himself.
It was to be three years before an exploratory well was drilled on the
ranch, and the alluring image of "liquid gold" was to prove an expensive
mirage.

In 1912 three wells were drilled along Sheep Creek near Black
Diamond.[2] Gas, accompanied by a showing of volatile oil, was discovered. But expansion was slow until the formation of the Royalite Oil
Company in 1921, and the success of their fourth well in 1924. This was
the first shaft to penetrate the major oil and gas bearing strata, the
Rundle Limestone.[3] The well came in at 3,740 feet, which was close to
the limit of contemporary technology. It became clear that this strike was
of a completely different order of magnitude to those which had
preceded it. Soon Turner Valley was linked to Calgary and nearby com-

---

1 *High River Times*, July 2, 1936.

2 D.I. Istvanffy, "The History of Turner Valley," *Alberta Historical Review*, Vol. 2 (October
1954), p. 30.

3 David A.A. Finch, "Turner Valley Oilfield Development, 1914–1945" (unpublished M.A.
Thesis, University of Calgary, 1985), p. 10.

munities by a gas line, and markets, rather than production capability, became the limiting factor to further growth. Gradually, exploratory drilling spread from the immediate vicinity of the early strikes. By 1929, a well was being drilled within one and a quarter miles of the E.P. Ranch buildings.[4] This was the Western Alberta No. 1 (Norden) well (Map 10). Drilling was finally suspended in May 1930 when it had reached 3,878 feet, but not before quite a lot of oil had been "baled" and sold by the crew in payment of their wages. It was the advent of this well that encouraged Carlyle to take steps to protect the seclusion of the ranch.[5] In another part of the Turner Valley field, "Home No. 1" struck naphtha in great quantities and stimulated another boom which lasted well into the depression. When Carlyle wrote to his friend George Hoadley, the local member of the House of Assembly, he suggested that he should visit the district:

> . . . if you are going to be in the south sometime soon we would be glad to see you and discuss with you the possibilities of getting the gravelled road west from High River. The Highwood people are depending on you for this and it is something needed because of the great development of oil well interests all through our territory, even south of the Highwood River.[6]

During June 1936 a whole new era was inaugurated when crude oil gushed for the first time at Turner Valley Royalties' well. For the next twelve years Turner Valley remained the major oil field in Canada, producing a peak volume of ten million barrels in 1942.[7] This breakthrough resulted from better geological theory and improved drilling technology, using the second generation of rotary drilling rigs.

Naturally prospective buyers of the E.P. Ranch knew that it was located immediately to the south of the expanding Turner valley oil basin, and were interested in the status of the underrights.[8] These mineral rights, covered by Miscellaneous Mineral Mining Lease No. 6, were, with the exception of the quarter section on which the ranch house was built, not transferrable from H.R.H. However, it seemed fair to assume that some accommodation could be worked out with the Alberta Government in the event of a sale.[9] Certainly, Newton felt that the

---

4 GA M2398 f. 151, Barnum Brown, "Geology and Occurrence of Petroleum, E.P. Ranch, Pekisko, Alberta," March 1945.

5 The first letter in this protracted exchange was dated September 1929.

6 GA M2398 f. 42, Carlyle to Hoadley, April 20, 1935.

7 Istvanffy, "History of Turner Valley," p. 34.

8 GA M2269 f. 257, Porter to Beatty, September 16, 1936.

9 GA M2269 f. 257, Porter to Beatty, November 4, 1936.

possibility of an oil strike enhanced the value of the property. Apropos of the possible sale of the ranch he wrote to Halsey:

> It is unfortunate that the well being drilled close to the ranch has for the time being ceased drilling due to lack of funds. It is an interesting test. The question of the 160 acres of mineral rights owned by the ranch should be considered.[10]

The well Newton referred to was the Pekisko Hills No. 1 Well. It was "spudded" in January 1934 and drilled to a depth of 4,400 feet before it was capped in September 1936. The well struck pockets of gas and a show of oil.[11] The astute Calgary agent of Canadian Pacific summed up the situation in a letter to his chairman, Sir Edward Beatty:

> The prospects for oil in that district are attracting considerable attention. . . . If the structure on which the ranch is located, known as the Highwood Structure, should develop into an oil producing area, the oil rights on the ranch would of course have considerable value.[12]

In his opinion the improvements made to the ranch and the ranch house itself meant that the property was overvalued if it was to be used for ranching purposes. On the other hand, if oil were discovered things would be very different. This exciting possibility seemed more realistic when a surface evaluation was completed by Stanley J. Davies, a consulting engineer from Calgary. He mentioned the encouraging results from the Pekisko Hills well, and referred to some work done in the area by Dr. G.S. Hume, of the Canadian Geological Survey. "The report is a favourable one as far as the east side of the E.P. Ranch is concerned." He went on to mention the likelihood that exploration companies would drill two further wells directly to the south of the ranch.[13] Thus it was clear that more and more information was being amassed on the complex geological structures which underlay the ranch, and all indications suggested that oil was present.

Early in 1939, the Duke of Windsor asked Malcolm Mackenzie, the British High Commissioner to Canada, to visit the ranch and talk to Newton. Between them they decided that the only hope for recouping some of the capital invested in the ranch lay in an oil strike. Therefore, the strategy for the next few years was to hang on to the ranch, reduce losses to an unavoidable minimum, and to watch the local developments

---

10 GA M7005, Newton to Halsey, November 20, 1936.

11 GA M2398 f. 151, Brown, "Geology," p. 11.

12 GA M2269 f. 371, Porter to Beatty, December 20, 1937.

13 GA M2398 f. 57, Stanley J. Davies, "Memorandum re E.P. Ranch," May 2, 1938.

in the oil industry carefully.[14] Only six months later the outbreak of war enormously increased the strategic value of Canadian oil. As H.R.H. commented to Newton, "One thing is certain; that if the prosecution of the war does not further the development of the Alberta oil-fields, nothing ever will."[15] At the same time the war turned the Duke's life upside down, as it did those of millions of other men and women around the globe. H.R.H. was forced to manage the search for oil on his Canadian ranch from Nassau in the Bahamas rather than from France.

The outbreak of war in September 1939 found the Windsors in their rented villa, La Cröe, at Cap d'Antibes in the south of France.[16] They closed up the house as best they might and motored across the country to Cherbourg, where they were met by Lord Louis Mountbatten on his new command, the destroyer H.M.S. Kelly. In London, they stayed with "Fruity" Metcalfe and his wife. After a few days of meetings and anxious discussion, the Duke received an appointment as a liaison officer at the British Military Missions at Vincennes. The Windsors returned to Paris and spent the phoney war "camping out" in part of their house at 24, Boulevard Suchet. It was from there that H.R.H. wrote Newton what was to be his last letter for eighteen months:

> I must apologize for the long delay in answering your letter of August 19th. However, not only has this wretched war upset all the mails, but my military duties now keep me pretty busy, and my private correspondence has suffered in consequence.[17]

In the spring, as the German blitzkrieg burst through the allied lines and turned toward Paris, Wallis moved to Biarritz. Toward the end of May, she was joined by the Duke, and together they drove to La Cröe. By mid-June the Germans were pushing down the Rhone Valley, and the British Consul in Nice was ordered to burn his papers and evacuate his post. The Windsors joined a diplomatic convoy headed toward the Spanish border. On this journey the party experienced some of the shattering realities of war, crowds of refugees, long delays at check points, and unaccustomed impotence in the face of overtaxed authorities. Finally, with the help of the Spanish ambassador to France, the party reached Barcelona, and moved on to Madrid. The British government was concerned that H.R.H. was in a neutral country friendly to Germany, and urged the royal party to proceed without delay to Lisbon, whence they could fly to England.

---

14 GA M843 f. 58, H.R.H. to Newton, February 24, 1939.

15 GA M7005, H.R.H. to Newton, October 20, 1939.

16 Frances Donaldson, *Edward VIII* (London: Sidgewick and Jackson, 1986), p. 346.

17 GA M7005, H.R.H. to Newton, October 20, 1939.

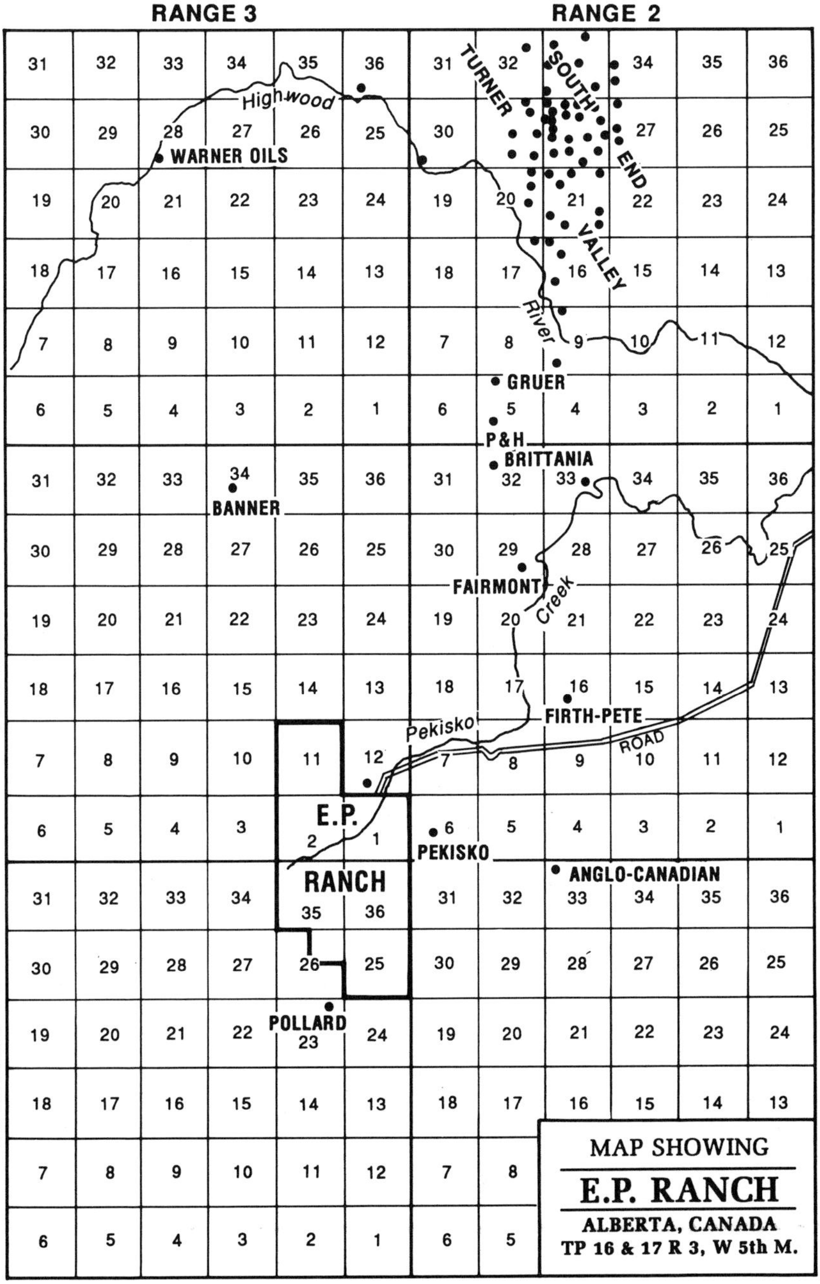

Map 10. Stanley J. Davies' map showing the E.P. Ranch
in relation to oil exploration, May 2, 1938.

Turner Valley, 1920s, showing size and density of oil derricks and collecting tanks.

The Windsors spent the next month in Lisbon. The actions of the Duke during this period have been interpreted in various different ways.[18] It is clear that his unwillingness to accept orders from London without quibbling, and his expressions of anti-war sentiments, coloured the British Government's attitude toward him for the remainder of the war, and indirectly affected his access to his Canadian property.

There can be no question that "in June and July, 1940, a good deal of Winston Churchill's attention had to be given to the recalcitrant Duke."[19] On his arrival in Lisbon, H.R.H. refused to take flight to England until his requests about the status of his wife were met. This impasse was resolved when he was offered the Governorship of the Bahamas. The Duke immediately accepted this appointment. However, during the following days, two further rows erupted and both required the intervention of the Prime Minister to solve them. The first concerned the desire of the Duke to spend some time in the U.S.A. before proceeding to his new job, and the second involved his request that both his valet and his chauffeur

---

18 For a careful analysis of the available evidence, see Michael Bloch, *Operation Willi* (New York: Weidenfeld and Nicolson, 1984).

19 Donaldson, *Edward VIII*, p. 359.

should be released from active service to accompany him to the Bahamas.[20]

This was not all. German intelligence made an effort to entrap the Duke of Windsor during this period, their hope being to entice him back into Spain where he could be held until peace negotiations with Britain might make him a useful figurehead for a new regime. If negotiations and persuasion failed to produce results, plans for abduction were also made.[21] A telegram from Churchill to the Canadian Prime Minister, Mackenzie King, informing him of the Duke's appointment suggests that the British government suspected something of these plans:

> The position of the Duke of Windsor on the continent in recent months has been causing his majesty and his majesty's government embarrassment as, though his loyalty is unimpeachable, there is always a backwash of Nazi intrigue which seeks to make trouble about him. The continent is now in the enemy's hands. There are personal and family difficulties about his return to this country.[22]

It was therefore with considerable relief that British diplomats in Portugal reported the departure of the Windsors on board the American ship Excalibur. The government in London hoped that they had heard the last of the Duke for some time. However, it was only a week after landing at Nassau on August 17, 1940, that H.R.H. telegraphed his superior, Lord Lloyd, in London and reported that Government House needed substantial renovations. He went on:

> I shall therefore have to rent another house but as there can be no official entertaining during that period and the heat is now intense, I propose, with your concurrence, to take advantage of the hot weather season to go to my ranch in Canada which I shall anyway have to visit for business purposes sooner or later.[23]

---

20 Donaldson, *Edward VIII*, p. 370; Lloyd telephoned to Churchill's office: "Lascelles and Sir Walter Mockton both agreed that H.R.H. had to be treated as a petulant baby, and that there was a by no means remote possibility that he was prepared to face a break on this subject, and that he was unable to appreciate how ludicrous the affair would appear when made public." Sarah Bradford, *The Reluctant King* (New York: St. Martin's Press, 1989), p. 439.

21 Bradford, *Reluctant King*, p. 437.

22 PAC MG26, J1, Vol. 284, p. 240379, High Commissioner to Mackenzie King, July 5, 1940; the original draft of this telegram written by Lloyd used stronger language. It was modified by Churchill. The original read, "The activities of the Duke of Windsor on the continent in recent months has been causing H.M. and myself grave uneasiness as his inclinations are known to be Pro-Nazi and he may become a centre for intrigue." Bradford, *Reluctant King*, p. 436.

23 Donaldson, *Edward VIII*, p. 381.

It was true that many matters concerning the future of the ranch needed resolving, but Lloyd regarded the request as a last-ditch attempt on the part of the Duke to get his own way and visit the United States before settling down in the Bahamas. The request was refused on the grounds that it would cause disappointment and anxiety to the people of the Bahamas. Instead it was H.R.H. who was disappointed. In his next letter to Newton he wrote:

> I had Mr. Allen write you at the end of last July when I was appointed Governor of the Bahamas, that the Duchess and I hoped to be able to visit the "E.P." Ranch in August on our way to take up this appointment. Unfortunately and inconveniently, we never passed by America, as I was very anxious to discuss various matters with you and see the property again after a lapse of thirteen years.[24]

The Windsor spent the next year making the best of their banishment and their life in what the Duchess called "the Elba of 1940." By the summer of 1941, they could feel some satisfaction that the Bahamas had enjoyed a record tourist season, and the Duke had demonstrated his determination to stand up to "the Bay Street Boys," as the clique of Nassau merchants were called. Wallis had organized some clinics for children, and was an energetic president of the local Red Cross. They felt they deserved a holiday, and hoped to get away during August and September, to escape the worst of the hot season. The prospect of spending some time in the centre of affairs, surrounded by people of their own kind, was alluring. The Duke wrote to Wallis' aunt Bessie:

> We can't plan anything definite for the summer yet and can only hope that nothing will prevent us from getting away at the end of August to America and my ranch in Canada.[25]

H.R.H. could justifiably argue that he had business to perform on the colony's behalf in Washington. He also needed the opportunity to put his own affairs in order and to make some decisions about his ranch.

That the Duke of Windsor should be granted permission to take some leave in the United States and Canada was by no means a foregone conclusion. A key facet of Churchill's policy at this desperate stage of the war was to do everything he could to bind Britain to the United States and to establish a close relationship with President Roosevelt. One reason why the Duke had not been allowed to visit the United States in 1940 was that the President was seeking re-election, and it was feared that

---

24 GAI M4843 f. 58, H.R.H. to Newton, April 7, 1941.

25 Bloch, *Duke of Windsor's War*, p. 203.

H.R.H. might have expressed views which would have strengthened the isolationist opposition. Some of the actions, associations and attitudes expressed by the Duke during his first year in the Bahamas had done nothing to dispel official suspicion. On one occasion the Duke and Duchess cruised to Miami on the Southern Cross, owned by the mysterious Swedish businessman Wenner-Gren. This action earned them the headline, "Windsors sailing on Goring pal's yacht."[26] They associated with other influential figures who were anti-British and pro-Nazi, even if their sentiments were cloaked in the laudable desire to foster peace. Early in 1941 the Duke gave an interview to Fulton Owsler, which was published in *Liberty Magazine,* and reproduced in Britain in the *Sunday Dispatch.* In it he seemed to support a negotiated peace, and he discouraged the Americans from entering the war.[27] This indiscretion could not have occurred at a worse time, for the crucial Lend-Lease Bill was being considered by the House of Representatives in Washington, and still had to face the Senate. Churchill telegraphed the Duke, telling him to avoid Wenner-Gren, who, he wrote:

> . . . according to reports I have received, [is] regarded as a Pro-German financier, with strong leanings towards appeasement, and suspected of being in communication with the enemy. Your Royal Highness may not, perhaps, realize the intensity of feeling in the United States about people of this kind and the offence which is given to the Administration when any countenance is given them.[28]

The Prime Minister went on to say that the Duke's *Liberty* interview had been interpreted as "defeatist and pro-Nazi . . . and approving of the isolationist aim to keep America out of the war."[29] With all these black marks against him, how could permission to visit the United States be granted?

---

26 John Parker, *King of Fools* (New York: St. Martin's Press, 1988), p. 245.

27 Michael Bloch, *The Secret File of the Duke of Windsor* (Reading: Bantam Books, 1988), pp. 226–28; and Bradford, *Reluctant King,* p. 441.

28 Bradford, *Reluctant King,* p. 442.

29 Bradford, *Reluctant King,* p. 442. The U.S. Assistant Secretary of State, Adolf Berle Jr., summarized the disquiet about the Duke in a letter to Lord Halifax: "Quite aside from the more shadowy activities of this family, it is to be recalled that the Duke and Duchess of Windsor were in contact with Mr. James Mooney, of General Motors, who attempted to act as mediator of a negotiated peace in the early winter of 1940; that they have maintained correspondence with Bendaux, now in prison in North Africa and under charges of trading with the enemy; that they have been in constant contact with Axel Wenner-Gren, presently black-listed for suspicious activity. . . ." Bradford, *Reluctant King,* p. 441.

Three months later the Duke wrote to Churchill again. This time he was much more placatory. He assured the Prime Minister of both his loyalty and his discretion, and expressed the hope that something could be done "to dispel this atmosphere of suspicion that has been created around me, for there is a good deal more I could do to help on this side of the Atlantic."[30] These protestations rang a chord with his old friend, who wrote to the Colonial Secretary:

> I see no reason why the Duke of Windsor should not, towards the end of September, visit Canada and the United States if he so desires. Such a request would not be denied any governor of Nassau. . . . I presume that he would go to New York where he would stay at a hotel rather than with society people and do any shopping which the Duchess may require. Thereafter they would go to the E.P. Ranch of which I expect they would soon tire and after that return to Washington where the President has promised to give them luncheon. . . . There is no reason why this tour should not be worked out and everything done for the comfort and honour of the former King-Emperor and his wife. But all must be planned before hand.[31]

Everything was to be thought out and arranged to avoid potential embarrassment. "We won't be allowed much playing around America, so we must confine everything as much as possible," wrote the Duchess to her aunt.[32]

The Duke wrote to Newton to direct him to prepare the ranch for a visit. "Although we are prepared to rough it up to a point, we would expect a clean, if modest, comfort which the house provided the last time I occupied it."[33] Carlyle sent a list of repairs judged necessary to make the ranch house habitable, and the Duke and Duchess discussed it and requested that "samples of colour in Kalsomine and design of wall paper should be submitted for the different rooms, stating the colour in which the rooms were originally painted."[34] The men on the spot were authorized to spend $300 immediately to put things in order. Subsequent letters dealt with domestics, linen, the refrigerator, the problem of the press, and the allocation of rooms.[35] Apart from this meticulous planning of details, the Duke made it clear that he was looking forward to discussing the future of the ranch face to face with his advisors.

---

30 Bloch, *Secret File*, p. 229.

31 Bloch, *Duke of Windsor's War*, p. 203.

32 Bloch, *Duke of Windsor's War*, p. 204.

33 GA M4843 f. 58, H.R.H. to Newton, April 7, 1941.

34 GA M4843 f. 58, H.R.H. to Newton, July 11, 1941.

35 GA M4843 f. 58, H.R.H. to Newton, August 7 and August 28, 1941.

The Windsors arrived in Washington on September 25. They stayed at the British Embassy, and were entertained that night at a dinner party. The guests included the Vice-President and several other dignitaries from the U.S. government. It was a good beginning.

The next day they left on their journey to Canada. Instead of travelling northward to Montreal and thence westward on the Canadian Pacific Railway, the Windsors were routed via Chicago and St. Paul, and entered Canada through North Portal, Saskatchewan. This route avoided the major centres of population and government in central Canada, and made it easier to pass off the visit as a purely private journey to the Duke's property in Alberta.[36] The Prime Minister of Canada was well aware that the memory of the abdication crisis was still very much alive among Canadians, and that a residue of hostility toward the Windsors remained. The Archbishop of Quebec, Cardinal Villeneuve, wrote to the Minister of Justice in Ottawa, concerning rumours that the Duke and Duchess might be "received" in some official way after their visit to the ranch. He suggested that this would be an affront to the reigning monarch, and that in the best interests of "la religion et du pays," the journey through Canada should be unofficial and discreet.[37] Another letter, purporting to voice "the opinion of nearly all the better type of Canadians," was more outspoken:

> I think it is disgraceful, after his [the Duke's] assurance that he would lead a retired and private life when he abdicated that he should have badgered the English Government ever since for some important position where his wife would be recognised; but of course it is her desire to shine in the limelight. . . . There are hundreds of Canadians who either of curiosity or from loose principles, would flock to see her and make a fuss over her, and it would give the rest of the world quite a false impression of what Canadians as a whole really think.
>
> I have deep sympathy for the awkward position in which you are placed, but I believe firmly that you have the skills and the diplomacy to keep the Duchess in her place.[38]

This kind of sentiment had been widespread during December 1936, and Mackenzie King had weighed it carefully as he responded to Baldwin's telegrams concerning the abdication. Since that time the Prime Minister had played a major role in both the planning and the execution of the royal tour by George VI and Queen Elizabeth in 1939. He had fallen

---

36 Bloch, *Duke of Windsor's War*, p. 210; and *Secret File*, p. 231.

37 PAC MG26 J1 Vol. 307, Villeneuve to LaPointe, September 27, 1941.

38 PAC MG26 J1 Vol. 298, Wadsworth to Mackenzie King, August 10, 1940.

The Duke and Duchess of Windsor at the E.P. Ranch, September 1941.

completely under their spell.[39] This relationship had been renewed the previous month when Mackenzie King had visited war-torn London.[40] He would not have been disposed to do anything which might have embarrassed the King and Queen of Canada. Indeed, in July, he had made it clear to the High Commissioner in London that he would prefer that the Duke should not come to Canada.[41] However, he received a telegram from Winston Churchill on September 28, 1941, which read, "I should be glad if you could give a friendly hand to the Duke of Windsor during his visit to western Canada."[42] He replied without delay, "Everything we can do is being done to make the visit to Canada of the Duke and Duchess of Windsor as pleasant as possible, and I have reason to believe that they are thoroughly enjoying their stay."[43] The Windsors were met at the Canadian border by Colonel C.H. King, who presented a handwritten letter of greeting from the Prime Minister. It started:

> Sir, May I express to your Royal Highness my personal greetings on your arrival in Canada. Not withstanding the anxiety which all bear these days, I hope your stay at your Canadian ranch may be restful and enjoyable for the Duchess of Windsor and yourself.[44]

The letter was carefully worded to exclude the Duchess from the "official" welcome to H.R.H., but not to leave her out altogether. It went on to introduce Colonel King, who had served with the Royal Canadian Mounted Police in the Calgary district for years, and who it was thought might be useful in making local arrangements. At the same time the colonel was commissioned to keep an eye on the Duke's activities, and to report to the Prime Minister's office.

A welcoming editorial in the *High River Times* stressed the private nature of the visit, and expresses rather well the feelings of the region for the Duke. It is therefore worth quoting in full:

> Expressions of welcome which undoubtedly will be tendered to him and the Duchess will be more in the nature of a spontaneous gesture. They will be a tribute to the man not the Duke, nor the former King of England, or former Prince of Wales. In the past he came to his E.P. Ranch as a Prince but he remains in the memory of all who saw him and

---

39 Tom MacDonnell, *Daylight Upon Magic: The Royal Tour of Canada, 1939* (Toronto: MacMillan, 1989).

40 PAC MG26 J1 Vol. 302, Mackenzie King to Churchill, September 30, 1941.

41 Bloch, *Duke of Windsor's War*, p. 211.

42 PAC MG26 J1 Vol. 309, Churchill to Mackenzie King, September 28, 1941.

43 PAC MG26 J1 Vol. 309, Mackenzie King to Churchill, September 29, 1941.

44 PAC MG26 J1 Vol. 320, Mackenzie King to H.R.H., September 22, 1941.

The Duchess of Windsor in Calgary, 1941.

spoke with him, not as a link with royalty, but as a man of charm, simplicity, and great friendliness. In this practical and candid land, we still place higher value on what a man is, than on what his ancestry and titles may be. Although an inevitable glamour surrounds any member of the Royal Family, no one could have capitalized less on that attribute than the Prince of Wales. In all his contacts he was direct, natural, and considerate of everyone. There are a hundred little incidents and experiences which bear this out. From visit to visit he recalled acquaintanceships he had formed previously and wished to renew. And the people he remembered best and whose society he enjoyed, were not those of wealth and power, but plain people who had done their quiet part in the arduous task of building up one small corner of the Empire. Those who associated with him most closely, and knew him best, found in him a warmth of understanding and an appreciation of the ordinary man's problems. . . . It is in that spirit that a warm welcome from the Alberta Public will be assured to him and the Duchess of Windsor as opportunities may develop.[45]

The Windsor's train reached Calgary early on Monday, September 29. They were welcomed by a friendly crowd of some 1,500. First to greet them were Newton and Carlyle. "Well here we are at last, after supervising my ranch all these years by correspondence," commented the Duke.[46] It took rather more than half an hour to shunt the private car from the main line onto the southern branch line. The Windsors pleased the crowd by leaving the station and pushing their way through the people out into 9th Street. All too soon the party climbed aboard and headed for the small village of Aldersyde where they were met with cars. During the preceding days, heavy rain followed by snow had threatened to make the dirt road leading to the ranch impassable, but hard work dragging and draining had improved the worst places in the road, and the convoy of cars and two baggage trucks made it through without difficulty.[47] The slow progress provided opportunities for the Duke to point out the oil derricks of Turner Valley, and other more familiar features of the countryside. Warm sunshine greeted them as they splashed through the ford and up to the ranch. Mrs. Carlyle ushered them into the house, and the Duke led the Duchess on a brief tour. Fred Kennedy, the veteran reporter from the *Calgary Herald*, was greeted as an old friend, and had a chance to chat with the Duke for a few minutes. He found him "younger and fitter" than in 1927. "He is direct in speech, self assured, and, from the time he arrived in Calgary in the morning until

---

45 *High River Times*, September 25, 1941.

46 *Calgary Herald*, September 29, 1941.

47 PAC MG26 J1 Vol. 302, King to Coleman, October 1, 1941.

he arrived at the ranch in the afternoon, he was always in command of the situation."[48]

During the afternoon and the next day the Windsors explored the ranch on foot and were shown the remaining stock. A pony had been readied for the Duchess to ride, but the brisk weather and the unfamiliar saddle deterred her. On Wednesday, reporters from fourteen newspapers were welcomed to a press conference. The Duke was non-committal as to his plans for the ranch; he was not sure if he would sell it, or if oil exploration work would be carried out. The Duchess impressed the reporters with her natural and friendly manner. She refused to be drawn into a discussion of clothes and fashion, and instead told them about her infant-welfare clinics in the Bahamas, and her work for the Red Cross.[49] In the afternoon the couple drove to Turner Valley and, guided by Bob Trammell the field superintendent, they toured both drilling rigs and processing facilities. "Workers remarked on his constant flow of pertinent questions," noted a reporter.[50]

A highlight of the holiday for the Duke was the long tramps he took hunting "prairie chickens" and ducks. On these expeditions his guide was "Dougie" Newton, Alick's son, who was on leave from the Navy. The young lieutenant had travelled all the way from Halifax to surprise his parents, but when he arrived home he found that everybody was down at the ranch. Douglas knew every coulee and pond on the property and was a natural choice as guide. In 1988, a year before he died, Douglas Newton still remembered that leave as being very special.[51] The Duke was trying out a new gun with an unfamiliar double trigger, and his hand was paining him, perhaps as a result of "working" the crowds. The first day he missed a lot of birds, much to his disgust. Gradually, however, his timing came back and he began to hold his own with his young companion.

On Saturday the Windsors left the ranch for a few hours to drive to High River for a special screening of Gary Cooper's new film "Sergeant York" at the Wales Theatre.[52] The next day they went to Claresholm, where a cheering crowd of 5,000 watched the Duke present "wings" to the graduating class of the Claresholm Service Flying Training School. In his speech, the Duke recalled his own period of flight training and remarked on the amazing speed with which the airfield and the school

---

48 *Calgary Herald*, September 30, 1941; J. Harry Smith, who was handling the press relations for the Secretary of State's Office, also commented on the excellent health of the Duke. PAC MG26 J1 Vol. 302, Coleman to Heeney, October 9, 1941.

49 *Calgary Herald*, October 1, 1941.

50 *Calgary Herald*, October 2, 1941.

51 Interview, Douglas Newton, Calgary, June 1987.

52 *High River Times*, October 9, 1941.

had come into being.[53] This visit, which certainly had all the trappings of an official event, was arranged between the Commandant of the RCAF Station and the Duke at the ranch. Colonel King wrote to the Prime Minister's office the next day:

> I knew nothing about it until it was arranged and, since it seems to have gone off very well, I must say that I am glad that I did not have the job of discouraging it by saying that it was not intended that there should be any official functions . . . the Duke went to Claresholm in an ordinary suit. He was delighted with the arrangements.[54]

On the last day of his stay in Alberta the Duke made a similar visit to the Elementary Flying School at High River.[55] He and Carlyle arrived rather earlier than was expected, and a zealous guard, who did not recognize the Duke, refused to admit them to the base! After the brief ceremony, the Duke went on to Calgary for lunch and a round of golf before visiting the Ranchmen's Club, where a large crowd of members turned out to welcome him. The Duchess visited a school in High River, and had tea with Mrs. Newton. Later that night an enthusiastic crowd sang, "For He's a Jolly Good Fellow," and "There'll Always be an England," and cried "Come back soon" as the train left.[56] Colonel King could report thankfully:

> The whole visit was without incident unless the surprise packet visit to the air station at Claresholm must be excepted. They wanted to be quiet and seemed to enjoy their visit to the ranch in spite of a lot of bad (wet) weather. They seemed to be well received, and I observed . . . no adverse comment in the Canadian papers. I must add that they were extremely kind and hospitable to me.[57]

Mackenzie King wired Churchill, "I should like you to know that I have just had a most cordial and appreciative message from the Duke of Windsor on his departure from Canada for the U.S.A. By all reports his visit has gone very satisfactorily."[58]

The royal couple had thoroughly enjoyed their holiday. The Duke had at last had the opportunity to show Wallis a treasured part of his glorious past, and she had relished the warm welcome of the crowds.

---

53 *Calgary Herald*, October 6, 1941.

54 PAC MG26 J1 Vol. 302, King to Coleman, October 6, 1941.

55 *Calgary Herald*, October 8, 1941.

56 *Albertan*, October 8, 1941.

57 PAC MG26 J1 Vol. 302, King to Coleman, October 13, 1941.

58 PAC MG26 J1 Vol. 309, Mackenzie King to Churchill, October 10, 1941.

Duke and Duchess of Windsor with Mark and Moses, two Stoney Indians.

From a business standpoint, however, the visit was not a success. The Duke had hoped to resolve all his dilemmas about the future of the ranch. He spent long hours closeted with Newton and Carlyle. Harry Smith, who was responsible for press relations for the visit, reported that:

> H.R.H. was engaged in business at the ranch and has apparently accepted the resignation of Dr. Carlile [sic] as his agent. Dr. Carlile is now managing some coal mines in Alberta and can no longer give attention to affairs at the ranch. There is some suggestion that drilling for oil may take place on the ranch property and apparently there were some negotiations concerning licenses and the like. Some suggestions had been made to H.R.H. that he himself should have a well drilled, but . . . he intimated that he was not embarking on any enterprise of that kind, although he might consider suggestions of licensing others who might desire to drill.[59]

On the one hand, the Duke wanted to sell the ranch, even at a loss, so that no further funds would have to be found for maintenance. On the other hand, he wanted to make sure that if anybody got rich from oil strikes, it would be him. His advisors pressed him to sell, and he accepted that this was probably the prudent course of action. At the same time, he remained vulnerable to every rumour about developments in the "oil patch." He never laid his dream of oil wealth to rest, and his actions in this arena were never cooly rational. The strategic value of "safe" oilfields to the allied war effort was immense, and the Canadian government embarked upon a vigorous oil exploration program. Their interest in the E.P. Ranch finally triggered the Duke of Windsor to take action on his own behalf, and it is to trace these developments that we now turn.

---

59 PAC MG226 J1 Vol. 302, Coleman to Heeney, October 30, 1941.

VII

Dry Wildcat: Disappointment and Survival, 1941–50

> It would indeed be a pleasant surprise to wake up finding oneself an oil magnate instead of the impoverished owner of a mere cattle ranch.[1]

It was hard for the Duke of Windsor to ignore the heady atmosphere of optimism which surrounded oil developments in the Turner Valley in the early 1940s. Even as he made preparations in the Bahamas to get away for his holiday to New York and Alberta, the Duke received a letter from N.E. Tanner, the Alberta Minister of Mines. In it, Tanner reported that government geologists had examined many promising areas in the province and had recommended that drilling operations should take place in the Pekisko area, "as the structure gives every indication that oil will be found."[2] He went on to suggest that as the exploration would contribute to the war effort, the Duke should surrender his special lease.[3] To the Duke, this letter was the most exciting evidence so far that there was indeed oil under his land. Immediately, he wrote to his lawyer in London:

> I am sure you would advise me against consenting to withdrawal, for in view of the large sums of money expended on the E.P. Ranch, for which I have as yet had no return, I do not consider it fair to ask me to withdraw . . . the first time it looks like a part of the property becoming a source of revenue to me. While I am naturally anxious to help the war

---

1 Philip Ziegler, *Edward VIII: The Official Biography* (London: Collins, 1990), p. 487.

2 Michael Bloch, *The Duke of Windsor's War* (New York: Coward McCann, 1983).

3 This was not an unreasonable request, as the lease contained provision number 11, which stated: "If in the opinion of the minister the said petroleum or its products or any portion thereof should at any time during this demise be required for the use of His Majesty's Canadian Navy, the minister shall have the right of pre-emption of all crude petroleum oil or its products gotten or won under this demise."

effort, one has to think of the future. . . . I may have to rely on the ranch
as an important asset.[4]

While he listened carefully to the sensible evaluations presented by his
advisors, Edward still hoped against hope that oil riches might dispel his
financial nightmares once and for all.

The conclusion of the meetings at the ranch had been that it was time
to sell. Neither Newton nor Carlyle had any hope that the ranch could
break even, and they agreed that "the financial aspect is far from promising."[5] The best of the pedigree cattle had been sold in 1938; those that
remained had been suffering from Bang's disease at the time of the
disposal sale. Although they had fully recovered, they were not the pick
of the herd. At the same time, there was practically no demand for
horses, and the flock of sheep was small. In these circumstances his
advisors predicted that the Duke would have to find about $2,000 a year
to maintain the ranch. Carlyle was authorized to write to Lincoln
Ellsworth, with whom he was acquainted, to see if the explorer was still
interested in buying the ranch. He wrote:

> His Royal Highness has been at the ranch for the past week and the
> future plans in connection with it have been discussed at some length,
> and in strictest confidence I can tell you that H.R.H. has decided to
> dispose of the property.[6]

However, the terms were such that the Duke would retain the mineral
rights to the one quarter section which he now held in fee simple, and
would receive 50% of any royalties that might result from oil exploration
by the new owner on the remainder of the ranch. Carlyle concluded his
letter by explaining that the Duke would be in New York during October,
and would be glad to discuss the matter. As it happened, Ellsworth and
H.R.H. did not connect, and the Duke was inclined to think that
Ellsworth was avoiding him. He reported to Newton:

> Lincoln Ellsworth is indeed a slippery customer and he was away from
> New York the whole two weeks we were there. I finally located him in
> Florida and suggested his meeting me in Miami, but he flew back to
> New York the day we left.[7]

---

4 Bloch, *Duke of Windsor's War*, p. 214.

5 GA M2398 f. 3, Newton to Allen, June 19, 1941.

6 GA M7005, Carlyle to Ellsworth, October 5, 1941.

7 GA M7005, H.R.H. to Newton, November 9, 1941.

Barnum Brown, working on geological core samples in the office at the E.P. Ranch, 1944.

It seems likely that if they had met, and if Ellsworth had responded positively to the offer, the Duke would have blown cold, for he was already pursuing another option enthusiastically.

During his hectic "working holiday" in New York, the Duke had chanced to meet Dr. Barnum Brown, a palaeontologist at the Museum of Natural History. The conversation turned to oil exploration and the Duke's hopes concerning the E.P. Ranch. Brown explained that, through his long association with fossils, he had learned how to "smell oil." Without more ado, H.R.H. asked him to carry out a surface survey of the ranch. The Duke wrote confidently to Newton about his new acquaintance, "Dr. Brown is a very eminent geologist and there is very little he does not know about the Alberta oil fields."[8] Brown was told of the offer that had been made to Ellsworth, and of the Alberta Government's request that the lease be surrendered. He proceeded to Calgary with instructions to keep the purpose of his visit secret. The Duke wrote: "I

---

8 GA M7005, H.R.H. to Newton, November 9, 1941. The Duke consistently believed that somebody he had met and talked to was superior to an anonymous expert, whatever his or her paper credentials. Another good example of this belief was his misguided decision to involve Miami detectives in the murder investigation that followed the death of Sir Harry Oakes in 1943. See John Parker, *King of Fools* (New York: St. Martins, 1988), p. 259.

repeat that Mr. Newton is the only man in my confidence in the Calgary district and that officials of the Department of Lands and Mines of the Province of Alberta are to be avoided at all costs at this stage."[9]

During the first week in December, H.R.H. received a preliminary report from Brown which assured him "that the E.P. Ranch is decidedly in a favourable position and that your Royal Highness will be well advised to retain it as a possible oil producing property."[10] Negotiations with Ellsworth were allowed to "run their natural course," and plans were put in hand for the vital geophysical subsurface survey which alone would pinpoint the optimum location for an exploratory well.[11] This kind of work could not proceed until the spring. The Duke planned to get to New York early in the year to make arrangements with Brown. In June he telephoned Newton from New York, but no definite plans had been made. Newton was not convinced that the search for oil was a good risk, or that it was being carried out in the most efficient manner. He voiced some of his doubts with delicacy and tact:

> I indeed hope that the Doctor's [Brown] investigations will prove satisfactory. I understand that it is more difficult to obtain accurate information in the broken foothills area that it is in the eastern and less broken formation.
>
> I realize that the proving of this area is a gamble which may give rich results, it also may well result in heavy and fruitless expenditures as has every area adjacent to, but outside, the Turner Valley. The district known as the Northern Extension of the Turner Valley in the last few weeks has seen many wells closed down and labelled (temporarily at least) as costly ventures [sic failures?] I have no doubt that oil will be found outside the present proven structures. I am also sure that there will be much money lost in finding it.
>
> I am firmly of the opinion that testing by drilling should only be done by corporations or individuals who are able to complete what they undertake. I have in general no faith in "wild catting" but realize that is how new fields are found and much made or lost.[12]

In spite of this cautionary note the Duke decided to finance a geophysical subsurface survey to be carried out by M.S. Blackburn. The work was completed during the summer, and the subsequent report established the position of an elongated dome in the strata underlying the southern

9 GA M7005, H.R.H. to Brown, November 23, 1941.

10 GA M7005, Brown to H.R.H., December 1, 1941, quoted in H.R.H. to Newton, December 7, 1941.

11 GA M7005, H.R.H. to Newton, December 7, 1941.

12 GA M2398 f. 19, Newton to H.R.H., June 24, 1942.

margins of the property. A location close to the lake was identified as the best site for an exploratory well.[13]

In May 1943, the Duke once again visited New York. He managed to interest two wealthy acquaintances in joining him in a project to drill for oil on the E.P. Ranch. Charles G. Cushing was an investment broker and a frequent golfing companion of the Duke's when they met in Palm Beach. Elisha Walker was a member of the banking house of Kuhn, Loeb and Company, of New York City.[14] They formed a company which they called "ECUSHWA," a name formed by combining a few letters from each of their names.[15] Putting together financing for the venture proved relatively simple compared to working out the legal niceties with Mr. Tanner and the Alberta Government.[16] A lawyer had to be retained and the relevance of lease provision number eleven, "that the lessee shall not will, assign, transfer, or sublet . . . the mineral rights," to the new company's organization, had to be established. Edward had already talked over his plans with the Canadian High Commissioner for the United Kingdom, and now the Right Honourable Malcolm MacDonald was enlisted to expedite the company's application.[17] Finally, a drilling licence was forthcoming, much to the relief of the Duke, who explained:

> I am staking everything on the discovery of oil for the present I have no alternative. In the event of victimization on the part of Edmonton or the failure of drilling operations, we will have to think again and very hard indeed.[18]

No sooner had one obstacle been removed than another arose. The Duke's partners drew his attention to clause number fifteen of the lease, which read, "in case the surface rights of the said lands cease to be used for ranching or farming purposes by the lessee or members of the Royal Family, these presents shall there upon become and be null and void."[19]

---

13 GA M2398 f. 151, Barnum Brown, "Geology and Occurrence of Petroleum, E.P. Ranch, Pekisko, Alberta" (unpublished report: March 10, 1945).

14 Bryan and Murphy, *The Windsor Story*, p. 475.

15 Edward, *CUSH*ing, and *WA*lker.

16 GA M7005, H.R.H. to Newton, July 1943. Before the war, relations between the Duke and Tanner had been cordial. When the minister visited Europe in the summer of 1939, he had a long talk with H.R.H., and explained what steps should be taken should the Duke wish to carry out oil exploration. Carlyle and Tanner were acquainted, and Mr. and Mrs. Tanner had been guests at the ranch. Edward's refusal to surrender his lease or to cooperate in a government exploration program had led to feelings of suspicion and hostility. GA M2398 f. 3, Newton to Allen, June 19, 1939.

17 GA M7005, H.R.H. to Newton, July 25, 1943.

18 GA M7005, H.R.H. to Newton, July 25, 1943.

19 GA M2398 f. 150, Miscellaneous Mineral Lease, Number 6.

What would happen, they asked, if the Duke died while drilling was going on? Would their right to drill be revoked? These were reasonable questions to ask before investing $100,000. The Duke's sole heir was the Duchess of Windsor, but was she considered part of the Royal Family? This question raised, in a new context, the issue that had been a bitter bone of contention between the Duke of Windsor and his brother, King George VI.[20] The latter had consistently refused to grant the title "Her Royal Highness" to the Duchess since he felt that this would render the trauma of the abdication meaningless. In this chapter of the ongoing battle, the Duke wrote to his brother and requested that his wife should be officially designated as a member of the Royal Family.[21] At the same time his lawyer discussed legal niceties with Lascelles, the King's private secretary. Lascelles saw the request as yet another ploy to gain recognition for the Duchess. He passed the matter on to the law officers of the Crown. They concluded that there was no reason why the Duke's heir had to be a member of the Royal Family in order to retain the lease, and anyway, they said, it was a matter for the Canadian courts to decide. King George was able to reply to his brother, "No action on my part can affect the issue."[22] Political and legal hindrances were finally cleared away; all now hinged on the men in the field manning the derrick.

Whatever his olfactory gifts in locating hydrocarbons, Dr. Barnum Brown was not the most energetic or forceful "executive officer" to push forward with the drilling. All he achieved during the summer of 1943 was the selection of a site for the proposed well (Map 11). He dithered over the choice of a contractor, and had to return to New York for consultations because he had radically underestimated drilling costs. Moreover, he had predicted a shallow well, presumably to make the increased costs of drilling more palatable. In May 1944, the Duke reported that:

> My associates seem to be experiencing a lot of difficulty in finding a driller who combines the essential attributes of reasonable charges and integrity. . . . I hesitate at this long distance to interfere with whatever oil drilling arrangements my associates, who are after all putting up the money, deem it expedient and convenient to make and therefore, I feel I should pursue the policy of leaving the matter in their hands.[23]

The well was finally started on August 23, 1944. Drilling went on continuously day and night. There were three shifts, each of five men, under

---

20 Michael Bloch, *The Secret File of the Duke of Windsor* (London: Corgi, 1988).

21 Bloch, *Duke of Windsor's War*, p. 318.

22 Ziegler, *Edward VIII*, p. 486.

23 GA M7005, H.R.H. to Newton, May 24, 1944.

Drilling on the E.P. Ranch, the Ecushwa No. 1 well, October 1944.

the efficient direction of Mr. E.R. Snyder, the son of the contractor. The cores revealed beds that were dipping at a high angle, and that were frequently fractured and faulted. It was a considerable achievement to keep a comparatively straight hole.[24] At about 1,500 feet, the drillers reported traces of oil in the sandstone, and an extraordinary directors' meeting was held amid considerable excitement to approve deeper drilling. The Duke agreed to contribute half of the cost of drilling operations over and above the $25,000 already committed by each of his partners.[25] He wrote to his mother, Queen Mary, "It would indeed be a pleasant surprise to wake up finding oneself an oil magnate instead of the impoverished owner of a mere cattle ranch."[26] By the end of October 1944, the bit had reached 2,710 feet, and there seemed to be a considerable showing of oil in the Fernie Shales. Finally, the Madison Limestone was reached, the strata which had yielded commercial oil finds in the Turner Valley. While the Ecushwa partners tried to contain their excitement, technical difficulties suspended drilling. It was not until February 1945 that further progress was possible. On the 14th, at 4,124 feet, the reservoir was

---

24 GA M2398 f. 151, Brown, Geology Report.

25 GA M4843 f. 58, H.R.H. to Newton, October 2, 1944.

26 Ziegler, *Edward VIII*, p. 487.

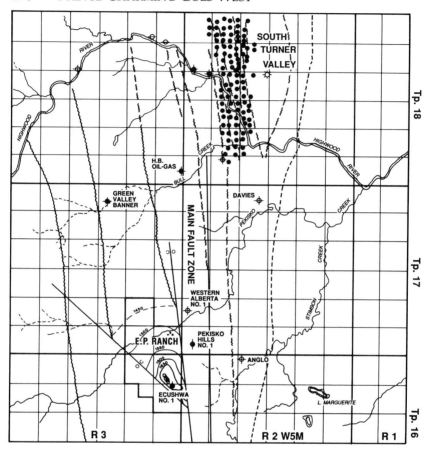

Map 11. Barnum Brown's map showing the location of Ecushwa Well No. 1.

breached and oil began to flow, only to turn to water after a few minutes.[27]

The Duke took this disappointment with remarkable fortitude. He telegraphed his partners, "a great disappointment for all of us, but thank you and Charles for fine cooperation and faith in the project." H.R.H. had committed some $45,000 to the venture, more than double what he had originally agreed to.[28] Barnum Brown's report recommended continuing Ecushwa No. 1 well another 2,500 feet, at an estimated cost of $62,000. Brown argued:

27 GA M2398 f. 151, Brown, Geology Report; and Bloch, *Duke of Windsor's War*, p. 345.

28 Bloch suggests a figure of $100,000, but the accounts only mention two cheques to Ecushwa Oils Ltd., one for $22,500 in 1944, and a second for $20,000 in 1945.

... in view of the well's showing and position the expenditure is justified. The excessive amount of carbon in the drilling fluid below the grit bed, corroborated by the volume of pyrobitumen in all the cores and naphtha in some and live oil stains in cuttings is proof of a vast amount of hydrocarbons under this area.[29]

H.R.H. instructed his lawyer, Hannah, to attempt to interest one of the major oil companies in further drilling operations on the basis of this favourable report, but there were no takers. With the end of the war, the Duke felt that the demand for oil would slacken, and he was not optimistic. The spectacular oil finds at Leduc in the following year finally sealed the fate of the Ecushwa Company.

It was during this period of turmoil in the affairs of the E.P. that Professor Carlyle severed his connection with the ranch. As was so often the case with resignations from Prince Edward's household, Carlyle's retirement was marred by suspicion, rancour, and a callous disregard for twenty years of loyal service and vigorous leadership.[30] Between 1922, when he resigned his position with Lane Ranches, until 1938, Carlyle had devoted all his time to managing the ranch. He had turned down other employment for fear that it might lead to some conflict of interest, or to embarrassment of his royal employer. Under his leadership, the E.P. had become the most famous ranch in Western Canada, and he had brought the outfit through the trials of the depression unscathed. Mrs. Carlyle had also provided invaluable unpaid service, as she had supervised the ranch house and had dispensed hospitality to a constant stream of visitors, with very little help.[31]

After the death of Burns in 1937, the ranch advisory committee had ceased to operate. H.R.H. came to rely more and more on the advice of Alick Newton. Relations between Newton and Carlyle were somewhat strained, and throughout their long association they never ceased to address each other in formal terms. In spite of his intense loyalty to the Crown and the Empire, Newton was very much a western Canadian and a Calgarian. Perhaps he was somewhat suspicious of a man with a very different background, many of whose far-flung contacts were in the United States. Moreover, "the Professor" was a technocrat, an acknowledged expert in the field of animal husbandry; Newton was an executive, a manager, he never forgot Carlyle's somewhat cavalier attitude toward bookkeeping.

---

29 GA M2398 f. 151, Brown, Geology Report, Part VIII, p. iii.

30 "This trait in H.M.'s character of no sign of gratitude for past work is a very nasty one," wrote John Aird. The dismissal of Halsey and the treatment of "G" Trotter are the most frequently cited examples. See Ziegler, *Edward VIII*, pp. 255 and 235.

31 GA M2398 f. 12, Carlyle to Newton, March 15, 1940.

PURE BRED

After the bulk of the thoroughbred shorthorn herd was disposed of, in 1938, there was less need for constant supervision of the ranch. Carlyle reduced his salary as manager, and began to develop other interests. During 1938 he worked part-time supervising the Hillcrest-Mohawk coal-mines in the Crow's Nest Pass, and, at the end of 1939, he accepted a position as managing director of the mines, on the understanding that he would be free to spend a day or two each week at the ranch.[32] In August 1941, Carlyle offered his resignation to the Duke so that he could devote all his attention to his mining interests. H.R.H. persuaded Carlyle to stay in his employ until after his visit to the ranch, which was scheduled to take place the following month. His letter to Newton reporting this exchange entirely omits any acknowledgement of Carlyle's long service; instead it suggests that the Duke was determined to squeeze the last drop of useful counsel from the Professor before letting him go. He wrote:

> I quite agree with your diagnosis of the man, who while an expert on cattle, has always been difficult to work with and has suffered from a swelled head. Although I shall ultimately accept his resignation, he will be useful to have around when we are discussing business, and as a contact with Lincoln, should I require it.[33]

During the visit, the decision was made to proceed with an approach to Lincoln Ellsworth. Carlyle was delegated to write the letter.[34] As has already been mentioned, the Duke missed meeting the prospective buyer both in New York and in Miami. By November 1941, H.R.H. and Newton were convinced that Carlyle was involved in a conspiracy. The Duke wrote that he had had a letter from Ellsworth's lawyer which, he said:

> . . . confirms our worst fears regarding Carlyle and it is unfortunate that he and Ellsworth are such close friends and that Carlyle is not shooting straight in concealing their correspondence on the transaction from you. The worst feature in my mind is that Carlyle has not written to me either. In the hope of improving matters with respect to Carlyle, I have written him that he must show you all correspondence with Ellsworth. . . . This procedure should strengthen your hand.[35]

Carlyle indignantly responded that he had indeed kept Newton informed of telegrams between himself and Ellsworth, which anyway only dealt

---

32 *Calgary Herald*, March 2, 1942.

33 GA M7005, H.R.H. to Newton, August 28, 1941.

34 GA M7005, Carlyle to Ellsworth, October 5, 1941.

35 GA M7005, H.R.H. to Newton, November 23, 1941.

with details of the mining lease on which he was an expert. Any delays in forwarding letters had been caused by his absence at the mine. In view of the letter he had received from the Duke, "very seriously censuring me for not co-operating with you [Newton] in your negotiations with Mr. Ellsworth," he asked that his letter of resignation be accepted forthwith.[36] The Duke commented:

> As I was only retaining Carlyle's services during these negotiations, and as you recommended dismissal in your last letter, I propose writing him accepting his resignation as manager as soon as you wire that you advise me taking this step.[37]

This should have ended the affair. Carlyle's resignation was accepted from February 28, although he was paid for the month of March, so that he could help the new manager take over.

There remains, however, a nagging thread of evidence which is not entirely compatible with this interpretation of events. In January 1942, while his plea to resign was being considered, Carlyle wrote to the Duke and offered to buy the E.P. for $25,000.[38] H.R.H. and Newton interpreted this as a ploy to gain control of the oil rights and suspected that Ellsworth was behind the offer. However, Carlyle knew better than anyone that the special rights which he had negotiated for the Duke were not transferrable, and would lapse if the ranch was sold. When Ellsworth renewed his offer the following year, H.R.H. once again wrote that he "Could not but detect the Professor's hand in the renewal of his wealthy friend's interest."[39] The final evidence of Carlyle's continuing interest in the E.P. dates from 1944, when he suggested that the ranch be sold to a trust which would preserve the ranch and operate it for the benefit of the public. He offered his services as manager. The Duke interpreted this suggestion as clear evidence that oil underlay his property![40]

What lay behind Carlyle's offers to purchase the ranch, and his reluctance to sever his connections with the E.P.? Perhaps he dreamed of retiring there. He was over seventy years old and had spent the last twenty years nursing the ranch through good times and bad. Certainly, he would have been anxious to do anything in his power to reverse the inevitable decline in the property brought on by a largely disinterested absentee landlord. But Carlyle was undoubtedly an imaginative "wheeler-dealer"; he must have been thoroughly frustrated by the inability of the

---

36 GA M7005, Carlyle to Newton, November 27, 1941.

37 GA M7005, H.R.H. to Newton, December 7, 1941.

38 GA M7005, H.R.H. to Newton, January 3, 1942.

39 GA M7005, H.R.H. to Newton, February 16, 1943.

40 GA M7005, H.R.H. to Newton, May 24, 1944.

Duke to decide on a course of action and then to pursue it vigorously. Perhaps he did dream that he, with Ellsworth's help, could find the elusive "black gold."

During the late 1930s and the 1940s, the Duke of Windsor maintained his ownership of the E.P. Ranch only because he hoped to benefit from the discovery and exploitation of a commercial oil field. His major preoccupation was to reduce losses to an inescapable minimum. Again and again he reiterated this theme. "How much would you be able to reduce my expenses from what they are now?" He inquired of the new management, and he went on:

> I fully realize that under the existing set up and conditions, the upkeep of the ranch must inevitably cost me money, but I place full confidence in you [Newton] and Mr. Farrell that you will keep the red figures at a minimum.[41]

For his part Alick Newton, who had inherited the overall supervision of the ranch from the defunct management committee, tended to take personal responsibility for the annual losses incurred by the ranch. He wrote, "I feel very deeply the lack of success of the property financially."[42] In his view:

> It is not possible to operate such a property without loss. It is neither a ranch nor a farm. . . . In a general way such properties even when fully stocked do not pay; certainly where the owner is not actually residing on the property and all labour etc. must be hired. If the experience of such properties were that they paid I would have one or more myself. The past history of the place will confirm to your Royal Highness what I have written.[43]

Newton advocated getting rid of all the purebred stock and making a switch to commercial beef cattle. These could be operated far more cheaply and would not require any farming activity to grow feed grains. Even then, he felt, the E.P. would be too small to make money.[44] Thus, because of its size and the diversity of its operations the ranch was expected to lose money. The concern of the absentee landlord was to reduce these losses to a minimum.

Judged against these pessimistic expectations the actual operations of the E.P. during the 1940s were surprisingly successful. Stock sales grew

---

41 GA M7005, H.R.H. to Newton, February 20, 1942.

42 GA M4843 f.58, Newton to H.R.H., April 16, 1950.

43 GA M7005, Newton to H.R.H., April 13, 1944.

44 GA M7005, Newton to H.R.H., April 1, 1948.

from $1,500 in 1940 to $7,500 in 1947, and book losses diminished to a mere $400 in 1945 and $340 in 1946. In 1947, losses of $3,000 were reported, but during that year $4,500 was invested in substantial and much-needed repairs to the ranch house. This was reported as an operating expense, so that stock rearing actually showed a profit of $1,500. Between 1939 and 1949, the Duke remitted a total of $23,848 to underwrite ranching, close to the estimate made by Newton that it would take about $2,000 a year to keep the ranch going.[45]

After the retirement of Carlyle in 1942, the E.P. Ranch was run by Alick Newton from his Calgary office. Tom Farrell, who was general manager of ranches for the Burns Foundation, was appointed manager, while J.T. Gray continued to manage the books and records as he had done for years under the management committee.[46] The man who lived at the ranch and looked after the day to day decisions was the foreman, William Elliott. He had joined the ranch staff in 1923 as a shepherd, and had served a long apprenticeship under Carlyle. Every month or so he sent the pay-roll and receipts for expenses to Farrell in Calgary, and his handwritten notes provide an intimate if sketchy picture of life on the ranch during and after the war. They include commentary on business matters, stock, crops, and the weather, as this example shows:

> I enclose bills and pay roll and cheques for horse pasture and eggs. We still have pretty near 60 head of horses here which will be here for the winter. I enclose the new bulls' registration papers which were sent out here. Horse pasture this year has brought in about a thousand dollars. I killed the black steer yesterday and I figure he dressed 700 lbs, which is pretty good for a steer 17 months old. He must have dressed 60%. Cows out on straw stacks and looking very well. We have used very little hay yet. Had one bull got pneumonia but he is better now but lost a little flesh. The sow has 10 in her fall litter. Could you get me 4 one inch turn bolts and four clamps for one inch cable.
>
> Yours truly, Wm. Elliott
>
> P.S. Don't forget the fifty bucks.[47]

Under Elliott's care the two purebred flocks became, for the first time, major and reliable contributors to the ranch income. Natural increase allowed yearly sales of forty to fifty sheep which earned an average of $1,500, this equalled or exceeded the receipts from cattle sales during the

---

45 These figures and those which follow were taken from the audited accounts of the E.P. Ranch, GA M2398 f. 103, 104, 105.

46 GA M7005, H.R.H. to Newton, February 20, 1942.

47 GA M2398 f. 26, Elliott to Farell, December 2, 1946.

early 1940s. Prices remained firm throughout the period and peaked in 1948.

The forty or so shorthorn cattle on the ranch consisted of those animals which could not be sold in 1938 because they had failed to pass a test for Bang's disease. This condition was, however, temporary and the herd gradually improved and grew in numbers.[48] By 1944, Elliott reported a visit from a Calgary-based auctioneer and shorthorn expert:

> Bill Durno was out looking at the bulls and I think he got a surprise. He expects to get an order for more bulls about the 15th. I suggest not taking less than $300 per head for the eight.[49]

The following year twelve cattle realized $3,310, and the earnings of the small herd reached $4,000 in 1946 and $5,000 in 1947. This period of steady growth and upbreeding in the shorthorn herd was brought to a brutal end by a major fire which destroyed the main cattle barn and killed twenty pedigree beasts in February 1948.[50] The fire was thought to have started in the electrical wiring, and it was fanned by violent westerly winds. Only eight bull calves were rescued from the southern end of the barn. Twelve of the victims were heifers and the breeding program was therefore completely disrupted. This must have been a heavy blow to Elliott and his men. Ironically, the fire earned windfall profits for the ranch, and this was the only year that the books showed a clear profit.[51] The two insurance companies involved paid the maximum compensation provided for by the policies, each of the heifers being valued at $500, instead of the $150–200 which they might have realized at a sale. The barn itself was valued at $6,000, and the total settlement was for $15,290.[52]

Horses contributed less and less to the ranch during the 1940s. The stallions were old and returns from service fees dwindled to nothing. At the same time the demand for horses and ponies weakened. Sometimes it was possible to trade a pony for fence posts, but, as the foreman remarked, "we will have to do an awful lot of fencing to get rid of these ponies."[53] Fortunately, the robust Dartmoor ponies required a minimum of care. As he mentioned in his letter, Elliott had started to take in horses

---

48 GA M7005, Newton to H.R.H., April 1, 1948.

49 GA M2398 f. 26, Elliott to Farell, December 7, 1944.

50 GA M7005, Newton to H.R.H., April 1, 1948.

51 GA M2398 f. 105, Income and Profit and Loss Account for year ending December 31, 1948.

52 GA M2398 f. 34, Hunt and Watt Ltd. to P. Burns Agencies, April 16, 1948.

53 GA M2398 f. 27, Elliott to Farell, February 28, 1943.

from the neighbourhood to winter over on the under-used rough pasture of the outlying portions of the ranch.

Unlike the run of the mill cow-calf ranching outfits in the vicinity, the E.P. continued to grow feed crops of oats and barley, as well as putting up hay. In May, Elliott reported that the land was ready to seed; in July he wrote, "grain is growing good but we are having light frost almost every night"; and in September he explained that "we are cutting steady. The ten acre field of barley took more time than I expected as it was badly tangled by wind."[54] The crop returns varied enormously according to the weather; a really good crop could reduce feed purchases to a few hundred dollars instead of the $1,500–2,000 that had to be bought in adverse years.

Domestic help was hard to get and keep on the isolated ranch. Moreover, wartime activity in the district had increased opportunities for employment and wage levels. Elliott reported:

> You will notice that I have put Ida down on the pay roll for $50. She has been pestering me for more money or she is going to quit. I am well pleased with her but it is up to you.[55]

Next year he tried the same strategy, "I gave Mrs. Levins the house-keeper a raise, because I wanted to keep her."[56] Sometimes a woman hired in Calgary found conditions at the ranch very different from what she had expected. Mrs. Tate wrote to Tom Farrell:

> Unlike what you told me re work here I am expected to look after whole house also do washing for bedding and all without washing machine. So it is too much for me.[57]

Elliott had to take what help he could get. He commented, "This cook is leaving on the 15th, but I managed to get another one. I don't know how good she is but I've hired her for $60 a month."[58]

Coping with rationing was an additional hassle for a busy ranch manager. The Calgary office wrote, "we note you have sent in your butter coupons only up to and including number 5 . . . we are returning herewith no. 14 butter coupon which you apparently cut in error."[59] On another occasion Elliott requested, "would you ask Mr. Gray to send a

---

54 GA M2398 f. 26, Elliott to Farell, May 31, 1948; July 4, 1949; and September 1, 1949.

55 GA M2398 f. 27, Elliott to Farell, November 3, 1943.

56 GA M2398 f. 26, Elliott to Farell, March 1, 1945.

57 GA M2398 f. 26, Tate to Farell, April 9, 1947.

58 GA M2398 f. 26, Elliott to Farell, October 1, 1947.

59 GA M2398 f. 27, Gray to Elliott, February 4, 1943.

yellow ration sheet as I must have burnt the one that was sent by mistake."[60] With staff coming and going, keeping track of ration coupons became a nightmare, and mistakes were inevitable:

> Mrs. Haldane got away from here without her ration book and I could not mail it to her without her address, I did take some canning sugar coupons from it but that was while she was here and she signed the form from the office before I took them.

> P. S. I have destroyed Mrs. Haldane's address.[61]

Elliott's correspondence with Farrell depicts a busy ranch differentiated from its neighbours by the diversity of its operations and its concentration on purebred stock. These differences meant that feed had to be put up or purchased, and this in turn implied a larger labour force. The size of the ranch community varied according to the season, but Elliott usually had two or three men to help him and a housekeeper/cook. The total wage bill rose from $2,200 to $5,478 during the 1940s. A large garden, a dairy cow, and some chickens, helped to reduce household expenses. To Elliott and his men, the comings and goings of Barnum Brown, the geophysical exploration team, and finally the drilling rig, were merely intriguing diversions in the seasonal round of seeding, lambing, calving, and harvesting. From their perspective the ranch was busy and flourishing; a far cry from the pessimism of the Duke and his advisors.

---

60 GA M2398 f. 26, Elliott to Farell, January 20, 1946.

61 GA M2398 f. 26, Elliott to Farell, October 10, 1947.

VIII

Last Hurrah:
The E.P. Ranch Company Limited,
1956–61

They planned an ocean liner and launched a pig-boat.[1]

In 1950 the Windsors once more decided to visit their ranch. The Duke had been busy, in fits and starts, writing his memoirs, first for a series of articles which were to appear in *Life* magazine, and then for his auto-biography, *A King's Story*,[2] Final arrangements for publication had been concluded with G.P. Putnam's, and a holiday seemed in order. Starting from New York at the end of January, the couple progressed from one set of friends to another. The pilgrimage culminated with a three day visit with President Miguel Aleman, in Mexico City. Thence they moved on at a leisurely pace via Texas to Alberta, arriving on April 11.[3]

As soon as he met the press, on Calgary station, the Duke scotched rumours that he might be selling the ranch. "Indeed no," he said, "It is the only piece of property I've ever owned."[4] He went on to explain that he planned to get out of purebred shorthorns and to replace them with a commercial herd of Herefords. Clearly, he had put some thought into the future of the ranch before his visit, and had come to Calgary to take stock, and to implement some changes.

The Duke and Duchess were met by Mr. and Mrs. Newton and escorted to the Palliser Hotel, where they were ensconced in the vice-regal suite with their valet and lady's maid. Some suitable furniture and decorations had been hurriedly transferred from the Banff Springs Hotel

---

1 Roy Griswold, Interview, June 1991.

2 *Life*, December 8, 1947 and following; and H.R.H. Edward, Duke of Windsor, *A King's Story: The Memoirs of the Duke of Windsor* (New York: G.P. Putnam, 1952).

3 Charles Higham, *Wallis: Secret Lives of the Duchess of Windsor* (London: Sidgewick and Jackson, 1988), p. 468.

4 *Calgary Herald*, April 11, 1950; and *Time*, Vol. 55, No. 17, April 24, 1950.

to the Palliser, including a picture of the Duke taken when he was Prince of Wales. The royal couple spent the day recovering from their long train journey, and the Duke worked spasmodically on the proofs of his book.[5] The next day they made an early start, and, driven by their young friend Douglas Newton, they reached the E.P. Ranch at about 10:30. There was still some snow on the ground, the remains of a long hard winter, and the roads were greasy and soft. It was not the most auspicious time for a visit, as the *High River Times* commented: "the outlook over the countryside is bleak indeed. Patches of snow still linger and everything is at lowest pre-spring ebb. It is difficult to picture the ranch setting as it is in summer."[6] However, the Windsors appeared to be in buoyant spirits, and hurried through their press conference so that they could get on with their tour of inspection; William Elliott took them from barn to barn, showing off the remaining shorthorns, and his particular pride and joy, the flocks of sheep. The Duchess was particularly taken with the young lambs. After a couple of hours outside, the party enjoyed a blazing fire in the ranch house, and got down to business over a picnic lunch. The house had been aired and cleaned, and the dust sheets which protected the furniture had been spirited away, but there was never any question of staying the night in the unheated cabin.

The Windsors were delighted to find the house less dilapidated than they had feared it would be after nine years without a permanent occupant. "Our ranch house is much less run-down than we expected," said the Duchess, "it really is in surprisingly good shape." She went on to explain that they planned to renovate the house so that they could spend more time there during the summer months, using it as a base for fishing, hunting, and sight-seeing.[7] On their way back to Calgary in the afternoon the royal party paid an impromptu visit to the High River Memorial Centre, where they caught a number of faithful committee persons cleaning up and preparing for a visit which was expected to take place next day.[8] In point of fact, the Duke spent Thursday in Calgary. He had lunch at the Calgary Petroleum Club, and was the first to sign the guest book of that august body. The president of the club said: "Like every other oilman you have learned that the road to discovery is marred by disappointments." He went on to say that he hoped that, "you will try again in the oil search and that discovery will be your reward." The Duke told reporters afterwards that he would certainly not "go it alone"

5 *Calgary Herald*, April 10, 1950.

6 *High River Times*, April 13, 1950.

7 *Calgary Herald*, April 12, 1950.

8 *High River Times*, April 20, 1950.

again, but that if he got backing from a major corporation he would be prepared to consider further exploration.[9]

Surprising though it may seem with the benefits of hindsight, it is hard to avoid the conclusion that, at this time, the Windsors sincerely believed that they would be visiting the ranch on a regular basis, as part of their yearly round from Europe to New York and Florida. Such visits would fit into their schedule particularly well during the months when both Florida and New York were uncomfortably hot. In remarks to the press in Medicine Hat during the journey eastward, the Duke and Duchess stressed again that they were considering making the E.P. Ranch their home for at least two or three months each year. The Duke commented: "Our only permanent home for mail is the Waldorf Towers in New York City, so you can see why we cling to the ranch. It is our landed tie with the Empire and it would be nice to have a permanent address in Alberta."[10]

One correspondent interpreted this sudden surge of interest on the part of the Windsors in their Alberta property rather differently. He argued that the economic and management changes which had been instigated during the visit could have been handled by the Duke's agents. He went on to point out that it was a most unsuitable time to come to southern Alberta for a holiday. If the motive for a visit was not for business or pleasure, what could it be? Perhaps, he suggested, the Duke was interested in the Governor Generalship of Canada, and was seeking to assure Canadians of his continued interest in and regard for the Dominion.[11] In fact the reporter, Andrew Snaddon, was resurrecting a possibility which had been raised in the U.S. press two or three years before, but both the Canadian government and Buckingham Palace had squashed it.[12]

The Windsor's perception of their Alberta home at this time must have been coloured by a series of rebuffs which they had suffered; indeed, during 1950 they must have wondered just where they would ever be able to put down roots. The Duke's overtures to his family, and his attempts to find worthwhile employment in an official capacity, had

---

9 *Calgary Herald*, April 13, 1950. The Duke did enter into an arrangement with Socony Vacuum Company of the United States to explore for oil once again. This attempt was also a failure and the connection with Socony was dissolved when the Ecushwa Oil Company was disbanded. See GAI, M2398, f. 152, Agreement dated August 3, 1953. See also the following quote in a letter from the Duchess to her Aunt Bessie, October 3, 1952, "The oil [well] they were drilling turned out a dud so that is very discouraging news." Michael Bloch, *The Secret File of the Duke of Windsor* (London: Corgi Books, 1988), p. 315.

10 *Calgary Herald*, April 14, 1950.

11 *High River Times*, May 11, 1950.

12 Philip Ziegler, *King Edward VIII: The Official Biography* (London: Collins, 1990), p. 493.

Duke of Windsor at the Canadian Legion in Calgary, April 1950. He is displaying
the spade that he had used to turn sod for the memorial hall in 1919.

been rejected by the British government.[13] Anyhow, he had seen enough of the egalitarian austerity of post-war England to be quite sure that he did not want to live there.[14] The United States seemed to be the obvious place to settle, and a house on Long Island caught their eye, but, without an official appointment, the tax burden would have been intolerable. France was emerging only slowly from the economic and political turmoil which followed liberation. The Duke was so concerned by the spectre of spreading communism that he shipped thirty crates of his most valuable possessions back to London.[15] When they visited La Cröe, they found the Riviera overrun with the brash new rich. In Wallis' beloved Paris, they had had to give up their house on the Boulevard Suchet, and the replacement they rented in the Rue de la Faisanderie was far from ideal. Thus, when they arrived at the ranch in April 1950, they had not made a major commitment financially or emotionally to a home. The ranch was a finite link with the Empire, which the Palace could not interfere with. The visit had made it abundantly clear that they were still welcome, which was a pleasant contrast to the reception which they had suffered elsewhere. On their return to Paris, the Duke wrote an interesting note to the Duchess, in which he tried to spell out the various options open to them. The immediate question was whether they should buy the La Clairiere estate outside Paris. H.R.H. pointed out that this would mean committing all their capital, and would limit their ability to travel. He went on:

> The alternative form of life would revolve around cities, travel, and the ranch. A small house or apartment in Paris: no country. A hotel or apartment in New York: no country. Travel, boats, hotels: no country. The E.P. Ranch would provide the only form of country life. A lovely place, but only habitable from July to September, and very isolated from all the comforts and amenities and social life.[16]

At this time it is clear the ranch figured largely in the Windsor's plans, and when their friend Lord Brownlow made an offer for the ranch, it was rejected. The Duke wrote that he would not sell now, and did not believe he ever would.[17]

---

13 Ziegler, *Edward VIII*, p. 494.

14 Ziegler, *Edward VIII*, p. 516. His attitude to his homeland was also coloured by the fact that there was a Labour government in power; by the crushing effects of death duties on the traditional aristocracy; and perhaps too by the theft of the Duchess' jewels during a stay with the Dudleys at Ednam Lodge near Sunningdale.

15 Ziegler, *Edward VIII*, p. 514.

16 Bloch, *Secret File*, p. 292.

17 Ziegler, *Edward VIII*, p. 536.

The decision taken during the visit to change from pedigree short-horns to a herd of commercial Herefords was implemented during the summer and fall of 1950. In August, eighty head of registered shorthorns were sold by auction. Top price of $875 was paid for a herd bull, and the average prices earned were excellent; the sale realized $24,000.[18] Over the next few months Hereford cows were purchased. Some of the best were bought at a community auction of stock from the Bar U, which was being disposed of by Burns Ranches Limited. The local paper commented, "The Duke of Windsor was a substantial buyer purchasing 50 cows at $29.30, and a further 25 at $27.25."[19] These prices were close to the record price of $30.00 paid by another buyer. Altogether, a herd of some 200 head was built up, and the Hampshire and Suffolk flocks already on the ranch were retained. For the next five years the ranch was run as a small cow-calf operation under the careful eye of William Elliott. He ran the ranch with the help of one hired hand and a housekeeper, employing additional temporary help during the summer. Sales of fifty-seven calves in 1952 increased to eighty-eight in 1955. Sales of dry cows, sheep, and rental of pasture, bolstered the ranch income to between $11,000 and $15,000.[20] In spite of Newton's fears that the switch to a commercial herd was taking place at a time when cattle prices were at the top of a cycle, prices during the period only softened marginally.[21] It was the rising costs of groceries, gas, and ranch supplies, which prevented the ranch from breaking even. Drafts totalling $17,000 were forwarded from the Duke's account with Baring Brothers Bank in 1952, 1954, and 1956. Thus, the cost to H.R.H. of indulging his whim to keep the ranch was some $3,400 a year, considerably less than £1,000 a year at current exchange rates, and a trifling sum to a man whose careful investments, guided by bankers and stockbrokers around the world, were valued in millions of pounds sterling.

In 1956, the E.P. Ranch was entirely reorganized, and it emerged once again as a rearing centre for pedigree stock. For a time it looked as though the prominent role played by the ranch during the 1920s would be duplicated in the late 1950s and 1960s. The chief architect of this renaissance was Lieutenant Colonel Edward Douglas Kennedy, late of the

---

18 *High River Times*, August 24, 1950.

19 *Canadian Cattlemen*, December 1950, p. 30; and *High River Times*, November 16, 1950.

20 One of the few sources of data on the ranch during the period 1950–56, when it was managed by Canadian Pacific, is a ledger book. The figures in the following paragraphs were abstracted from this ledger, but they do not have the authority of the audited accounts cited elsewhere. GAI, M2398, ledger 7, 1951–56.

21 GAI, M7005, Newton to H.R.H., March 16, 1950. In fact Newton had been urging the Duke to make the change over to a commercial herd since the early 1940s.

Royal Horse Artillery.[22] Kennedy was a well built, bluff, and vigorous man, who dominated most company not so much by his physical presence as by his dynamism and vitality. His active mind threw out ideas like fire-crackers, and some of them were excellent. He expected those around him to react as smartly and positively as he did, and he had no time for equivocation. It was typical of his character that when travelling in rural Alberta he liked to "bee-line it," or go across country on a straight line, even if this meant dirt roads and ferry crossings. This was the way they had moved in the army, and it was good enough for peacetime too!

Perhaps because of his experience as a British Officer in an elite regiment, Colonel Kennedy found it hard to accept that "colonial" stockmen from Canada and the United States really knew their business, and could teach him much about local conditions. His attitude tended to be condescending or downright dismissive. While well established local ranchers, men like Cross or Baker, were completely confident of their positions and could accept the Colonel and his "Imperial" manner with amused tolerance, others found it hard to take. Moreover, driven by his frenetic energy, Kennedy sometimes had rather a cavalier attitude toward the possessions of those with whom he came into contact: he would borrow a pick-up, or use the telephone for a long-distance call, without asking permission. The fact that he would be happy to reciprocate generously did not prevent this habit from souring relations with some neighbours. His attitude towards his employees was complex. While he was cordial and jocular with the young men and women with whom he shared a common social background, he tended to be authoritarian with the stock experts who managed the various departments. They were like non-commissioned officers, and, while he could respect their abilities, he found it difficult to accept their advice. Kennedy had the vision to see a multi-million dollar opportunity, and the drive and panache to transform the idea into a reality. Unfortunately he inherited certain ingrained social attitudes which were to lead to crucial mistakes in the management of the new venture.

Kennedy had served with distinction in the Italian campaign, and after the war he found himself in Italy attempting to help the allied effort to rebuild that country's shattered farm economy. When he was finally released from the army, Kennedy returned to London and established a company named British Exports Limited, which shipped pedigree livestock all round the world. Herds in Australia, Argentina, the United

---

22 The account of the activities of the E.P. Ranch Company Limited draws on a series of interviews with men and women who worked there, in particular, Mary Diebel, Colonel Kennedy's daughter, Roy Griswold, John Little, Nita Maga (Robinson), and Judge R.G. Black.

States, and Canada, had been isolated during the war years and now required infusions of new blood. Each region defined the ideal animal in rather different terms. In the hot dry grasslands of Queensland and Texas, leggy bulls which could travel far and fast were at a premium, while in New Zealand or Argentina, weight gain was more important. Kennedy had the knack of matching the needs of diverse buyers with the animals produced by his clients.

As he toured the livestock sales throughout England and Scotland, Kennedy noticed how frequently he ran into Canadian stockmen. Naturally some of these men were from the foothills; to cite but one example, Tony Cross was a regular at the Galloway sales in Perth, Scotland. The obstacles to moving pedigree stock to and from post-war Britain were formidable. Currency was controlled and the red tape involved caused frustrating delays. Moreover, the normal way to travel from Canada to the sales in Great Britain was by train and boat, and the costs in dollars and in time were also considerable. Thus, from many points of view, the advantages of building up a pool of pedigree stock in Canada were obvious. Kennedy was among the first to capitalize on this opportunity.

Exactly when and where the Duke of Windsor and Colonel Kennedy met has not been established. However, one can imagine that as soon as the Duke heard the nature of Kennedy's business, he would have regaled him with the story of the E.P., and its glory days as a centre for the dissemination of purebred stock. It cannot have taken long for the conversation to move from generalities to the idea of using the E.P. once again as a "holding tank" for pedigree stock in Canada.[23] The royal connections would be invaluable in stimulating business, while H.R.H. would have been enthusiastic about a scheme which offered the prospect of his ranch regaining some of its old importance. The Duke agreed to lease the land and buildings of the ranch to a company, to be called the E.P. Ranch Company Limited, of which Colonel Kennedy was to be the managing director.

The Duke and Kennedy drew together a truly international group of investors to support the venture. Count Filippo Corsini, of Florence, Italy, was a friend that Kennedy had made during his service in Italy. The Count was interested in livestock, and had several farms in the hills. He also welcomed a chance to invest some money outside Italy, with the prospect of earning Canadian or U.S. dollars. In Paris, some of the Duke's friends banded together as the "Société Civile de Gérance Particulière," and bought shares in the new company. Other investors included Colonel Sir Watkin Williams Whynn, a British member of parliament from Wales; Thomas McTurk, a Scottish farmer passionately devoted to Galloway

---

23 It was another example of a chance social encounter which had far-reaching consequences, like his meeting with Barnum Brown, the geologist. See Chapter 7.

cattle; and Victor Alfred Waddilove, who had been the Duke's personal secretary for three years. The initial authorized capital was soon oversubscribed, and some $60,000 was made available for capital investment.[24]

Kennedy and Waddilove spent some weeks at the ranch in October 1956, and were enthusiastic about the prospects and possibilities.[25] Work was in hand to refurbish the ranch house and to connect the buildings with the main electricity grid and the telephone system. The overall plan for development envisioned four different species at the ranch: cattle, ponies, pigs, and sheep. The initial shipment of pedigree stock from Britain included fourteen Herefords, ten Galloways, and nineteen Wessex pigs. Some Welsh ponies were expected to arrive in the fall. The stock wintered well, and, during a visit in the early spring of 1957, the managing director laid plans to build the herd up to about 200 beasts.[26] By May, the new manager, Peter Melvin, his wife Elizabeth, and their two children, were settled in the ranch house. Melvin was a native of Aberdeen, Scotland, and had had considerable experience with mixed stock enterprises in the Scottish border country.[27]

The growing herd of English horned Herefords impressed Canadian breeders with their size and weight gain characteristics. For some years there had been fears that Canadian Herefords had been losing quality. Their bones had become smaller and more refined, and they had lost some of their ability to rustle a living under harsh range conditions. It was felt that the imports from England might do much to improve things. The Galloways too were "big framed, level backed, and big enough to do credit to any breed."[28] There were also opportunities for shipping Canadian cattle to the United Kingdom, for polled Herefords were uncommon there and were proving to be a popular innovation. Thus, Colonel Kennedy made the rounds of Canadian sales buying cattle for England, while at the same time promoting the sales of E.P. stock.

One way in which the enterprise differed markedly from the early days of the E.P. was that pigs were a major focus for attention. There were some 600 pigs on the ranch split into two herds. The English "Large White" pig was the original parent strain from which the Canadian "Yorkshire" breed had been derived. Many experts felt that the Canadian offspring had begun to lose size, robustness, and fecundity. There was much interest in the idea of reintroducing the old English genes to the Canadian bloodlines. The prospects looked so good that the E.P. Ranch

---

24 GAI, M2398, ff. 152 and 158.

25 *High River Times*, October 18, 1956; and *Lethbridge Herald*, October 27, 1956.

26 *High River Times*, May 16, 1957.

27 *Farm and Ranch Review*, June 1957, "Famous E.P. Ranch being Restocked," p. 27.

28 *Farm and Ranch Review*, October 1958, "New Breeds at the E.P.," p. 8.

Company purchased 400 acres of land near Aldersyde to develop as a pig farm. This site had the advantages of being located in a grain growing area more accessible to the Calgary market.[29] The Wessex Saddlebacks, which were kept on the ranch, were rather smaller, and not as valuable as bacon producers. However, they proved to be exceptionally hardy and flourished on the underused rough pasture and willow brush close to the ranch buildings.

During the late 1950s and early 1960s, riding was undergoing a tremendous surge of popularity in the United States. Welsh ponies were much in demand as mounts for children. Animals which had roamed the flanks of Snowdon in a semi-wild state suddenly received recognition as valuable commodities. Of course, they were all genuine "Welsh ponies," but they had no papers whatever. Customs officials and buyers alike demanded pedigree papers; the problem was resolved by calling all ponies rounded up on the mountains "Foundation Stock." Their progeny would be designated F.S.2, and papers were made out using these terms. Another problem was to plan the shipment of ponies from the United Kingdom at the most opportune time. It was obviously not a good idea to throw the newly arrived animals on the range in the fall, and it was best that they avoid travelling while in foal, or during the hottest part of the summer. At the supply end in Wales, there was little understanding of these kinds of problems, and a week or indeed a month here or there meant little. One way round this difficulty was to send selected ponies to a farm in England to be "gentled" for a few months before shipment. Mary Kennedy remembered having bands of ten or twelve ponies sent to her in Shropshire for two or three months.[30] Demand for these hardy and likeable animals was consistent, and all that could be spared from the stud were sold. Buyers from the United States, like Owen Jacklin from Washington State and Al Hefte from Missoula, Montana, were frequent visitors at the ranch. The flock of Hampshire sheep had been retained, while the Suffolks had been replaced by a few head of North Country Cheviots. No wonder that knowledgeable stockmen who visited the ranch in the late 1950s were impressed with the variety and standard of the stock which they inspected.

The simple cow-calf operation had been replaced by a multi-faceted rearing farm which handled valuable pedigree stock of widely differing breeds and species. Each division required an experienced expert to run it, and the success of the whole operation depended upon attracting and keeping these key employees. Typical of this group was Roy Griswold. Born in a village in the English Midlands, Roy had studied animal nutrition and had gained some years of practical experience at a major stock

29 *High River Times,* July 3, 1958.

30 Interview with Mary Diebel, May 1991.

farm. A run-in with strikers from the Austin car assembly plant, the Suez crisis, and subsequent petrol rationing, convinced Roy that it was time to leave the United Kingdom. One Wednesday he went to the Canadian Pacific offices in Birmingham and registered as a prospective immigrant to Canada, who was looking for a sponsor. Only three days later, Colonel Kennedy, accompanied by his secretary and his daughter, arrived at the farm where Griswold was working to interview him. Later, it transpired that the E.P. Ranch Company had asked to be informed if anybody with expertise in animal husbandry enlisted in the sponsor program. Within a few weeks, Roy found himself in London reporting to the offices of British Exports Ltd., en route to Southampton and a boat to New York. At the office he was handed a three pound bag of seed to deliver to the ranch, and told to pop down to Buckingham Gate, just across the road from Buckingham Palace, to meet Victor Waddilove, the Duke of Windsor's secretary. It was quite a send-off. Roy was to spend three years with the E.P., and was in large part responsible for the establishment and success of the pig farm at Aldersyne.

John Little was another key member of the staff. He was raised on a dairy farm in Hampshire, England. In his teens he had travelled with top-notch cattle to shows in London and Toronto. When he was engaged to bring some cattle out to the E.P., he stayed on to work there. He took over as manager in 1959 and remained in charge of the ranch until it was sold. During the last thirty years he has carved out his own farm from the bush north and west from Leslieville, Alberta.

Mike Bullen, the son of a well known hunting and show-jumping family in England, was recruited to bring out the original band of Welsh ponies, and he stayed on to see them settled in. He was succeeded by Gary Beesley and Brenda Evans, while the Colonel's daughter, Mary, who had been a frequent visitor to the ranch, took over management of the ponies in 1960.

A diverse operation of this kind was necessarily labour intensive. To some extent this had been anticipated by the Duke, who had stipulated that the ranch be used to train young Englishmen who were hoping to get a start in agriculture. These "apprentices" handled much of the unskilled labour on the ranch. They usually numbered four or five, but at times their ranks swelled to ten. This system of providing an opportunity for "young gentlemen" to try ranch life, recalled the heyday of the Bradfield Ranch or the Military Ranch during the 1880s and 1890s.[31] Some recruits, like Chris Newton, came for a summer only; others stayed a year or more. Some arrived with letters of recommendation from the Duke or one of the shareholders; others turned up in High River looking

---

31 See Chapter 2; and Patrick A. Dunae, *Gentlemen Immigrants* (Vancouver: Douglas and McIntyre, 1981), Chapter 5.

for work and were sent to the E.P. because of their English accents! David Guinness, of the Irish brewing family, arrived with only the clothes he stood up in, and worked until his hands were a bloody mess from carrying bales, when he joined the field gang straight from the train.

One colourful character was Jim Peeden. His father ran a major transport company in England and often moved stock for Kennedy. Jim used this connection to get himself a job. Before travelling to the E.P. he went to the Ferguson Tractor Company in Coventry for an intensive short course on tractor maintenance. As he began to enjoy the freedom and isolation of the ranch, Jim reacted strongly against his genteel upbringing. He grew a huge beard, wore the oldest cast-off clothing that he could find, and did not wash too often. He learned to roll his own cigarettes, and would stop his tractor in the middle of the field and place his tin of tobacco on the tractor tyre while he took a pinch or two of tobacco to place on the paper. Having triumphantly lit his "weed," he would engage gear and roar off, only to flip the tobacco onto the ground under the wheels. On his return to England the gang at the ranch sent him a carefully gift wrapped memento, a tin of Player's tobacco which had been ceremonially run over!

Victor Mulligan brought a consignment of stock over from Ireland to New York and then took a Greyhound bus across the continent to the E.P. Ranch. Later, he was much envied by his colleagues because he owned an ancient car. He was wont to dress up on Friday nights and go to dances in Longview. One night, while he was changing, his "friends" lifted the car bodily and parked it tightly between two huge cottonwoods, rendering it completely immobile. On another occasion, while Victor was out tripping the light fantastic, the boys built a formidable barrier across the bridge to prevent his return in the small hours of the morning. Somehow the old Dodge butted its way through, and Victor appeared none the worse at breakfast. Colin Dunlop, and Elizabeth, Rosemary, Paul and Sally Beezley were among others who served at the ranch in one capacity or another. Most of the young people worked hard and earned their keep, but of course the turnover was rapid, and each new arrival had to be taught afresh. This made for excitement and an interesting social mix, but not necessarily for the smooth running of a working ranch. During the summer months when work was at a maximum, the community at the ranch was like a large, noisy, and poorly integrated family. Nita Robinson, a seventeen-year-old from Black Diamond, was cook. She remembered feeding twelve or fourteen around the big table in the ranch house. Elizabeth Melvin would do the shopping in High River, and take a turn at cooking. As soon as lunch was cleared up, "Cookie" would head for the corral and get an hour or two of riding before it was time to face making another meal.

Naturally, there were some memorable parties. Peter and Elizabeth Melvin would seek refuge with the neighbours and leave the old ranch house to the mercy of the revellers. Frequent and popular visitors were the nurses from the hospital in High River. One night they brought an experimental libation of dandelion wine, which proved so mellow that Antony Fleetwood Wilson, "Plonks" to his friends, walked straight through the closed French windows without really noticing it. Later, attempts to throw Victor in the creek were thwarted by the fact that it was frozen over, and the party had to be content with leaving him in a snow bank to cool off.

Of course, such amateur help, however willing, was hard on the machinery and on the tempers of the foremen. When one of the tractors got mired in a slough, it did not take long for the young driver to walk back to get the larger tractor. Half an hour later, both were stuck fast. He returned for help, and before long the Landrover and the truck were also out of commission. Much to the embarrassment of the assembled company, the help of the neighbours had to be enlisted to retrieve the vehicles one at a time.

The energy and drive of Colonel Kennedy and the initial investment of the board had achieved much in a short time. However, some deep-seated problems underlaid all the bustle and achievement. The first was the role of the managing director. Kennedy's outstanding attribute was his ability to create a network of friends, customers, clients, and colleagues, wherever he went. Like the Duke, he had abundant charm and never forgot a name or a face. He would happily plunge off down section roads to find out how a particular farmer had made out with a bull from the E.P. However, because of his world-wide business, Kennedy could only spend a few weeks a year in western Canada. Although he packed an enormous amount into those short visits, it was difficult to build durable bonds of mutual respect with his neighbours in the foothills. He was better known by international stockmen than he was in Calgary or High River. The new company really needed somebody on the spot to promote its interests and to insure efficient interaction between the demands of Canadian ranchers and farmers on the one hand, and the production of pedigree livestock on the other. For all his energy and charm, Kennedy could not fill this role.

The new enterprise was an organizational nightmare. All major purchases of equipment or stores had to be approved by the London office. This meant lengthy delays, which were compounded by the managing director's hectic travel schedule. Moreover, the diversity of the operation made it unwieldy; there were two breeds of cattle, two of pigs, and two of sheep. Each had to be segregated from the others, while breeding cycles of each animal had to be carefully recorded. The paper work alone was a daunting task. Weekly reports on the progress of each litter of pigs was required by both London and the Canadian government. Mary Kennedy felt that it was like working for five different bosses, as each major investor demanded to be kept informed of developments in his area of interest. The English never really grasped the realities of the Canadian winter. When Kennedy took Griswold to Edmonton to gather the latest information on the construction of pig-barns, before building one at Aldersyne, the party was shown how to lay a self-heating floor by burying electric cables in the concrete. When they returned, Kennedy insisted on installing only half the density of wires in order to save money. This meant that auxiliary space heaters had to be purchased, and that more piglets than necessary were lost due to cold.

To some extent it was inevitable that the different enterprises on the ranch should compete with one another for space, scarce resources, and labour. It would have needed strong leadership from somebody with a clear vision of the wider goals to bind the separate parts into a cohesive and cooperative whole. Kennedy could have provided this leadership had he been on the spot, but Peter Melvin could not. In the absence of a strong local manager who knew every facet of the business, Kennedy—during his brief visits—was apt to interfere with the day to day operations of the ranch, sometimes with disastrous results. Two examples will illustrate this.

After nearly two years of operation, and good progress in crossing the Large White pigs with the local Yorkshires, the company made a major breakthrough. Paul Leeney, a pre-eminent breeder from the Corn Belt of the United States, called to order a consignment of gilts (young female pigs). The price offered was very good, and to receive attention from a breeder of that calibre was something of a coup. However, there was a condition attached to the deal: Leeney wanted to purchase the boar as well. Griswold replied that the boar was the foundation of his whole operation, and that he would not dream of parting with him, but he said that he would check with Kennedy to get confirmation of his decision. To his surprise Kennedy told him to go ahead and clinch the deal. This was a bit like killing the goose which had begun to lay golden eggs, for the quality of the pigs deteriorated after the departure of the boar. Worse was to follow. Leeney called again and ordered another major consignment. Griswold made a careful selection of his best stock and loaded them in preparation for shipment. At the last minute, Colonel Kennedy insisted that the truck be filled up, even if it meant sending some piglets of less outstanding quality. When the truck arrived in Iowa, Leeney immediately spotted the few substandard gilts, and refused to accept the whole consignment. As the shipment had passed through the U.S. sealed as bonded cargo to a particular destination, there was no question of selling to another breeder, and the best of the E.P. pigs ended up in an American slaughterhouse.

The major shareholders had unreasonable expectations concerning the rate and timing of returns from their investment. Unlike Kennedy's export business, where he bought, shipped, and sold animals with a very rapid turnover, the breeding operations at the E.P. were by their very nature long-term and slow to mature. John Little considered that breeding animals could take as many as three years to acclimatize to new conditions. Grass, water, feed, and altitude, were all factors that required getting used to. The idea was to preserve the breeding herds intact and to sell only the progeny. It was bound to take time for a rearing farm like this to begin to garner profits. The investors found this logic difficult to accept and looked askance at cost overruns for new barns and machinery. They were reluctant to put up any more money until some returns were forthcoming, and this meant that there was always a shortage of ready cash. It was probably this atmosphere of crisis management which led to some of the mistakes which were made. When Mary Kennedy arrived in the spring of 1960 to take over management of the Welsh ponies, she found that the pick of the bunch had been sold to a dealer from Washington State, on the authority of Thomas McTurk, a director of the company who was visiting from England. She was able to get back most of the animals, but a valuable stallion was lost.

In spite of these organizational difficulties, the E.P. Ranch Company Limited came close to being a triumphant success. The only regret expressed by those I talked to who were involved in the enterprise was that the bold and timely concept—a million dollar idea if ever there was one—had not been given a little longer to succeed. Of course, the situation in 1956–61 was very different from what it had been in the 1920s. There was a well established Canadian breeding industry. The E.P. could no longer be expected to sweep all before it as it had done in an earlier era. Nevertheless, the company did show animals, not only in High River and Calgary, but also in Montana and elsewhere in the United States. By 1960 both Herefords and Galloways were winning prizes and gaining recognition throughout the west, while pigs and ponies were sought after by both Canadian and U.S. breeders.[32] The record prices paid when the E.P. Ranch stock were sold in 1961 and 1962 were clear evidence that the ranch could have made money. The 1950s were a time of experimentation and rapid technological change in the livestock industry. Kennedy had the vision and experience to insure that the company remained an innovator and a leader in the field. The foremen who actually managed the breeding programs on the ranch were well informed and dedicated

---

32 See, for example, *High River Times*, June 1, 1961, which reports that the bull Earl Noble of Okotoks, was highest selling Hereford. Also *High River Times*, February 15, 1962, which recorded the fact that two bulls from the E.P. were judged grand champion and runner-up in Billings, Montana.

to their stock. And yet, som how, the enterprise never really fulfilled its potential. In retrospect, so... blamed this on the managing director and his entrenched assumption f British superiority. But of course the whole idea was his, and without Kennedy there would never have been a E.P. Ranch Company. I think the key weakness lay in the financial structure of the company and the attitudes of the major investors. A group of rich men had been persuaded to commit relatively small sums to the project. Probably, one motive for their participation was the social cachet of being involved in a venture with the Duke of Windsor. There is no evidence that the precise aims of the enterprise had been spelled out, nor had the expectations of the shareholders been identified. From the beginning it was a loosely organized amateurish affair between friends and acquaintances. But the investment was being made in a pedigree breeding operation where returns, if any, were bound to be slow in coming. After the initial capital had been spent, there was not sufficient interest or commitment to insure an adequate flow of operating funds. "They planned an ocean liner and built a pig-boat," commented one observer. The opportunity was there, and the concept was brilliant. The implementation of the idea was marred by human and organizational shortcomings, but the E.P. Ranch Company touched the lives of many Canadians, and is remembered with affection and nostalgia.

After four years of operation, it became clear that the E.P. Ranch Company would be in no position to pay regular and handsome dividends to its shareholders. The principles on which it was founded were sound, but the complexity and labour intensity of the operation weighed against it; every dollar earned had to be ploughed back. The participants became increasingly disenchanted as the prospects of recouping their investments became more remote.

During the spring of 1961 the Duke empowered his solicitors in Calgary to carry out an appraisal of the property. E.B. Nowers visited the E.P. and toured the fields and pastures in a jeep. He was already familiar with the general lay-out, having spent a weekend with the Carlyles thirty-five years before, and having been responsible for valuing the buildings for insurance during the interim. Having made an inventory of the lands and buildings, Nowers prefaced his report by explaining that it was very hard to make a precise evaluation:

> While the value of any real property results from the profitable use that can be made of it, sales of real estate, particularly in good times, are often made at prices considerably in excess of sound values. While, in a general way, there is a noticeable recession in business both in Canada and the United States, ranches, particularly in the Pekisko district, have never sold at higher prices even allowing for the fact that our dollar is now worth only fifty cents in purchasing power in comparison with say the 1939 prewar dollar. . . . We have had in Alberta a number of well-off

people who are interested in ranching and who are not too much concerned with whether or not a ranch can be made to pay. Largely from this source, there has developed a demand for attractive ranch properties at prices above those justified by the cattle market and the fact that government leases of land are no longer obtainable.[33]

In his opinion, the value of the E.P. Ranch could be summarized as follows: 4,000 acres at $25, which amounted to $100,000; and improvements valued at $50,000; for a total of $150,000. Perhaps, he added, with some luck and taking into account the fame of the ranch, the Duke might obtain $30 an acre, for a total of $170,000.

Early in November, a packed news conference was told that the E.P. Ranch was to be sold and the stock dispersed. *The Globe and Mail* headline read: "Royal Ranch Saga Ends."[34] Lawyer R.G. Black handled the arrangements in Calgary and followed H.R.H.'s instructions to advertise the sale of the ranch in prestigious journals around the world. There was an immediate surge of interest. "We've had many inquiries from people all over," Mr Black said, "We've even had one from someone on the high seas travelling to Australia."[35]

The stock was sold with surprising speed. Only three weeks after the announcement, the English Herefords were on the auction block at the Calgary Stampede and Exhibition Grounds. The excellence of the animals, and the interest whipped up by the media, combined to stimulate the bidding. Before the end of the day, twenty-eight cows with calves, ten young bulls, three yearling heifers, and two imported herd sires, were sold at an average price of $700.[36] A few days later it was the turn of the Welsh ponies; forty-three were sold for more than $22,000. Buyers came from Oregon, Washington, and Idaho, as well as from Saskatchewan and British Columbia. The average price of $534 was thought likely to stand as a Canadian pony sale record for some time.[37] During the next month, the Galloway herd was sold privately to A.R. Cross, of Midnapore, who already had an internationally famous herd of Shorthorns.

The ranch land and buildings had been advertised since November, with a closing date for bids set at January 15, 1962. A number of groups came forward to suggest possible ways of keeping the royal ranch going, in one way or another.[38] Some Calgary business men offered to buy it as a present for Prince Charles, the current Prince of Wales. This offer

---

33 GAI, M2398, f. 159, Nowers to Black and Co., June 13, 1961.

34 *Globe and Mail*, December 7, 1961.

35 *Edmonton Journal*, December 7, 1961.

36 *Farm and Ranch Review*, May 1962, "End of a Chapter for Famous Ranch."

37 GAI, M2398, f. 159, List of Ponies Sold, December 2, 1961.

38 *Calgary Herald*, September 6, 1980.

was declined by the Palace. Another group suggested that the ranch could be used as a place where juvenile offenders could be rehabilitated through a regime of hard work in beautiful surroundings. Others suggested that the government should purchase the ranch for use as a public park. Rumours went the rounds suggesting that two groups from the United States had put in high bids in order to obtain the property for use as a "dude ranch" for rich holiday makers. Alternative stories had any number of famous people as prospective buyers, and the rumoured price crept upwards as the weeks passed, from $60 an acre to $90.

It seems likely that the Duke of Windsor's expectations concerning the sale were just as inflated. He felt that there would be a flood of people making bids because the ranch had been the focus for so much attention, and because he had received so many inquiries over the years. Judge Black recalled that there was indeed a lot of interest, but very few serious bids. He pointed out that there really was not anything exceptional to sell, once the publicity had been stripped away.[39] The ranch house, originally built at the turn of the century, and enlarged and remodelled in the 1920s, was more like a cabin than a permanent residence, when judged by the standards of the 1960s. The land was superior grazing land, and a proportion of it had been cleared and cropped for decades, but the "going rate" for comparable land elsewhere in the region was around $25 an acre.[40]

After a month of mounting tension, the news that the ranch had been sold broke on February 27, 1962.[41] The successful bidder was Jim Cartwright, who owned the D Ranch, and whose family had been a neighbour of the E.P. throughout its existence. There was a sense of relief and quiet jubilation among ranchers in the foothills. An editorial in the *High River Times* was headlined, "A Popular Purchase." Charles Clark explained that there was a "feeling akin to keeping a prized and historical possession in the family. The family in this case, comprising the neighbouring ranchers in the broad Pekisko valley."[42] Elsewhere, Clark summed up local sentiment when he remarked, "we are glad a local man had the opportunity and ability to buy it; we know it will be used as a working ranch, to good advantage."[43] The Cartwrights' roots ran deep in the neighbourhood. Jim's father, E.A. Cartwright, had come out from eastern Canada around 1900 to join an Englishman named John Thorp in

---

39 Interview, Judge R.G. Black, May 1990.

40 See Nowers' evaluation above.

41 *Calgary Herald*, February 28, 1962; and *Albertan*, February 28, 1962.

42 *High River Times*, March 8, 1962.

43 *Calgary Herald*, February 28, 1962.

a ranching venture.[44] At that time they had been neighbours of the Bedingfelds. The purchase of the E.P. meant that the landholdings of the D Ranch could be consolidated. "Up to now we have been running our cattle over other people's land, and things haven't been handy," explained Cartwright.[45] The price paid for the land, improvements, and brand, was $180,000.[46] This figure was a compromise for both the buyer and the seller. It was $10,000 more than the most optimistic estimate of the Duke's appraiser; on the other hand, it was a huge reduction from the $250,000 mentioned in an option which Cartwright held during the fall of 1961. Once the main ranch was disposed of there were only a few loose ends to be tidied up. In March 1963, the Aldersyde pig farm was sold for $50,000, and in July, it was resolved by the shareholders that the E.P. Ranch Company be wound up. [47]

After forty-three years the royal link with the foothills was broken. The Prince of Wales had considered disposing of the ranch in the early 1930s; King Edward had pursued this objective seriously during his brief reign; the Duke of Windsor had blown hot and cold, always hanging on to his Canadian property in the end, almost as if it were a talisman against future contingencies. Why did he finally decide to sell the E.P. in 1961? Probably the key factor behind the decision was the Duke's health. In 1958, H.R.H. had suffered a long and debilitating attack of shingles. This painful and prolonged set-back had forced him to face up to his own mortality. He was sixty-four; his younger brother, George VI, had died six years before, and his mother a year later. Suddenly, he was unable to maintain his spartan regime of physical exercise. It was completely unrealistic to continue to dream that either he or his wife would willingly subject themselves to the rigours of a cross continental railway journey to visit their ranch.[48]

In a more positive vein, the Duke and Duchess had, by the late 1950s, established a comfortable and secure way of life. It centred round their home on the Bois de Boulogne, which Wallis had transformed into a mini-palace of impeccable taste, and the Mill at Gif, where Edward could enjoy gardening in the country. They usually spent two or three months away, visiting New York for the social life and somewhere warm where the Duke could play golf. The hypothetical role for the E.P. Ranch

---

44 *Albertan,* February 28, 1962; see also *Canadian Cattlemen,* May 1950, "Edwin Aubrey Cartwright of the D Ranch," p. 12.

45 *Calgary Herald,* February 28, 1962.

46 GAI, M2398, f. 159, Black to Cartwright, February 27, 1962.

47 GAI, M2398, f. 159, Resolutions, March 22, 1963 and July 15, 1963. This land was sold a year later for use as a gravel pit for $1 million.

48 Ziegler, *Edward VIII,* p. 554; it was only three years later that he underwent open heart surgery.

visualized by the Duke in 1950 had never become a reality, and the niche it might have played by providing a "place in the country" had been usurped by the Mill. Indeed, when one reads of the elegance and sophistication of the Windsor's French houses, and the luxury with which they surrounded themselves when they travelled, it is hard to explain why they held onto the ranch for so long.

The answer must be that the Duke of Windsor retained an abiding affection for his Alberta ranch which was rooted in his experiences in western Canada as a young man. Judge R.G. Black was sent to New York by his firm to have some papers to do with the sale signed by the Duke. He remembered arriving at the Waldorf-Astoria and being met by Sydney Johnson, the Windsor's Bahamian butler and major domo. Over a protracted lunch the Duke chatted animatedly about Calgary and the ranch, and asked after several individuals and families. Black produced some photographs and promotional pamphlets which the Duke enjoyed perusing, and kept for further reading. The interview had gone so well that Black was invited back the next day. He formed the strong impression that the Duke was still reluctant to sell the ranch, even though he realized that he was unlikely to visit it again. This evaluation corresponds closely with that of Colonel Kennedy, who used to enjoy reporting to the Duke in Paris about the affairs of the E.P. Ranch Company. Kennedy told his daughter that H.R.H.'s tired eyes would light up as they discussed the happenings at the ranch, and that the Duke retained an accurate image of the ranch house, the creek, and the cottonwoods, in his mind's eye. Just as Edward was to prove himself faithful unto death to the woman for whom he had relinquished his throne, so too he had shown himself capable of a long-lasting relationship with a corner of the Alberta foothills with which he had once fallen in love.

Epilogue

This book has been about a ranch and its owner, Prince Edward. Perhaps we can focus some concluding remarks by attempting to answer three or four questions about the place and the person. The simplest question is, "What happened next?" Much more difficult to evaluate is the second: "What was the impact of the E.P. Ranch?" and the linked supplementary question, "Was it successful?" Finally, we must struggle to respond to the inquiry, "What has our study of the ranch revealed to us about its royal owner?"

After the sale of the E.P. in 1962, the land was integrated into the operations of the giant "D" ranch, and the barns and outbuildings were modernized as they were needed. The ranch house, however, remained unoccupied, although full of the original furniture. With Jim Cartwright's approval, the building was used for occasional events by the parishioners of St. Aidan's Anglican Church, and local families were served tea on royal china. The mystique of the ranch continued to draw the curious from far afield, and the steady trickle of summer visitors interfered somewhat with the efficient operation of the ranch. Cartwright was by no means indifferent to the historic value of the E.P., and he approached Heritage Park in Calgary with the suggestion that they should move the ranch house to the park.[1] He felt that the historic building deserved to be preserved and made available to a wider public. When his offer was refused, he seriously considered demolishing the building, which was deteriorating badly and was becoming a target for vandals. Cartwright's son John, and his wife Lynn, took up residence in a new ranch house very close to the E.P. in 1974, and began to take an active interest in the old building. There was much to do. The house was overgrown and the roof was sagging. In the musty interior, the presentation editions of books

---

1 Harry A. Tatro, *Survey of Historic Ranches*, study prepared for the Historic Sites and Monuments Board of Canada, 1973, p. 185.

by Canadian authors, like the novels of Ralph Connor, were growing mould. The blue Spode dinner service was cracked and dusty, and the familiar pictures of Kings and race horses needed rematting.[2] When Jim Cartwright died suddenly in 1976, plans were already being made to rescue the structure before it collapsed. Under the direction of Lynn Cartwright, and with the support of her husband and his brother Gordon, who had inherited the ranch, a local contractor, Mr. Leo Heywood, proceeded to carry out a far-reaching transformation. Over half of the old house was removed, for the logs used in the original cabin, around which the larger structure had been built, had rotted badly. Heywood built a narrow rectangular house around the core of the old living-room fireplace. The exact dimensions of the old structure were adhered to and the original fittings were used in the reconstruction wherever possible. A wide glassed-in verandah along the west end of the building preserved some of the spacious charm of the original. When the curtains were rehung, the bookcases filled, the pictures restored to their accustomed places, and the fire lit, the illusion was complete and the atmosphere of the old drawing room was recreated.[3]

John and Lynn planned to turn the house into a small museum, a focus for the attention of the visitors who still found their way across Pekisko Creek. However, the demands of a young family, and the challenge of managing a major ranch, meant that their dreams were not realized immediately. It was not until 1984 that Lynn entertained some sixty guests to a pre-opening party at "The Prince of Wales Tea House." This invitational event was a triumphant success in spite of the rather cramped and old-fashioned kitchen facilities available. It did not prepare the tiny staff for the overwhelming public response to the new venture. They struggled to look after more than 500 visitors the first weekend. Over the following years the Tea House went from strength to strength, the season was extended to cater to fall hunting parties, and the number of visitors continued to increase. It was with regret that the public heard that the popular facility was to be closed in the spring of 1989.[4]

The second question asked, "What was the impact of the E.P. Ranch on the livestock industry of Alberta?" Contemporary observers welcomed the royal purchase in 1919, and had high hopes that it would produce both tangible and indirect benefits to the region. They anticipated that it would provide a pool of first-class blood stock within easy reach, both

---

2 Private communication with Dr. Donald Smith, who visited the ranch in November 1975, in connection with an article he was writing on the Prince of Wales' visit to Calgary in 1919.

3 Lynn Cartwright, "The Prince of Wales Tea House," unpublished paper, University of Alberta, 1990.

4 *High River Times*, May 8, 1989.

geographically and financially, of Albertan ranchers. During the 1920s the ranch lived up to these expectations, but the scale and scope of its impact was limited by the size of the undertaking. A few dozen thoroughbred bulls, a few score prime heifers, and a few hundred sheep could at the most enrich the bloodlines of a handful of ranches. The indirect effects of the ranch were probably more far-reaching. The spotlight focused on the cattle industry by the patronage of the popular young Prince had a considerable impact, and the importance and utility of stock rearing was impressed on a wider public. However, it is only fair to remember that southern Alberta had enjoyed a long history of breeding excellence which reached back to the 1890s. From time to time, market trends and tariff changes had led to the importation of inferior stockers from eastern Canada and Mexico, but even during these periods of general regression in stock quality, the slow process of establishing and improving purebred strains had proceeded on selected ranches. It would be totally wrong to think of the E.P. as the only breeding farm in the foothills; it was one of several.

One way to measure the success of a business enterprise is to study the account books (Appendix A). Prince Edward was always quick to stress that the E.P. was a working ranch, and was expected to pay its way. In fact, this proved to be a vain hope because of the nature and the size of the operation. First, the ranch was run as a breeding farm for purebred stock; it was therefore particularly susceptible to every quirk of the market and was necessarily labour intensive. Even when the decision was finally made to change to a commercial beef herd, it was clear that the ranch was too small to offer any real hopes of substantial returns.

All things considered, it is not the fact that the E.P. Ranch lost money which is remarkable; it is the fact that the losses were not greater. Those who managed the ranch were successful in limiting the losses to a level at which they were acceptable to the royal owner. During the "build-up" in the 1920s, the Prince's enthusiasm was unbounded and there was a steady flow of cash and stock to the ranch. A comparison of expenses and income shows that considerable losses were sustained during the early years of the depression, but these were recouped to some extent by the extraordinary stock sales of 1936 and 1938. Through the war years and the early 1950s, under the careful management of William Elliott, expenses were slashed and cash transfers from London were kept to a minimum. The losses sustained over the years, amounting as they did to between $2,000 and $5,000 annually, were insignificant when measured against the Prince of Wales' huge income from the Duchy of Cornwall and the Civil List. Similarly, by the 1950s the Duke of Windsor had a multi-million dollar stock portfolio, and the daily fluctuations in the prices of gold and commodities were of far greater significance to him than the annual losses of a few thousand dollars sustained by his property in Alberta. However, during the decade between the abdication in 1936 and the aftermath of World War II, the Duke was tortured by financial worries. This state of mind lay behind his determination to keep expenditures at the ranch to a minimum, while at the same time he harboured unrealistic dreams of what the property would fetch on the open market.

The accounts make it clear that Edward did not hold on to the ranch for forty years as an investment. His motives must have been a complex mixture of nostalgia and sentiment. Those who managed the ranch were successful in that they made sure that his whim to hold on to the ranch was not an extravagantly expensive one.

The two outstanding biographers of Edward VIII, Donaldson and Ziegler, are both reluctant to attempt a brief epitaph for their complex subject.[5] His every virtue was complemented by a corresponding vice. While he was a loyal friend to many, he ruthlessly abandoned others for some trivial or imagined slight. In some instances, H.R.H. displayed striking generosity, and yet he was notoriously mean. But both authors would accept the sentiment, if not the simile, proposed by a reviewer recently, that Edward was "the Peter Pan of the British Monarchy"; he never really grew up.[6]

This book has looked at Edward, the Prince, the King, and the exiled Duke, from the narrow perspective of the purchase and subsequent management of his ranch. What conclusions emerge? First, it is clear that Edward remained "Prince Charming" to Albertans throughout the four decades that he owned the ranch. The crowds which welcomed him and his Duchess in 1941 and 1950 were warm and enthusiastic. Foothills families felt a direct and personal attachment for Edward VIII. They respected his decision to abdicate and admired the dignity with which he handled himself. To them he was a victim rather than culprit. They had their own image of the man, and if they idolized him, it was on the basis of their contacts with him. They were far from being "victims of a shameful hoax perpetrated by the establishment and the media."[7] Perhaps the Canadian west brought out the best in him, for he captivated the people at the RCAF base near High River in 1941, with the same effortless charm and easy grace which he had displayed in 1919. Even those who worked for the ranch and were drawn into closer contact with H.R.H. remained his loyal supporters. Pat Burns, Alick and Douglas

---

5 Frances Donaldson, *Edward VIII* (London: Weidenfeld and Nicolson, 1974); and Philip Ziegler, *Edward VIII: The Official biography* (London: Collins, 1990).

6 *Daily Telegraph*, September 15, 1990. The "Weekend" section of the paper had the banner headline, "The King who never grew up."

7 Pierre Berton, *Toronto Star*, July 6, 1991. Berton's remark, made in his review of Ziegler's book, referred especially to the way the press handled the abdication crisis.

Newton, the Carlyle family, and Colonel Kennedy, all fell under Edward's spell, and willingly tried to do his bidding even when the requests were unreasonable and presumptuous.

And yet, in some instances at least, Edward revealed some of the less attractive facets of his character in his dealings with his ranch. He appears to have been somewhat feckless and incapable of sustaining his enthusiasm. He thoroughly enjoyed the 1923 visit, but the following year he could not wait to move on to the more sophisticated pleasures offered in Vancouver and Victoria. In 1927, he was frankly bored by what the ranch had to offer. He was happiest when absorbed in physical action, planting trees, laying out a garden, or entertaining the "aristocracy" of the cattle industry, but his interest was capricious and many plans laid with excitement never came to fruition. In the long term, too, he appears to have had difficulty in reaching a decision and then sticking with it. Throughout the 1930s he would explore the notion of selling the ranch only to pull back at the last moment. His choice of Barnum Brown as the man to supervise the search for oil on the ranch, and the way he made it, indicate that Edward was sometimes immature in his judgement of people. Finally, the callous way in which he first used, and then summarily dismissed, his loyal manager, Professor Carlyle, was entirely inexcusable.

Hector Bolitho was unusually prescient when he wrote, soon after the abdication, "authors of the future will not write upon the romantic theme of a king who gave up his throne for love, so much as upon a theme of the man of promise who came to disaster through the slow disintegration of his character."[8] But Albertans enjoyed for the most part the endearing side of Edward's personality. They would endorse the kinder words of his lawyer and friend, Walter Monckton. "There is still and always will be a greatness and a glory about him. Even his faults and follies are great."[9]

---

8 Hector Bolitho, *Edward VIII: An Intimate Biography* (London: Eyre and Spottiswoode, 1937), p. 306.

9 Lord Birkenhead, *Walter Monckton* (London: Weidenfeld and Nicolson, 1969), p. 154.

Appendices

The appendices provide some statistical underpinning to the description and analysis presented in earlier chapters. Appendix A charts the financial fortunes of the ranch. Appendix B presents some agricultural statistics which, taken together, provide an indicator of the economic health of agriculture in general and of cattle raising in particular. Appendix C gives the climatic averages for Pekisko, and illustrates the variability of the climate by contrasting the observed data for selected years.

Appendix A

Figures 1 and 2, drawn for the most part from the audited accounts of the E.P. Ranch, provide an overview of its financial fortunes.

The first graph plots expenses against income, and shows that the ranch "broke even" only occasionally, and in exceptional circumstances. In 1948, for example, receipts were bolstered by a major stock sale and by a generous insurance payment after a fire. The gap between expenses and returns was greatest during the early years of the depression; however, sales deferred until 1936 and 1938 did much to narrow the gap. During the war years, expenses were slashed and remained remarkably steady while returns increased; this reflected William Elliott's good stewardship.

Figure 2 shows the steady flow of cash to the ranch during the 1920s. This culminated in 1927, when the ranch house was enlarged and remodelled. In fact, the graph does not show the extent of the Prince's investment during this period, for valuable stock was moved from his English estates to Alberta. The total value of these animals amounted to some $100,000. During the uncertain years of the 1930s, the cash flow from London dwindled. The only exceptional year was 1931, when the deeded acreage of the ranch was doubled by a purchase from the government.

Table 1 illustrates how estimates of the value of the E.P. Ranch varied over the years. Both the value of the land and the value of livestock were overestimated in 1927. This was the end of the build-up period, and the high value put on the stock reflected the "book prices" of animals transferred from the United Kingdom. The high land value reflects a ten-year period during which the ploughed acreage had been extended and the buildings enlarged and modernized. The effects of the depression are shown in the drop in the value of stock from $73,000 in 1927 to $45,000 in 1935. Estimates of "fixed assets" remained relatively constant between 1930 and 1950, and it is interesting to recall that the figure Edward was told to expect, if he sold on the open market during the late 1930s, was $40,000 for both stock and land. This was less than half what the books suggested the property was worth. The figures in column 4 show the estimated values of the ranch in terms of the buying power of the dollar, 1935–39. They were worked out using the General Wholesale Price Index. See F.H. Leacy (ed.), *Historical Statistics of Canada* (Ottawa: Statistics Canada, 1983).

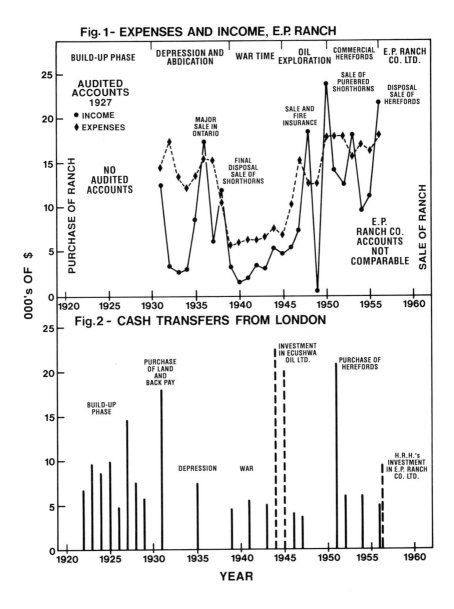

Fig. 1- EXPENSES AND INCOME, E.P. RANCH

Fig. 2 - CASH TRANSFERS FROM LONDON

Table 1: Estimated Value of the E.P. Ranch,
Selected Years, 1920–61

Year	Land and Fixed Assets	Stock and Current Assets	Total Value	Value in Standardized Dollars
1920	40,000	50,500	90,500	39,000
1927[a]	97,553	73,035	170,588	134,000
1931	92,053	47,165	139,217	148,000
1935[b]	86,721	44,660	131,381	140,000
1939[c]	86,787	13,180	99,967	101,000
1942	87,320	12,936	100,257	81,500
1946[d]	86,568	17,332	103,901	74,500
1950[e]	83,582	18,119	101,701	47,000
1961[f]	180,000	90,000	270,000	112,500

a End of build-up phase, high book value.
b Midst of depression, but prior to sale.
c After sale of pedigree stock.
d Post-war value of stock recovering.
e Cattle sold later actually realized 24,000.
f Current assets divided among shareholders. H.R.H. received whole value of land.

Sources: 1920, Ledger books and letters; 1927–50, From audited balance sheets, E.P. Ranch, GA M2398 f101, 102, 103; 1961, Agreement of sale; Newspaper accounts of stock sales, see text.

Appendix B

These figures are included to support and illustrate various comments made in the text concerning the economic context in which the E.P. Ranch was doing business. The impact of the depression on ranching is best shown in column B, although the decline in total value of cattle and calves in Alberta (column A) and the prices offered for bulls (column C) emphasize the same thing. In contrast, the 1950s were a time of relative stability and uniformly high prices for the livestock industry. The figures do suggest that the switch to a commercial herd of Herefords in 1950 was made when prices were near a peak, but the sale of the pedigree short-horns also benefited form this. (N.B. Bull sales, 1949 and 1950.) The indicators suggest that the E.P. Ranch Company did not have to contend with any marked market downturns during its brief existence between 1956 and 1961.

TABLE 2: AGRICULTURAL STATISTICS: INDICATORS OF THE ECONOMIC CLIMATE

Year	A Total Value of Cattle and Calves in Alberta	B Average Yearly Farm Price for Cattle, Calgary per cwt.	C Bull Sales Average per Head, Calgary Number	C Price	D Market Prices Cents per Bushel Wheat	D Oats	E Indexes of Farm Prices 1961 = 100 Grains	E Livestock
1919					217	100		
1920					199	54		
1921		$5.77			130	47		
1922		4.82			110	47		
1923		5.06			107	41		
1924		5.10			168	60		
1925		5.82			152	50		
1926	$17,255,000	5.95	404	$162	146	59		
1927	16,334,000	7.06			146	65		
1928	19,441,000	9.09			124	59		
1929	18,171,000	8.71	501	219	124	59		
1930	9,006,000	7.68	531	217	64	30		
1931	6,560,000	4.71	570	173	60	31		
1932	4,084,000	4.02	644	127	54	26		
1933	3,842,000	3.27	638	110	68	33		
1934	5,892,000	3.68	674	118	82	43		
1935	11,067,000	4.89	674	128	85	34	37.3	26.4
1936	12,039,000	4.30	554	126	123	53	43.1	26.4
1937	17,088,000	6.28	522	129	131	50	66.0	30.4
1938	13,565,000	5.18	434	145	62	29	48.0	30.5
1939	15,344,000	6.08	442	203	76	36	32.9	31.2
1940	18,018,000	6.72	623	190	74	35	35.6	33.1
1941	19,064,000	8.29	670	196	77	49	37.3	39.0
1942	23,566,000	9.90	723	246	94	49	43.5	48.0
1943	28,525,000	11.30	625	414	123	51	56.4	54.3
1944	35,611,000	11.13	843	351	125	51	73.5	54.2
1945	49,136,000	11.37	799	457	125	51	84.7	56.2
1946	48,613,000	12.08	953	392	138	56	96.5	60.9
1947	45,974,000	13.85	850	478	158	84	99.5	67.1
1948	79,612,000	18.75	879	471	205	78	103.1	90.6
1949	84,403,000	20.05	1002	639	206	91	101.1	97.6
1950	93,711,000	26.13	1162	540	191	96	100.2	109.8
1951	95,390,000	32.50			188	91	98.5	138.4
1952	72,366,000	24.12			186	80	97.7	106.8
1953	69,061,000	18.89	Purebred		186	73	91.8	95.8
1954	74,391,000	18.56	Stock at		173	90	82.4	92.0
1955	77,012,000	18.25	E.P. Sold		174	84	81.5	86.1
1956	85,731,000	17.90			168	81	83.4	86.0
1957	108,883,000	17.41			162	76	78.0	91.8
1958	146,419,000	21.72			166	78	80.1	100.6
1959	130,542,000	23.29			166	82	82.5	100.4
1960	142,136,000	20.60			167	82	86.8	95.1
1961	157,038,000	20.98			190	96	100.0	100.0

Sources:
Column A. J.K. Woychuk (ed.), *Alberta Agriculture: A History in Graphs* (Edmonton: Queen's Printer, 1972), p. 90
Column B. Woychuk, *Alberta Agriculture*, p. 108.
Column C. Alberta, *Department of Agriculture*, Annual Reports, 1926–1950.
Column D. F.H. Leacy (ed.), *Historical Statistics of Canada*, 2d ed. (Ottawa: Canadian Government Publication, 1983), Series M228–238.
Column E. Leacy, *Historical Statistics of Canada*, Series M196–205.

Appendix C

These statistics are included to support the description of the climatic environment of the E.P. Ranch undertaken in Chapter 2. The figures for the single years, 1926, 1933, and 1935, illustrate the seasonal variability of rainfall. The departure from the mean of the figure for total rainfall may be quite moderate, but drought in the critical growing season is not made good by above average rainfall at other times of the year. Nevertheless, the figures make it clear that Pekisko did not experience chronic and severe drought during the "dirty thirties" as did places further east away from the mountains.

TABLE 3: CLIMATIC STATISTICS FOR PEKISKO, ALBERTA LATITUDE

	1926		1933		1935		1951–80	
	°C	mm	°C	mm	°C	mm	°C	mm
January	−3.3	0	−6.7	17.5	−12.5	58.9	−11.1	37.3
February	−2.8	15.2	−10.5	17.5	−2.2	11.4	−7.0	39.2
March	0	43.2	−4.4	47.7	−8.5	55.9	−5.3	47.9
April	2.8	22.4	−0.5	101.3	−2.4	38.9	0.9	78.6
May	6.7	7.6	6.1	35.6	9.4	67.3	6.6	80.9
June	9.4	94.5	10.5	53.3	10.5	54.1	10.3	115.1
July	15.0	52.8	14.4	6.6	14.1	75.9	13.2	61.6
August	13.3	97.5	12.8	109.9	11.7	49.3	12.3	71.8
September	2.2	210.8	7.2	30.2	8.9	27.2	8.4	57.9
October	5.0	15.0	2.2	73.1	2.5	90.2	4.2	34.5
November	−3.8	24.1	1.1	9.1	−3.8	5.6	−3.2	30.3
December	−7.7	5.8	−13.9	86.6	−1.9	21.3	−7.4	41.0
Ū		591.1		588.8		556.0		696.1
Departure from average		−14%		−14%		−19%		

Sources: Dominion of Canada, Meterological Service, *Monthly Record of Meterological Observations in Canada* (Ottawa: Queen's Printer, 1926, 1933, 1935) for the respective years, and Alberta Environment, Climate of Alberta, Report for 1985 (Edmonton: Queen's Printer, 1986) for the 30-year mean.

Bibliography

A NOTE ON ARCHIVAL SOURCES

The most important body of archival material on the E.P. Ranch is in the Glenbow Archives in Calgary. The E.P. Ranch Papers consist of fourteen document boxes containing correspondence, financial papers and ledgers. After the Duke of Windsor died, the Duchess graciously bequeathed all the papers pertaining to the ranch, which had been held by his Calgary lawyers, to the Glenbow. Pat Burns helped the Duke of Windsor manage his ranch during the 1930s, and the Burns papers contain a full record of this correspondence and the minutes of the Ranch Management Committee. Alick Newton became the Duke's main agent in Calgary, and his correspondence is preserved in the Newton and Riveredge papers.

At the Public Archives of Canada the most significant files were found in the papers of the Department of the Interior, Timber and Grazing Lands Branch. The Borden, Mackenzie King, and Meighen Papers, all contributed something.

The publication of Sir Allan Lascelles' papers, edited by Duff Hart-Davis, was really exciting, for his letters to his wife from the ranch contain vivid descriptions which illustrate the impact that the site had on a visiting Englishman. The project was far advanced when Ziegler's "Official Biography" of Edward VIII was published. The unprecedented access that the author had to the Royal Archives means that his book is to some extent a "primary source" to other interested scholars. Fortunately, he quotes at length from letters from the Prince of Wales to his mother and to Freda Dudley Ward.

A SELECTED BIBLIOGRAPHY

BARR, J.J. "The Impact of Oil on Alberta: Retrospect and Prospect." In A.W. Rasporich (ed.) *The Making of the Modern West: Western Canada Since 1945.* University of Calgary Press, 1984.

BERTON, PIERRE. *The Great Depression, 1929–1939.* Toronto: McClelland and Stewart, 1990.

BIRKENHEAD, SECOND EARL. *Walter Monckton.* London: Weidenfeld and Nicolson, 1969.

BLOCH, MICHAEL. *The Duke of Windsor's War.* New York: Coward McCann, 1983.

_____. *Operation Willi.* New York: Weidenfeld and Nicolson, 1984.

_____. *Wallis and Edward: Letters, 1931–1937.* New York: Simon and Schuster, 1986.

_____. *The Secret File of the Duke of Windsor.* London: Corgi Books, 1988.

BOLITHO, HECTOR. *King Edward VIII: An Intimate Biography.* New York: Literary Guild of America, 1937.

_____. *A Century of British Monarchy.* London: Longman and Green, 1951.

BRADFORD, SARAH. *The Reluctant King: The Life and Reign of George VI, 1895–1952.* New York: St. Martin's Press, 1989.

BRADO, EDWARD. *Cattle Kingdom: Early Ranching in Alberta.* Vancouver: Douglas and McIntyre, 1984.

BREEN, DAVID H. "The Turner Thesis and the Canadian West: A Closer Look at the Ranching Frontier," in Lewis H. Thomas (ed.) *Essays on Western History.* Edmonton: University of Alberta Press, 1976.

_____. *The Canadian Prairie West and the Ranching Frontier, 1874–1924.* University of Toronto Press, 1983.

BROADFOOD, BARRY. *Ten Lost Years.* Toronto: Doubleday, Canada, 1973.

BRODY, ILES. *Gone With the Windsors.* Toronto: John C. Winston, 1953.

BRYAN, J. and MURPHY, CHARLES J.V. *The Windsor Story.* New York: William Morrow, 1979.

COLVILLE, JOHN. *The Fringes of Power: 10 Downing Street Diaries, 1939–1955.* London: W.W. Norton, 1985.

COOKE, ALASTAIR. *Six Men.* London: Bodley Head, 1977.

CRAIG, JOHN R. *Ranching with Lords and Commons.* Toronto: William Briggs, 1912.

DE MARIGNY, ALFRED. *A Conspiracy of Crowns.* New York: Crown Publishers Inc., 1990.

DONALDSON, FRANCES. *Edward VIII.* London: Weidenfeld and Nicolson, 1974.

DUNAE, PATRICK A. *Gentlemen Immigrants: From British Public Schools to the Canadian Frontier.* Vancouver: Douglas and McIntyre, 1981.

_____. (ed.). *Ranchers' Legacy.* Edmonton: University of Alberta Press, 1986.

EVANS, SIMON M. "Spatial Aspects of the Cattle Kingdom: The First Decade," in A.W. Rasporich and H.C. Klassen, (eds.) *Frontier Calgary: Town, City and Region, 1875–1914.* Calgary: McClelland and Stewart West, 1975.

_____. "The Passing of a Frontier: Ranching in the Canadian West, 1882–1912." Unpublished Ph.D. Dissertation, University of Calgary, 1976.

_____. "Stocking the Canadian Range." *Alberta History* 26 (Summer, 1978).

FINCH, DAVID A.A. "Turner Valley Oilfield Development, 1914–1985." Unpublished M.A. Thesis, University of Calgary, 1985.

FRANCIS, D. and GANZEVOORT, H. *The Dirty Thirties in Prairie Canada*. Vancouver: Tantalus Research, 1980.

FRANCIS, R. DOUGLAS. *Images of the West*. Saskatoon: Prairie Books, 1989.

FRIESEN, GERALD. *The Canadian Prairies: A History*. Toronto: University of Toronto Press, 1984.

GRAY, JAMES. *The Winter Years: The Depression on the Prairies*. Toronto: MacMillan, 1966.

_____. *Men Against the Desert*. Saskatoon: Western Producer, 1967.

GRIFFEN, FREDERICK. *Variety Show: Twenty Years of Watching the News Parade*. Toronto: MacMillan, 1936.

HARDINGE, HELEN. *Loyal to Three Kings*. London: William Kimber, 1967.

HART-DAVIS, DUFF (ed.). *In Royal Service: The Letters and Journals of Sir Alan Lascelles, 1920–1936*, Vol. 2. London: Hamish Hamilton, 1988.

HIGHAM, CHARLES. *Wallis: Secret Lives of the Duchess of Windsor*. London: Sidgewick and Jackson, 1988.

HIGH RIVER PIONEERS' AND OLD TIMERS' ASSOCIATION. *Leaves from the Medicine Tree*. Lethbridge Herald, 1960.

HORN, MICHAEL (ed.). *The Dirty Thirties: Canadians in the Great Depression*. Toronto: Copp Clark, 1972.

H.R.H. EDWARD, DUKE OF WINDSOR. *A King's Story: The Memoirs of the Duke of Windsor*. New York: G.P. Putnam, 1952.

_____. *A Family Album*. London: Cassell, 1960.

INGLIS, BRIAN. *Abdication*. New York: MacMillan, 1966.

ISTVANFFY, D.I. "The History of Turner Valley." *Alberta Historical Review* 2 (October, 1954).

JAMESON, SHEILAGH S. "Women in the Southern Alberta Ranch Community," in H.C. Klassen (ed.), *The Canadian West*. Calgary: Comprint, 1977.

_____. *Ranchers, Cowboys and Characters: Birth of Alberta's Western Heritage*. Calgary: Glenbow-Alberta Institute, 1987.

JONES, DAVID C. *Empire of Dust*. Edmonton: University of Alberta Press, 1987.

KINROSS, LORD. *The Windsor Years*. New York: Viking Press, 1967.

LONGFORD, ELIZABETH. *Elizabeth R: A Biography*. London: Weidenfeld and Nicolson, 1983.

MACKINTOSH, W.A. and JOERG, W.L.G. (eds.). *Canadian Frontiers of Settlement*, 9 vols. Toronto: MacMillan, 1934–40.

MACOUN, JOHN. *Manitoba and the Great North West*. Guelph: World Publishing, 1882.

MACDONNEL, TOM. *Daylight Upon Magic: The Royal Tour of Canada, 1939*. Toronto: MacMillan, 1989.

MAINE, BASIL. *The King's First Ambassador*. London: Hutchinson, 1935.

MANCHESTER, WILLIAM. *The Last Lion: Winston Spencer Churchill; Alone, 1932–1940*. New York: Dell Publishing, 1988.

MCEWAN, GRANT. *Pat Burns: Cattle King*. Saskatoon: Western Producer, 1979.

MENKES, SUZY. *The Windsor Style*. London: Grafton Books, 1987.

MIDDLEMAS, K. and BARNES, JOHN. *Baldwin: A Biography*. London: MacMillan, 1969.

MOSLEY, DIANA. *The Duchess of Windsor*. London: Sidgewick and Jackson, 1980.

NEATBY, H. BLAIR. *William Lyon Mackenzie King.* Toronto: University of Toronto Press, 1976.

NEWTON, W. DOUGLAS. *Westward with the Prince of Wales.* London: D. Appleton, 1920.

NICOLSON, HAROLD. *Diaries and Letters, 1930–39.* London: Collins, 1966.

O'NEILL, MOIRA. "A Lady's Life on a Ranch." *Blackwood's Edinburgh Magazine* 163 (January, 1898).

_____. *Songs of the Glens of Antrim.* London, 1910.

OSGOOD, ERNEST STAPLES. *The Day of the Cattleman.* Chicago: University of Chicago Press, 1929.

PALMER, ALAN. *Crowned Cousins.* London: Weidenfeld and Nicolson, 1985.

PARKER, JOHN. *King of Fools.* New York: St. Martin's Press, 1988.

PEARSON, JOHN. *The Selling of the Royal Family.* New York: Simon and Schuster, 1986.

PONSONBY, SIR FREDERICK. *Recollections of Three Reigns.* London: Eyre and Spottiswoode, 1951.

REES, RONALD. *New and Naked Land: Making the Prairies Home.* Saskatoon: Western Producer, 1988.

ROSENVALL, L.A. and EVANS, SIMON M. *Essays on the Historical Geography of the Canadian West.* Geography Department: University of Calgary, 1987.

SENCOURT, ROBERT. *The Reign of Edward VIII.* London: Gibbs and Phillips, 1962.

STAMP, ROBERT M. *Kings, Queens and Canadians.* Markham: Fitzhenry and Whiteside, 1987.

STAVELEY HILL, SIR ALEXANDER. *From Home to Home: Autumn Wanderings in the North West.* New York: Argonaut Press, 1966.

TATRO, HARRY A. *A Survey of Historic Ranches.* Historic Sites and Monuments Board of Canada, 1973.

THOMAS, L.G. "The Ranching Period in Southern Alberta." Unpublished M.A. Thesis, University of Alberta, 1935.

_____. *Our Foothills.* Calgary: Millarville, Kew Priddis and Bragg Creek Historical Society, 1975.

_____. *Rancher's Legacy*, Patrick A. Dunae (ed.). Edmonton: University of Alberta Press, 1986.

TOWNSEND, W. and TOWNSEND, L. *The Biography of H.R.H. The Prince of Wales.* London: E. Marritt and Son, 1929.

THORNTON, MICHAEL. *Royal Feud.* New York: Simon and Schuster, 1985.

VANDERBILT, GLORIA and FURNESS, LADY THELMA. *Double Exposure: A Twin Autobiography.* New York: McCay, 1958.

VERNEY, FRANK E. *H.R.H.: A Character Study of the Prince of Wales.* London: Hodder and Stoughton, 1926.

WARWICK, CHRISTOPHER. *Abdication.* London: Sidgwick and Jackson, 1986.

WINTER, GORDON and KOCHMAN, WENDY. *Secrets of the Royals.* New York: St. Martin's Press, 1990.

ZIEGLER, PHILIP. *Crown and People.* London: Collins, 1978.

_____. *Edward VIII: The Official Biography.* London: Collins, 1990.

Index

Simon Evans is a professor of geography at Memorial University of Newfoundland. He dates his interest in ranching to his experiences as a "tenderfoot" on a Montana ranch in the 1960s. His Ph.D. dissertation at the University of Calgary was on the ranching frontier in Canada, and he has published *Essays on the Historical Geography of the Canadian West* (with Lynn Rosenvall, 1987) and a dozen articles in *Prairie Forum*, *The Canadian Geographer*, *Great Plains Quarterly*, *Agricultural History*, and *Alberta History*. Dr. Evans lives in Corner Brook, Newfoundland.